The Service Sector: Productivity and Growth

Contributions to Economics

Albrecht Ritschl
Prices and Production
- Elements of a System - Theoretic Perspective -
1989. 159 pp. Softcover DM 59,-
ISBN 3-7908-0429-0

Arnulf Grübler
The Rise and Fall of Infrastructures
- Dynamics of Evolution and Technological Change in Transport -
1990. 305 pp. Softcover DM 85,-
ISBN 3-7908-0479-7

Peter R. Haiss
Cultural Influences on Strategic Planning
1990. 188 pp. Softcover DM 65,-
ISBN 3-7908-0481-9

Manfred Kremer/Marion Weber (Eds.)
Transforming Economic Systems: The Case of Poland
1992. 179 pp. Softcover DM 69,-
ISBN 3-7908-91415-3

Marcel F. van Marion
Liberal Trade and Japan
1993. 298 pp. Softcover DM 90,-
ISBN 3-7908-0699-4

Michael Carlberg
Open Economy Dynamics
1993. 203 pp. Softcover DM 75,-
ISBN 3-7908-0708-7

Hans Schneeweiß/
Klaus F. Zimmermann (Eds.)
Studies in Applied Econometrics
1993. 238 pp. Softcover DM 85,-
ISBN 3-7908-0716-8

Gerhard Gehrig/Wladyslaw Welfe (Eds.)
Economies in Transition
1993. 292 pp. Softcover DM 90,-
ISBN 3-7908-0721-4

Alfred Franz/Carsten Stahmer (Eds)
Approaches to Environmental Accounting
1993. 542 pp. Softcover DM 178,-
ISBN 3-7908-0719-2

János Gács / Georg Winckler (Eds.)
International Trade and Restructuring in Eastern Europe
1994. 343 pp. Softcover DM 98,-
ISBN 3-7908-0759-1

Christoph M. Schneider
Research and Development Management: From the Soviet Union to Russia
1994. 253 pp. Softcover DM 85,-
ISBN 3-7908-0757-5

Valeria De Bonis
Stabilization Policy in an Exchange Rate Union
1994. 172 pp. Softcover DM 75,-
ISBN 3-7908-0789-3

Bernhard Böhm / Lionello F. Punzo (Eds.)
Economic Performance
1994. 323 pp. Softcover DM 98,-
ISBN 3-7908-0811-3

Karl Steininger
Trade and Environment
1995. 219 pp. Softcover DM 75,-
ISBN 3-7908-0814-8

Michael Reiter
The Dynamics of Business Cycles
1995. 215 pp. Softcover DM 75,-
ISBN 3-7908-0823-7

Michael Carlberg
Sustainability and Optimality of Public Debt
1995. 217 pp. Softcover DM 85,-
ISBN 3-7908-0834-2

Lars Olof Persson / Ulf Wiberg
Microregional Fragmentation
1995. 132 pp. Softcover DM 75,-
ISBN 3-7908-0855-5

Andreas Foerster
Institutional Analysis of Development Administration
1995. 234 pp. Softcover DM 90,-
ISBN 3-7908-0853-9

Ernesto Felli · Furio C. Rosati
Giovanni Tria (Eds.)

The Service Sector: Productivity and Growth

Proceedings of the
International Conference
held in Rome, Italy, May 27-28, 1993

With 24 Figures

Springer-Verlag Berlin Heidelberg GmbH

Series Editors
Werner A. Müller
Peter Schuster

Editors
Ernesto Felli, Professor in Econometrics, University of Molise,
Faculty of Economics, Via Cavour 11 A, I-86100 Campobasso, Italy

Furio C. Rosati, Professor in Microeconomics,
University of Rome "Tor Vergata", Faculty of Economics,
Via di Tor Vergata, snc, I-00133 Rome, Italy

Giovanni Tria, Lecturer in Macroeconomics,
University of Rome "Tor Vergata", Faculty of Economics,
Via di Tor Vergata, snc, I-00133 Rome, Italy

Copyediting
Paola Ferranti, Giovanna Ramacci and Romana Torossi (co-ordinator),
ISCOM, P.zza G. G. Belli, 2, I-00153 Rome, Italy

ISBN 978-3-7908-0875-9 ISBN 978-3-642-49999-9 (eBook)
DOI 10.1007/978-3-642-49999-9

Die Deutsche Bibliothek - CIP-Einheitsaufnahme
The service sector: productivity and growth; proceedings of
the international conference held in Rome, Italy, May 1993. -
Heidelberg: Physica-Verl., 1995
(Contributions to economics)

NE: Felli, Ernesto [Hrsg.]

88/2202-5 4 3 2 1 0 – Printed on acid-free paper

CONTENTS

PART II
International and Intersectoral Differences in Productivity: Catching-up or Divergence?

Preface

The economics of the service sector has recently attracted a large attention. At a macroeconomic level, the discussion has been focused on the issues concerning the relationship between the expansion of the service industry and the potential for a stable and sustained growth. Slow productivity growth, due to the largely non tradable nature of the output, lack of competition due either to regulations or to barriers to entry are among the "bads" sometimes associated with a "service led" growth. On the other hand new working places are created in the service industries at a rate much higher than in the industrial ones. Is a lower rate of technological change and the continuing of inflationary tensions the price to pay for a sustained expansion of employment in the service sector? These are in a nutshell the questions that led CEIS (Centre for International Studies on Economic Growth - University of Rome "Tor Vergata") to organize the International Seminar on "The Service Sector: Productivity and Growth" held in Rome in May 1993, whose revised proceedings are published in this volume.

The economists and academicians invited to the conference have faced the issues mentioned above from different perspectives, but they concentrated especially on the problems relative to growth and productivity.

A first group of contributions is devoted to the analysis of the interdependence among the service and the industrial sectors of the economy and to offer some evidence about the development of the service sector in the recent years. In particular the essay of Grubel concentrates on the role of producer services in the process of economic growth. While De Bandt and Felli and Tria deal with the problem of the influence of the services on the productivity of the

other sector of the economy. Manzini and Tivegna analyze the links between the growth of employment in the service sector and the inflation process, comparing the experiences of Italy and Germany. A more detailed study of the development of the service sector in Italy is, instead, carried out by Monducci and Pisani. Klodt reviews the problem of the convergence among economies by looking separately at the role of the service and non-service sector.
The second group of papers presented in this volume is instead mainly concerned with the problem of the possible differences in productivity among market services and manufacturing industries. While the paper of Ergas concentrates on the role of regulations in the retail sector at the EEC level, the paper by Scandizzo highlights the behaviour of industrial and service firms in the Italian economy. Finally, the works of Pellegrini and Atella-Rosati are devoted to the existence and causes of divergence in the productivity growth, the former presenting an analysis relative to the Italian economy and the latter studying the behaviour of productivity in the G7 countries.

Ernesto Felli
Furio Camillo Rosati
Giovanni Tria

Introductory Remarks

Luigi Paganetto
University of Rome "Tor Vergata"

The idea behind this seminar is to gather a wealth of opinions on both the global role of the services sector in the process of economic development and the role of each single service involved. It must be underlined that the settled belief according to which it is hardly possible to speak of the services as a global reality would have obliged us to address each service separately and, therefore, to organize this Seminar on a totally different basis. C.E.I.S., which has been undertaking systematic research activities in this sector for quite a while now, has decided to base this first Seminar on this subject on its concern for a discussion having the widest possible scope and addressing the most significant study and research orientations in our country and abroad, in order to determine the state of the art.

The Seminar has been financed by the "Tor Vergata" University of Rome and Confcommercio (Trading, Tourism and Services Enterprises Association), which I would also like to thank for its hospitality.

The research interests of C.E.I.S., concerning international economic interdependency issues, have determined that the Seminar pay great attention to the issue of international relations.

It is a well known fact that the role of the services sector in the last few years has focused mainly on the considerable increase of its share on GDP and employment, on its low productivity growth rate and increase of relative prices, which has frequently proved higher than the average rate of growth of prices.

The prevailing explanation is that the link existing between the low productivity growth rate of services and the greater relative growth of prices is the result of the need to pay wages of the same order and level of those of much more productive sectors. Recently, in Italy, there have been a lot of discussions as to if and to what extent services have had an inflationary role in this country. According to a study made by the Bank of Italy (Barca and Visco, 1991), between 1976 and 1990 the consumer price of services purportedly rose by 28 % with regard to other prices (non-energy products), compared to a growth differential equal to approximately one half in France and Germany. This differential seems even greater if we consider only the commercial distribution and transportation sectors.

The greater dynamics of the prices of services compared to those of manufactured goods, according to this analysis, stems from a lower productivity growth rate, which in turn is linked to a deficit of competition due to existence of public sector monopolies and economic and legal barriers barring access to the market.

Subsequent research has shown highly differentiated productivity trends for the various sectors confirming the existence of heavy delays, in respect of both efficiency and quality in the post office and railway sectors, slight delays in telecommunications and a relatively satisfying situation in the electricity distribution sector.

In this case also, the reduced dynamics of productivity in some sectors is related not only to technological differences, according to the hypothesis made by Baumol (1967), but is also affected by the different competition arrangements. Baumol's hypothesis is based on the idea that the production of services, especially those related to professional activities, does not allow actual productivity increases. The example is Beethoven's quartet, the time and work required to reproduce it having remained unchanged through the centuries. Baumol has pointed out that this is an extreme case and that there are differentiated productivity growth rates within the services sector taken as a whole, for each specific service.

In any case, scholars generally tend to highlight the limits rather than the potentials of the services sector, in respect of the issues of economic growth.

Grubel, see page 11, reminds us that Bluestone and Harrison (1986), in the United States, have underlined how the dualism of growth in the services sector (see, for example, the fast food - paying low wages - and computers - paying high salaries - sectors), combined with the reduction and compression of wages and salaries in the manufacturing sector, has considerable effects on income distribution, which in turn seriously affect growth.

It must be reminded that there are disagreements even with regard to the new technologies sector. In fact, the OECD states that despite widespread and growing investments in this sector, in particular in the information sector, there is no clear evidence of any increase of productivity linked to the use of these technologies, with the sole exception of the increase of the number of bank accounts managed by each clerical worker.

Another important issue is the role of services in international trade. In particular, there seems to be no stable relationship between trade surplus and deficit in the services sector. As pointed out by De Bandt, see page 149, countries such as the United States and France feature a surplus of services but a trade balance deficit with regard to manufactured goods. Germany and Japan have the opposite problem. The prevailing interpretation is that the excessive growth of services is occurring at the expense of a reduction of the production basis and this, in turn, could jeopardize the possibility of maintaining services exports in the long run.

In this case also, an assessment made on the basis of aggregate data only appears debatable. An analysis capable of distinguishing between the various types of services, i.e. communications, transportation, trade, credit, etc., would certainly be more convincing.

Moreover, a disaggregation based on functional rather than sectoral considerations, distinguishing between consumer services, government services and production services, would probably prove even more significant.

The growth of production related services is particularly strong in advanced industrial countries. It is largely related to the increase of quality of the human resources employed, besides to the growth of the number of employees.

This is the reason why it represents a different manner of introducing technology in the production process, through the increase of capacity and skill of the participants. The growth of consumer services, on the contrary, is largely related to the increase of female workers, with the consequent shift of current activities from the domestic en-

vironment to the market, as stated in the studies by Hammes and Grubel (1992).
In such a context, the services rendered by the public sector may achieve their objects if they are provided in accordance with the development currently under way in the production and consumer services. The issue at stake is not only the efficiency of the public sector services, but also the introduction of adequate rules governing competition in the private sector services, which is of decisive importance for the development of the economic system by guaranteeing the indispensable competitive boost in a sector which is not always adequately exposed to the stimuli of competition.
Moreover, I believe that in evaluating the efficiency and productivity of services at sectoral level, one must also carefully assess the manner according to which the necessary measures are made.
In particular, I find the observations by Felli and Tria, see pag. 41, on the relations between the trade and manufacturing sectors and the issue of the contribution of the former to the returns to scale of the latter, of particular interest. It is undoubtedly true, as Diamond says, that when there are many purchasers on the market, many clients visit the retail outlets and the opportunities of making the most suitable acquaintances increase; in this manner trade contributes to the growth of industrial output. The consequence is that the measurement of productivity is always unsatisfactory, unless one takes into due account all the variables which contribute to it; in this case one must evaluate the effects of the influence of trade on the manufacturing sector.
In other cases it shall be necessary simply to proceed with caution, but I am sure that such numerous and authoritative contributions to our Seminar shall enable us to make many steps forward.

References

Barca F. and Visco I., (1991), "L'Economia Italiana nella Prospettiva Europea: Terziario Protetto e Dinamica dei Redditi Nominali", *Temi di Discussione del Servizio Studi*, Banca d'Italia, 175.

Baumol W.J., (1967), "Macroeconomics of Unbalanced Growth: The Anatomy of Urban Crises", *American Economic Review*, 131, 57-70.

Bluestone B. and Harrison B., (1986) *The Great American Job Machine: The Proliferation of Low-Wage Employment in the US Economy*, Joint Economic Committee, Washington.

Hammes D. and Grubel H., (1992), "Home Production, Market Production and the Changing Allocation of Expenditures on Services", *The Service Industries Journal.*

PART I

Competitiveness and Productivity: The Link Between Manufacturing and Service Sectors

1

Producer Services: Their Important Role in Growing Economies

Herbert G. Grubel
Simon Fraser University

In this paper I present some empirical findings and theoretical explanations of the strong and growing importance of producer services in national income, all of which have significant implications for economic policy on the service industries. These ideas about producer services have been developed earlier by Momigliano and Siniscalco (1982) and discussed in previous publications (Grubel and Walker, 1989 and 1991). My reading of academic and especially of popular writings on the service industries suggests that these ideas have reached an increasing audience, but that they are far from universally accepted and deserve further attention and publicity.

The paper extends on the central theme contained in my earlier publication in three ways. First, it updates statistics on the growth of the service industries in Canada by adding information on the years 1987 to 1991.

Second, the data for the most important series in constant prices makes use of newly available estimates in terms of a 1986 base, replacing those with the 1981 base.

Third, I present a number of regressions which compare the historic correlation between national income and the three components of the service sector, showing that annual changes in GDP are most closely correlated and have the highest elasticity with respect to changes in producer services rather than consumer and government services.

1. Alleged Problems with the Growth of the Service Sector

The growth of the service sector as a percent of GDP between 1961 and 1989 in Canada is shown in Figure 1. As can be seen, between 1965 and 1989 the share of the service sector in current prices has risen from .54 to .64, or almost 19 percent in 24 years. While a projection of these data implies that ultimately the goods producing sector will disappear, this point will not be reached for another century, even if there are no fundamental changes in the economy. The data on the growth of the service sector share in constant 1986 dollars will be discussed below. These trends in the share of the Canadian service sector are found in most industrial countries and have been going on for a long time. They have induced a number of reactions in the literature which are important in the assessment of the main findings of the present paper. Some of the most important studies of the modern service sector are those of Bell (1973), Bluestone and Harrison (1982), Gershuny and Miles (1983), Ginzberg and Votja (1981), Ott (1987), Riddle (1986) and Shelp (1981). The main conclusions of this literature may be summarized briefly and selectively as follows. First, the service sector is believed to be subject to low productivity growth for reasons made prominent by Baumol (1967) and discussed further below. As a result of this fact, the rigidity of wages and increasing productivity in the manufacturing sector, modern economies are subject to a structural upward bias in inflation.

Second, a variant on this theme recalls the assertion by Adam Smith, echoed by Karl Marx, that the production of services involves an unproductive use of scarce resources. This view is based on the premise that with a population living at the subsistence level, any movement of labour into personal services for the aristocracy lowers the production of essentials like food, clothing and shelter and means a threat to survival. While this argument is irrelevant in the industrial countries of the world and in the light of modern economic theories, these ideas from the last two centuries linger in the minds of some analysts who use them to argue that goods producing industries are economically more beneficial than service producing industries.

Third, there are concerns that the shrinking of the goods producing sector implies increasing reliance on imports from abroad with accompanying problems of dependence and lack of defence industry capabilities. Fourth, Bluestone and Harrison (1986) argued that the recent US growth of the consumer service industries generated large numbers of low paying - high paying jobs, the former in the ubiquitous fast-food industries and the latter in the computer industry. Combined with the shrinking of middle income jobs in the manufacturing industries, the service sector growth is thus believed to result in the creation of a bimodal distribution of income and to require an industrial strategy to deal with this undesirable change in the income distribution.

Fifth, Browne (1986) emphasized that the growth of the service industries has been caused to a considerable degree by the shifting of household production into the monetary sector, as is clear from the example used in the paper's title "Taking in Each Other's Laundry - The Service Economy". The main implication of this fact is that the measured growth of national income is biased upward since such shifts in production do not result in a corresponding increase in total output of the combined household and market sectors.

Sixth, as a result of the growth of government spending and deficits, there is much public concern about the growth of government services as part of the total service sector in the economy. In Canada in particular there is widespread discussion about the detrimental effect of cuts in the provision of medical and educational services which might be necessitated by the current, large deficits and debt.

The following analysis is designed to analyze the size, productivity growth, composition and sectoral development of Canada's service sector with the aim to show that the concerns about the growth of service output are misplaced. It will show that, to the contrary, this is a necessary characteristic economic growth in a world in which human and knowledge capital play an increasing role in the determination of productivity of both labour and physical capital.

2. Productivity in the Canadian Service Sector

Figure 1 shows that the nominal and real share of the Canadian service sector in GDP have grown at the same rate, except for the earliest period 1961-1969, when the real share remained constant while the nominal share rose about .05 percentage points. This recent and rather long-lasting equality in the nominal and real shares is inconsistent with the conventional wisdom on this matter, which owes much to Baumol's influential (1967) study. In this paper Baumol argued that many personal service producing industries by their very nature do not permit increases in productivity. He illustrated his analysis with the well-known example of the live performance of a Beethoven quartet, which will forever have unchanging requirements of time and manpower and therefore unchanging labour productivity. He considered many other services like education, public transportation and medical care to be subject to the same limits on productivity growth.

In recent years, Baumol (1987) has argued that in fact these personal service industries represent an extreme on a spectrum of service industries with different rates of productivity increases. The telecommunications and air-travel industries are examples of service industries at the other end of the spectrum and have enjoyed very high rates of productivity growth. What is interesting about the Canadian data is that according to the best estimates of Statistics Canada, during the last 15 years or so the service sector on average enjoyed the same productivity growth as the goods producing sector. Concerns about the dampening effect on overall economic growth resulting from the increase in the service sector appear to be unfounded.

3. A Taxonomy of Services

Service industry statistics in most countries provide information about the value-added of narrowly defined industries like legal services, business services, health, recreation, hotels, education, retail trade, financial services, wholesale trade, transport and communications. These data are useful for a wide range of analytical studies. However, they do not lend themselves to a division into consumer, government and producer services. As will become clear later, an understanding of the nature and size of these three major categories of service industries sheds important light on the economic implications and welfare effects of the growth in the service sector.

Some studies on the service industry sector have noted that much of the growth has been due to the relatively rapid expansion of business and legal services, which in the United States in the period 1980-91 had the most rapid employment growth of all of the service industries with 70 and 105 percent, respectively. It is also possible to use the existing data and consider education and health as government services and recreation as consumer services.

However, in fact most of the industries for which output data are available sell their services to consumers as well as business and government. Financial services, legal, hotel, accounting and advertising services (the latter the main components of business services) are used predominantly as intermediate inputs by business and government. But they are also purchased by consumers. On the other hand, some industries producing predominantly consumer services like restaurants, laundry and dry-cleaning establishments are also patronized by business firms and government. As a result, some of the output of these industries should be as counted as producer services.

One method for estimating the value of the services used as intermediate inputs by business and government involves information contained in national input-output tables. This methodology has been used by Momigliano and Siniscalco (1982) in their pioneering study of Italy. It requires a detailed working knowledge of input-output tables and sophisticated computational skills to arrive at the required information. An additional disadvantage of using national input-output tables is that they are available only with a considerable time-lag, limiting the analysis to historic data.

The following empirical study uses instead a simpler technology to divide the value-added of the service producing sector into the three components of consumer, government and producer services. The method uses information, which in principle underlies the construction of input-output tables by statistical offices but without the need for manipulating these tables. It is available readily and with relatively short lags from publications of most national governments in the world. Much effort is devoted by national statistical offices in the preparation of these data.

Consumer Services National Income Accounts were designed on the basis of the Keynesian macro-economic model identity Y=C+I+G+(X-M). Consumer expenditures C are divided into spending on durables, semi-durables and services. In order to arrive at the value-added of the industries producing the consumer services recorded in these statistics, it is necessary to deflate the published spending series by a factor which represents the material inputs used in their production. In the case of the restaurant industry, for example, it is necessary to deduct from gross sales the value of the food and other material inputs. In the calculations presented below, value-added was considered to be 60 percent of all the services bought by consumers. The 60 percent figure was derived by an examination of the ratio of value-added to gross output of some major Canadian service industries in 1973. To simplify the calculations, this deflator was applied for all years. The bias resulting from this approach is not known, but I do not believe that it is serious.

3.1 Government Services

In the Keynesian equation above, G stands for exhaustive government expenditures. Statistics Canada provides estimates of this sum broken into current and investment spending. In the following analysis only data on current spending are used and there is no adjustment made for the use of intermediate goods inputs by the government in the provision of these services. It is assumed that all of these outlays result in the provision of government services to the public.

3.2 Producer Services

Statistics Canada publishes a long and consistent series on the value-added created by all service producing industries. Expressing this series as a proportion of national income creates the widely cited statistics shown in Figure 1.

The value-added of the consumer and government services described above is subtracted from the value-added by all service producing industries. The residual is called producer services. It contains the services which traditionally are considered intermediate inputs into the production of goods, like wholesale and retail services. Importantly, it also contains that share of hotel, restaurant, financial, legal, laundry, car-rental and similar services which is not purchased by consumers.

4. The History of Canadian Service Industries

Figure 2 shows the time series for the share of GDP represented by the value-added of the consumer, government and producer service industries, all in current dollars for the years 1961-89, the definition and measurement of which was discussed in the preceding section. The most outstanding facts apparent from this figure are, first, the quantitative dominance of producer services with 26 percent throughout the period.

Second, consumer services were 16 percent and 19 percent at the beginning and end of the period, respectively. At both points in time they represent the second largest service sector, though during the period 1970-88, government services constituted a larger share. Third, government services have grown most rapidly from 12 percent of GDP in 1961 to slightly less than 19 percent in 1988.

However, in economics the analysis of nominal figures is often misleading and it is more instructive to consider real magnitudes. Figure 3 does so and shows the share of the three categories of services in GDP in 1986 prices. Figure 4 focuses on the annual and cumulative changes of these shares considering 1961 equal to 100.

Figure 1

Total Services as GDP Share Canada, Nominal and 1986 Prices

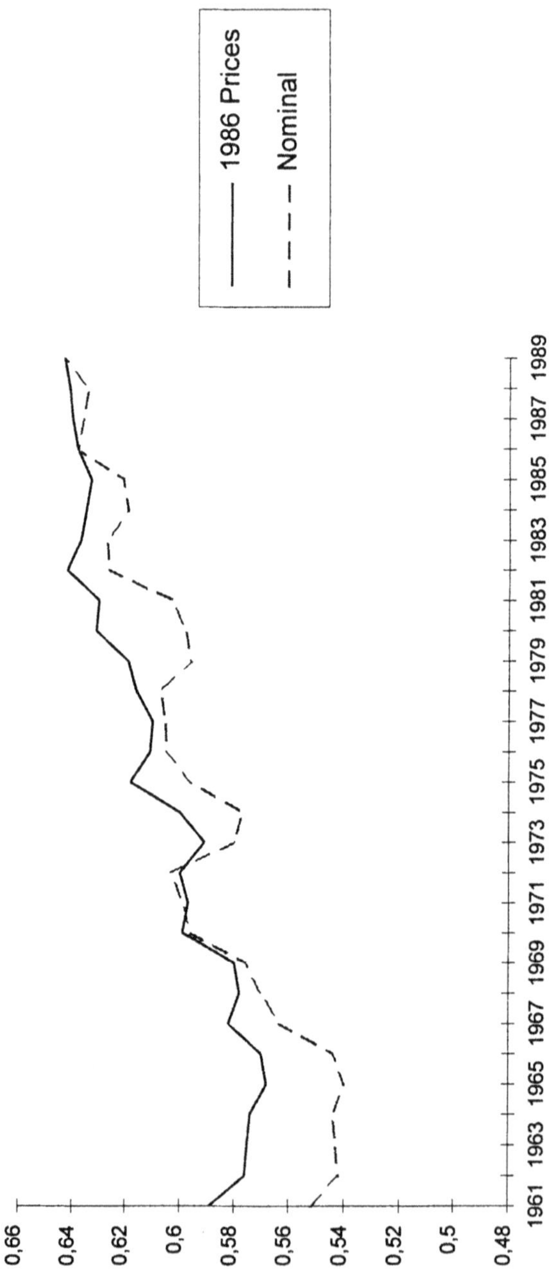

Source : Cansim Matrices 4663 and 4670

Figure 2

Services as Share of GDP Canada, Current Dollars

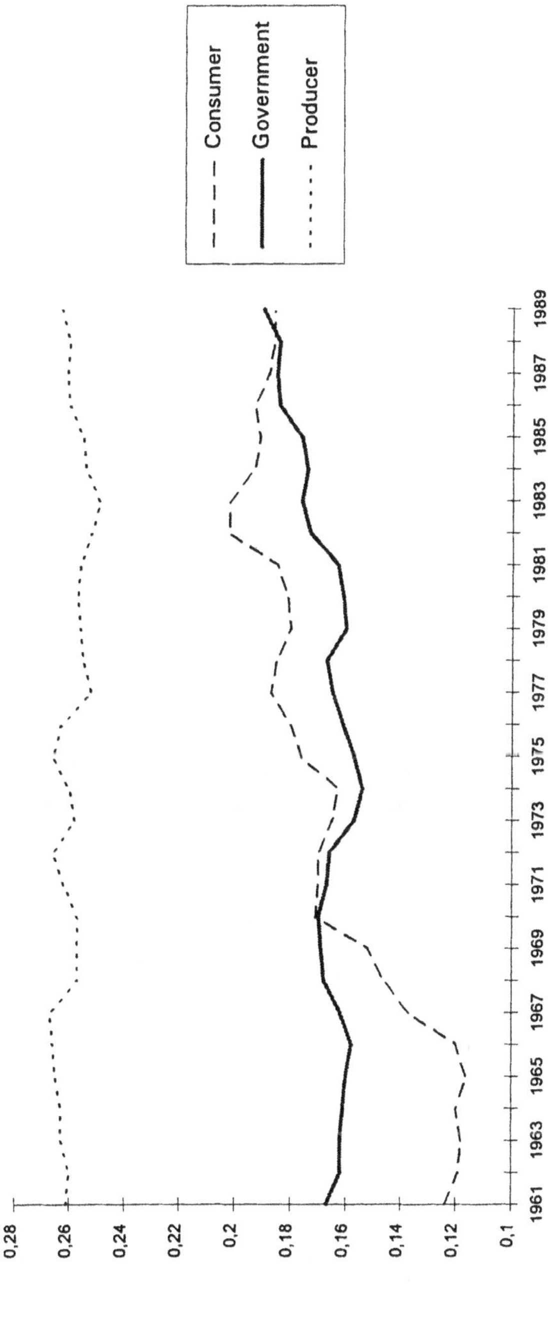

Source: Cansim Tape Matrices 6623 and 4668; see text for calculations

4.1 Problems of Measuring Real Magnitudes

The deflation of all price indices is subject to well-known difficulties associated with the assessment of changes in the quality and performance characteristics of the goods and services in these indices. In the case of some services these difficulties are particularly great. For example, the work of some private academic researchers has revealed the existence of serious upward biases in the government estimates of the cost of computer services.

However, for the purposes of our present analysis the most important problem arises from the well-known bias inherent in the present measurement of real government services. The data on government spending disregard all changes in labour productivity and instead measure output of the sector by the quantity of labour input. For example, the use of computers in the preparation of pension checks associated with a reduction in hours of labour required shows up in statistics as a decrease in the supply of government services, even though the number of checks prepared has remained constant or increased.

Figures 3 and 4 and the following discussion should be considered in the light of these limitations of the data on real services generally and especially on government services. If and when data on the real level of government services are revised and show that current estimates are downward biased, the share of producer services in national income will be smaller since these services are a residual. However, the actual impact on the size of producer services will depend on the size of the upward revision of the total service industry sector which will accompany the revision of the statistics on real government services.

4.2 Description of Trends

Figure 3 shows that the relative importance of the three types of services is the same in real and nominal terms. In 1991, producer services represent the largest share at 26 percent, consumer and government services are roughly the same at 20 percent of GDP. Between 1961 and 1988 the share of government services exceeded that of consumer services by a substantial margin, in some years as much as 4 points. While the consumer service share has been on a steady climb after 1973, the share of government services went into a strong decline between 1982 and 1988, from which it recovered slightly thereafter.

Figure 4 shows more clearly the rates of growth of the three components of the service sector. As can be seen, the producer services share grew 20 percent while those of the consumers and government services rose 13 and 3 percent, respectively.

Figure 4 also shows that the share of producer services fluctuated rather strongly around the growth trend. The relationship of these fluctuations to the cyclical changes in GDP will be examined econometrically in the next section.

The development of the consumer service share is dominated by the persistent, cumulative decline in the share by 10 percent between 1961 and 1973 and the subsequent strong and continuous growth. From 1973 on, the share of consumer services cumulatively rose more rapidly than that of producer services. Fluctuations around these trends are relatively minor.

The share of government services exhibits some major fluctuations, which appear during some periods to be negatively correlated to the fluctuations in producer services. However, the most dominant feature of the share of government services is the existence of 4 distinct, major trends. Between 1961 and 1965, the share fell 10 percent. It rose about 20 percent between 1965 and 1970, remained constant during the following 12 years, fell strongly by 13 percent between 1982 and 1987 and rose 5 percent thereafter.

Figure 3

Services as Share of GDP Canada, 1986 Prices

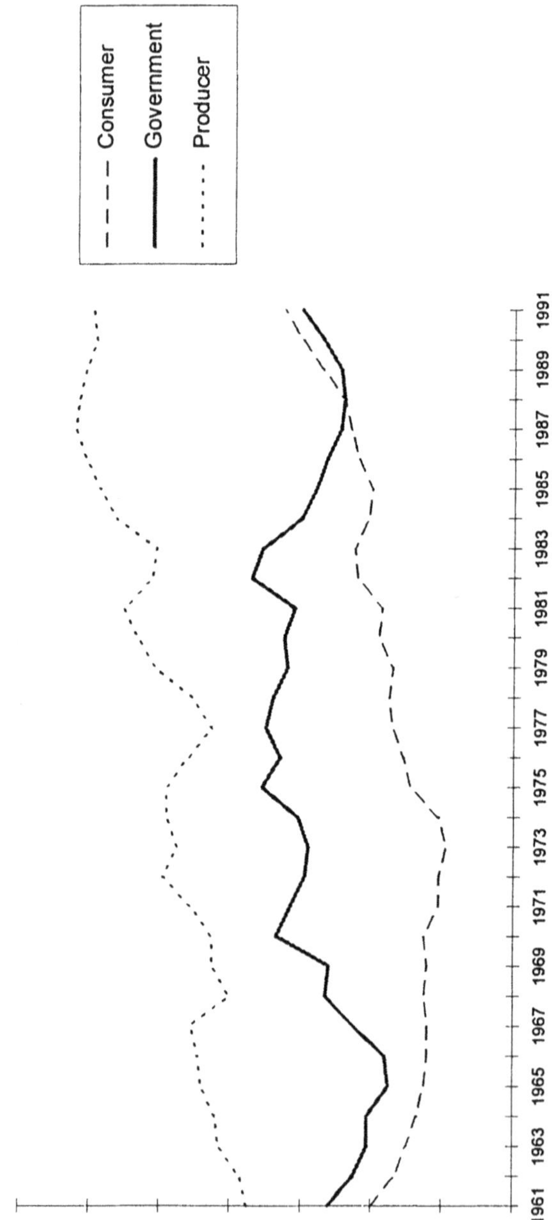

Source: Cansim Tape Matrices 4670 and 6840; see text for calculations

Figure 4

Growth of Share of Services Canada, 1986 Prices, 1961=100

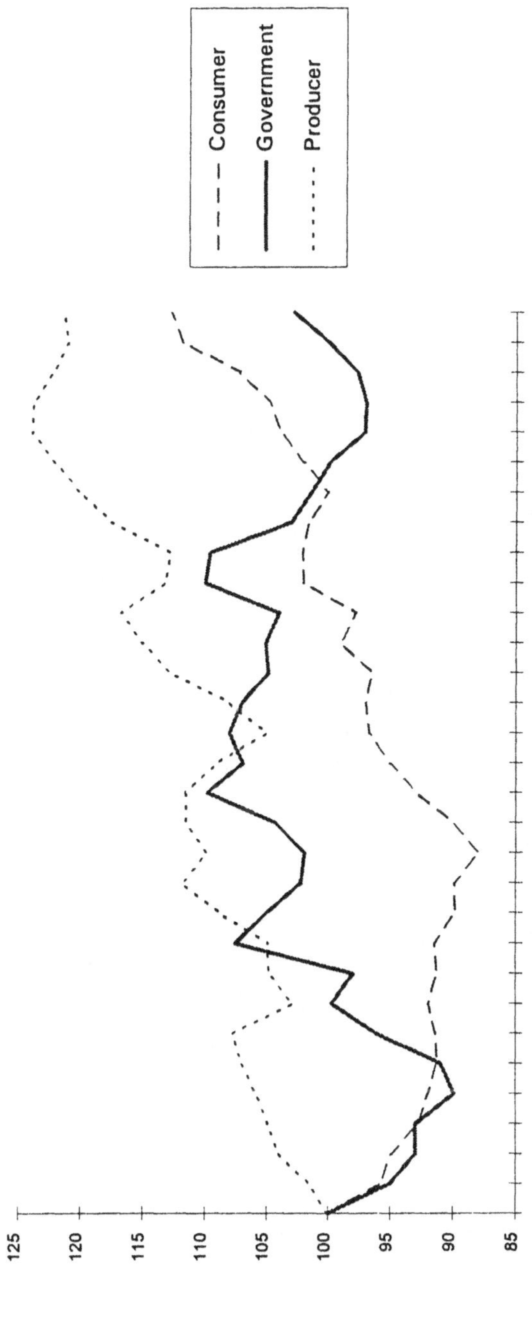

Source: Cansim Tape Matrices 4670 and 6840; see text for calculations

5. Correlation Analysis of Shares

To examine the influence of the different service sector on national income I estimated the following equation:

$$\begin{aligned} GDP = .001 + &.18\ Govt + .18\ Cons + .22\ Prod + .40\ Goods \\ &(38.5) \qquad (20.3) \qquad (48.5) \qquad (87.5) \end{aligned}$$

The variables are annual changes in real (1986) dollars covering the period 1961 to 1989: GDP = national income; Govt = government services; Cons = consumer services; Prod = producer services; Goods = goods producing sector. The r-squared is .99. The t-ratios are given in parenthesis. The Durbin-Watson statistic is 1.45.

The use of the GDP as the dependent variable can be justified on the grounds that the developments in the output of the four sectors determine aggregate output. The signs and size of the estimated coefficients on a priori grounds are as follows. The signs on consumer and producer services and goods sector should be positive since the value-added of these industries is the main autonomous determinant of GDP. The sign on the Government coefficient is indeterminate. It is negative under the assumption that these outlays are deliberately counter-cyclical. It is positive if the spending by government is determined by budgetary conditions, growing rapidly when booms create large tax revenues and growing more slowly during recessions and lower increases in tax revenues. The results of the estimation confirm my theoretical expectations for the goods producing, and consumer and producer service sectors. The signs are positive and the t-ratios are high and statistically significant. The results for the government service sector show that exhaustive government spending has been pro-cyclical. Presumably, the counter-cyclical spending has predominantly been through transfers to persons.

The elasticity between should be largest for annual changes in the dependent variable GDP and the independent variables goods sector and producer services. The reason for this expectation is that growth in goods production is known to be cyclically most variable. It therefore has the greatest influence on the annual changes in GDP. The producer service sector, on the other hand, depends heavily on the derived demand for producer services. The results of these calculations also support these a priori expectations. The elasticity at means is .34 for the goods and .26 for producer service sectors while it is .18 for government and .20 for consumer services. In other words, a onepercent change in spending on goods and producer services produces an 34 percent and 26 percent change in GDP, respectively. These effects on GDP are much larger than those produced by either the consumer or government services.

In sum, the regression analysis strengthens the findings of the analysis based on Figures 2-4 which showed that producer services represent the largest of the service producing sectors of the economy. Producer services have had the most rapid rate of real growth during the last 30 years. Annual changes in the real output of producer services are more highly correlated and have a higher elasticity with respect to changes in real GDP than changes in real consumer and government service output.

6. The Economics of the Consumer and Government Services

In this sector I present briefly an economic analysis of the facts about the development of the three service industry sectors presented above.

6.1 Consumer Services

The observed growth in the real demand for consumer services has been driven by three important factors. First, as a result of the growth in average incomes in Canada, the real demand for consumer services has risen. This is so mainly because a large proportion of these services have a relatively high income elasticity of demand, like for example restaurant, hotel, car-rental, travel, recreation and similar services. Historically, the consumption of these kinds of services has been a privilege of the rich whose average incomes have permitted a growing proportion of the population to enjoy them.

Second, the demand has been curtailed by the increase in the relative price of many consumer services. This increase in the relative price is due to the Baumol effect discussed above. The number of hourly wages of the average Canadian required to get a hair-cut or attend a live theatre performance has been on a rising trend.

Third, Canadian women in recent years have enjoyed increasing levels of education and have chosen to have fewer children later in their lives. As a result, the female labour force participation rate has risen considerably. With less time available for work in the household and more income available for the market purchase of the services no longer produced in the home, the demand curve for consumer services has been shifted upward. Canadian families increasingly eat their meals in restaurants, have their homes and laundry cleaned by commercial enterprises and send their children to private child-care facilities.

In a theoretical and econometric study of household behaviour Hammes, Rosa and Grubel (1989) and Hammes and Grubel (1992) have found strong support for the preceding arguments about the demand for consumer services. About 40 percent of this growth in demand is attributable to the shift of production from household into the market. This implies that if and when the rise in the female labour force participation rate slows or is reversed, the growth in the demand for consumer services will be decreased correspondingly. It is certain that this influence will have to become operative once the female labour force participation rate has reached 100 percent.

6.2 Government Services

The dramatic growth in the supply of government services in Canada between 1966 and the early 1970s was driven by left-leaning governments committed ideologically to increasing the role of the state in the provision of public goods and a comprehensive social security net requiring a substantial administrative staff. The high levels in the supply of real government services remained largely unchanged until the recession of 1982-83. During this period, rising income levels and automatically increases in government revenues made it possible to provide these services at unchanged levels and at the same time meet rising demands for transfer payments under the social security system.

The sharp drop in the share of GDP used in the provision of government services after 1982 has been due to fiscal problems of the government. On the one hand, transfer payments continued to increase. A rapidly growing debt required large interest payments. On the other hand, the growth of taxation revenue was limited to real growth as a result of the introduction during the late 1970s of taxation rates indexed to inflation. Increases in taxation rates were politically unacceptable.

As a result of these trends in outlays and revenues, the government initiated reductions in the growth of government services and privatized a number of crown corporations. These actions underlie the observed, substantial decrease of government services as a share of national income.

The decrease in the provision of these services is desirable to the extent that it is due to privatization and the normally accompanying increased productivity. It is undesirable to the extent that it is due to a decrease in the supply of public goods like public security, health, education, environmental protection and social overhead capital like roads and harbours. Decreases in the defence police forces, waiting lines for hospital admission and university enrolment and deteriorating roads and bridges are evidence of growing shortages in the provision of these public goods in Canada.

It is interesting to note that these spending cuts were accompanied by unrestrained continuing increases in transfer payments. These trends can readily be explained with the help of public choice theory. The benefits of public goods are widely dispersed and provide little incentive for the organization of interest groups lobbying for their maintenance. The number of workers involved in the production of these services is relatively small and their organizations have little political influence. Transfer payments, on the other hand, provide substantial benefits to individuals and correspondingly strong incentives for the formation of interest groups that lobby effectively for their preservation.

However, during 1993 Canada's fiscal deficits and government debt have become so large that reductions in transfer payments are all but unavoidable, at least after the election in the Fall of that year. Once the growth in these transfer payments is curtailed or reversed, the deficit can be eliminated and economic growth may eventually permit renewed increases in the supply of real government services.

7. The Economics of Producer Services

Producer services can be considered to lie along a spectrum, on one end of which we find retail, wholesale, janitorial, security and restaurant services. These services have been characterized by a relatively slow rate of technical change in their own production function. In addition, the characteristics of their output also has remained relatively unchanged. It therefore has contributed little to the increase in productivity of the goods and service producers using it as inputs.

At the other end of the spectrum we find industries like communication, computer and transportation services, which in recent years have enjoyed large increases in productivity due to the revolution in micro-electronics and aviation. In addition, the output of these industries has become technically more sophisticated and has become relatively less costly. As a result, more of these services were bought by the goods and other service producing industries and they enjoyed increased productivity.

In particular other producer service industries like finance, accounting, law, advertising, information generators and processors, tourism, shipping and courier services have increased productivity, lower relative prices and better and new types of services as a result of greater use of new and better communication, computer and transportation services. The increase in the productivity of these producer service industries has been raised also by deregulation and privatization, which were forced on governments because of the development of new services and increasing lack of relevance of traditional principles of regulation.

The result of these processes is evident from the data in Figures 3 and 4. The share of all producer services in nominal income has remained constant while their share in total output in real terms has increased.

7.1 Human and Knowledge Capital and Increased Roundaboutness

Of fundamental importance for the understanding of the role of producer services in the economy is the fact that the producer service industries with this high level of technical change use large quantities of human and knowledge capital. The role of these two forms of capital has been revealed first in Solow's (1957), now classic study. It has been reconfirmed in more recent studies by Jorgensen and Fraumeni (1987) and Mankiw et.al. (1992). The description above of the nature of the producer service industries, in particular the role they play in the application of modern electronics, makes it clear that these industries are the main vehicle through which the increasing levels of human and knowledge capital are introduced into the production of goods and consumer and government services.

Another interesting way of understanding the role of producer services involves the concept of the roundaboutness of production which is an integral part of the capital theory advanced by the Austrian school of economics. According to this theory, the deepening of capital through the availability of more capital per worker is inevitably accompanied by the growing specialization of production and layers of suppliers of inputs. Producer services have experienced such a process of increased specialization and their growth is itself a manifestation of growing roundaboutness.

For example, once a large company like General Motors might have been able to generate all needed legal services through a staff of company lawyers. Now, it is likely to buy in the market specialized services for which it has relatively little demand like, for instance, contract law of a Chinese province. Specialized services of this nature are in sufficient demand world-wide to keep their providers occupied. At the same time, it is likely that these specialized services reach General Motors through the intermediation of a less specialized firm of lawyers which regularly provides a wide range of other services to the car producer. In this example it is obvious how important for the delivery of the legal service are low costs of communication and travel.

The development of highly specialized producers of such human and knowledge capital intensive services is also encouraged by the rapid pace of technical change and the development of new services. Small firms have a comparative advantage in the adoption of new technologies. Typically they are not bureaucratized and unionized and therefore they have in comparison with large companies greater flexibility in the allocation and retraining of workers, levels of employment and compensation. As a result, the often large goods producers of the world find it more profitable to buy these services from small outside firms rather than produce them internally.

The falling costs of producer services has had an additional, important consequence. Small and medium-sized firms in the goods and service producing sectors have been induced for the first time to buy producer services like marketing, accounting, advertising, computing, financing and management consulting. These firms in turn have enjoyed corresponding increases in productivity.

7.2 Embodied Services

A final, noteworthy result of the growth of producer services in the economy is the increased share of services in the market price of goods. This phenomenon is especially pronounced in the case of electronic storage devices containing computer programs, music, films and information. These products are recorded statistically as the output of the goods producing sector. Yet it is clear that the share of the value of these products created by manufacturing is very small. The vast bulk of the value is made up of the embodied services of programmers, entertainers, intellectuals, wholesalers, retailers and many types of business services like finance, accounting, marketing and transportation.

Embodied services also account for very large proportions of goods other than those involving modern electronic storage devices. Books and other printed material always have had this characteristic. A wide range of goods is produced in automated factories where engineering, scientific and computing services represent a very large share of the total costs. For example, IBM produces the keyboards for all of its world-wide sales of computers in a factory in Tennessee which is almost fully automated and employs only a very small number of workers. Ley and Hutton (1987) found that in the early 1980s 75 percent of the exports of the province of British Columbia consist of primary products while 70 percent of all employment was in the service producing sector. Lee Iacocca (1985) reports that the Chrysler corporation now spends more per car on medical services for workers than on steel.

The concept of embodied services has some important implications for the interpretation of international trade in services. As noted above, some analysts have been concerned about the ability of a country to pay for needed imports as an increasing share of that country's resources is devoted to the production of services which, as a result of high transportation costs, cannot be traded. I have shown elsewhere (Grubel, 1987, 1989) that services embodied in goods traded internationally represent a multiple of trade in services defined conventionally. Services are in fact tradable after they have been embodied in goods. Countries will never run out of the ability to pay for the import of goods.

In sum, as a result of the accumulation of human and knowledge capital and the increased roundaboutness and specialization which it stimulates, the final value of goods, consumer and government services will contain increasing shares of producer services. Conceptually, this share of producer services in the value of final goods and services can approach 100 percent asymptotically. In such a state, goods production will take place in futuristic factories manned by very few workers. The large producer service industries of the world employing a large share of all workers will apply science and technology to ever more efficient robots run by computers.

8. Summary and Conclusions

The growth of the service sector in most countries of the world is seen by many analysts to be a development which leads to the prediction of slow economic growth, a loss of national export capacity and security and a host of other economic problems.

This study developed the taxonomy of consumer, government and producer services and manipulated published Canadian data to estimate the relative size and growth rates of these different types of service industries. The analysis of these data showed that in 1991 producer services represented 26 percent and consumer and government services represented an equal 20 percent of real GDP. Between 1961 and 1991 the growth of the share of producer, consumer and government services was 20, 13 and 3 percent, respectively. The relative importance of producer services was confirmed also by a regression analysis of the annual changes in the value-added of the three types of service industries and the goods producing sector.

A discussion of the determinants of the demand for consumer services showed the role played by the increase in the labour force participation rate of women and the implicit shift of production from the household into the formal sector.

The growth of government services was argued to have been relatively constant as a result of the growth in transfer payments under the social security system and the exhaustion of the country's taxation capacity. Public choice theory was used to explain this differential growth of transfer payments and the production of real government services.

The growth of producer services was attributed to the deepening of human and knowledge capital and the accompanying roundaboutness of the process of production. It does not require corrective government intervention and does not have any of the other alleged negative implications for economic growth, international trade and welfare. In fact it is evidence of a robust, growing economy.

The analysis has an important implication for economic development policies. Governments need to encourage producer services as well as goods producing industries if they wish to achieve an efficient use of scarce resources in the stimulation of economic growth and international trade. It is likely that in the achievement of these objectives in today's world after many years of almost exclusive focus on traditional industries, producer service industry subsidies have a higher social rate of return than subsidies to goods producing industries.

References

Baumol, William, (1967), "Macroeconomics of Unbalanced Growth", *American Economic Review*, 57, 415-26.

Baumol, William, (1987), "Productivity Policy and the Service Sector", *Fishman-Davidson Center for the Study of the Service Sector, Discussion Paper* no.1, April.

Bell, David, (1973), *The Coming of Post-Industrial Society: A Venture in Social Forecasting*, Basic Books, New York.

Blackaby, Frank, (1978), ed. *De-Industrialization*, Heinemann Educational Books, London.

Bluestone, Barry and Bennett Harrison, (1982), *The Deindustrialization of America*, Basic Books, New York.

Bluestone, Barry and Bennett Harrison, (1986), *The Great American Job Machine: The Proliferation of Low-Wage Employment in the US Economy*, Joint Economic Committee. Washington.

Browne, L.E., (1986), "Taking in Each Other's Laundry-The Service Economy", *The New England Economic Review*, July/August.

Gershuny, J.I. and I. Miles, (1983), *The New Service Economy: The Transformation of Employment in Industrial Societies*, Praeger Publishers, New York.

Ginzberg, E. and G.J. Votja, (1981), "The Service Sector of the U.S. Economy", *Scientific American.*

Gordon, Robert J., (1987), "The Postwar Evolution of Computer Prices", *NBER Working Paper no. 2227.*

Grubel, Herbert G., (1987), "All Traded Services are Embodied in Materials or People", *The World Economy*, 10, 3, September, 319-330.

Grubel, Herbert G., (1989), "Issues in Free Trade in Services Between Canada and the United States", *Economic Aspects of Regional Trading Arrangements*, David Greenaway, Tom Hyclak and Richard Thornton, (eds.), Harvester-Wheatsheaf, New York.

Grubel, Herbert G., and Michael Walker, (1989), *Service Industry Growth: Causes and Effects*, The Fraser Institute, Vancouver.

Grubel, Herbert G., and Michael Walker, (1991), "The Dominance of Producer Services in the US Economy", *Banca Nazionale del Lavoro Quarterly Review.*

Hammes, David, Jean-Jacques Rosa and Herbert Grubel, (1989), "The National Accounts, Household Service Consumption and its Monetization", *Kyklos.*

Hammes, David, Jean-Jacques Rosa and Herbert Grubel, (1992), "Home Production, Market Production and the Changing Allocation of Expenditures on Services", *The Service Industries Journal.*

Iacocca, Lee, (1985), *Iacocca: An Autobiography*, Bantam Books, Toronto.

Jorgenson, Dale and Fraumeni, Barbara, (1987), *The Accumulation of Human and Non-Human Capital 1948-84*, Harvard University, Cambridge.

Ley, D. and T. Hutton, (1987), "Vancouver's Corporate Complex and Producer Services Sector", *Regional Studies*, 21 (5), 413-22.

Mankiw, Gregory, David Romer and David Weil, (1992), "A Contribution to the Empirical Analysis of Economic Growth", *Quarterly Journal of Economics.*

Momigliano, Franco and Domenico Siniscalco, (1982), "The Growth of Service Employment: A Reappraisal", *Banca Nazionale del Lavoro Quarterly Review*, September, 269-306.

Ott, Mack, (1987), "The Growing share of Services in the U.S. Economy - Degeneration or Evolution?", *Federal Reserve Bank of St. Louis Review*, 69, 6, June-July, 5-22.

Riddle, Dorothy I., (1986), *Service-Led Growth: The Role of the Service Sector in World Development*, Praeger Special Studies, New York.

Solow, Robert, (1957), "Technical Change and the Aggregate Production Function", *Review of Economics and Statistics*, 39, 312-20.

Shelp, Ronald K., (1981), *Beyond Industrialization: The Ascendancy of the Global Service Economy*, Praeger Special Studies, New York.

Comment

Paolo Garonna
ISTAT - Rome

In commenting of this interesting paper, I will focus on the "tree", rather than on the specific "individual branches", because that is where the strength of the paper lies, i.e. in setting clearly into perspective the issues relative to producer services in the Canadian context, but also more broadly in the context of a developed industrial economy.

The issues can be analyzed under two main distinct but interconnected headings:

1. First, the interpretation of the role of services in general, and producer services in particular, in the growth of industrial economies.
2. Second, the implication of outstanding measurement and conceptual issues on the analysis of the service sector including there in the distinction between producers, consumers and government services.

On the first set of issues, I fully support the approach and the conclusions drawn by the Author. They appear persuasive and balanced. Besides they have prestigious and authoritative antecedents: as early as the 17th century, Sir William Petty referred to the relatively high standard of living of the Dutch in comparison with that of the French and the English to argue that "there is more profit to be made from industry than from agriculture, and much more to be made from commerce than from industry". The paper produces evidence that the nominal and real share of the Canadian service sector in GDP contradicts Baumol's hypothesis, showing that substantial productivity gains can be realized in the service sector. Cross sectional international comparisons confirm this finding. Italy therefore seems to have a special problem with its service sector, considering that in the 1970's the average differential in productivity increases between industry and service was 2,9% and that it climbed to 3,5% in the 1980's.

The growing importance of producers' services in terms of GDP share and high elasticity with respect to GDP, on which the paper dwells, is also well founded. It corresponds to similar developments in Italy: from 1982 to 1988 the share of producers services over total intermediate costs increased from 6,2% to 9%.

This process is certainly linked - as the Author argues - to the deepening of human capital, based on the immaterial factors of production, the growing knowledge intensity of production and to the increased integration and interdependence of production processes. On this, there is a growing literature in Italy dealing with vertical disintegration, "decentramento", the role of small and medium enterprises, subcontacting, new firms and business demography (creation and cessation of enterprises) (see Becattini, 1987, Brusco and Garonna, 1984).

A few issues however deserve a more careful consideration. I wish to point out two of them, which have recently attracted considerable policy attention.

First, it remains to be understood why in some countries (like the US and Japan), the service sector appears capable of absorbing existing unemployment and creating jobs; and why on the contrary in other countries this is not the case, or when it is, the process is seen as pathological, because it feeds dualism and the underground economy, creates an underclass of working poor, undermines skills and future performance, etc.

Second, in a diachronic perspective, it has to be explained why in all countries the service sector is becoming increasingly *less* capable of generating employment. The economic depression of the early 1990's has been particularly noticeable in signaling this worrying feature. Is it connected with increasing competition, and the resulting pressure on cost-competitiveness? or is it due to insufficient growth of demand?

A focus on the crucial link between services and employment could make the paper more comprehensive: this however would probably entail - I guess - a shift of emphasis from producers' to consumers' services. What is noteworthy in fact is not so much the considerable progress in producers' services, but rather the correspondingly remarkable lack of progress in consumers' services (Garonna, 1993). As Prof. Grubel rightly points out, significant developments have taken place on the supply side of the labour market, namely the aging of the labour force, the massive inflow of women into the employment structure, etc. Why then, those fundamental shifts in labour market behaviour have not produced, as we may have expected, a push in consumers' services, and a higher elasticity of demand for those services with respect to GDP?

On this issue, Grubel seems to suggest that the Baumol effect may be playing the decisive role as a constraining factor, while it is not taken to play any role for services as a whole.

The paper in fact makes reference to the classical Baumol cases, like hair-cuts or live theatre performance, and does not mention other more prominent, or advanced, consumers' services such as long-term care, children's care, business services to households. etc.

Further analytical work is required to shed some light on this aspect. What may be missing is an approach looking at cross.elasticities for consumers', producers' and business services, and more broadly at the interdependence between different kinds of services: governement services versus households services; producers' versus government service; even producers' versus consumers services, as it is implied by the increasing transfer of service production from the household or informal sector to the market.

The first set of interdependences is particularly relevant: the provision in fact of social services as public or quasi-public goods can become a source of large distortions. It drains considerable resources. It determines spurious redistributions, benefitting by-and-large the middle classes rather than those most in need. The institutional framework, such as the national systems for education, health insurance, etc. play an importance role in this context, and may account for improved performance or variations in performance.

Implications for policies can also be derived: government support for producers' services, in terms of incentives or subsidies, and the provision of services as public goods - as advocated by Prof. Grubel

- might have under certain conditions a dampening effect on demand rather stimulating the growth of the sector.
On a positive perspective, relying on a thorough understanding and a careful management of cross-elasticities and interdependence can open up promising directions for future research and policy action. In particular the inability of the current policy and institutional frameworks in the industrial economies to cater for the fundamental changes taking place in society and the economy may be hold responsible for the flatness of the consumers' services curve, or more broadly for the insufficient development of services. Social policy reform, therefore, if adequately designed and controlled, could provide a stimulus for the growth of a market for consumers' services. But this requires an "active" policy stand, some kind of "industrial policy for services" capable of supporting the necessary supply-side structuring and of substaining demand where needed.
Coming to the second set of issues raised by the paper, the interesting results obtained by Grubel are based on an analysis of data, which - as the Author acknowledges - present problems in relation to well known conceptual and measurement issues.
The definition of "services" itself is rather hazy and has led to controversy. Adam Smith's conventional definition: "Services perish in the very instant of their performance, they cannot be stockpiled nor incorporated into any other production", is based on the notion of lack of material existence. This definition has been largely responsible for the development of the classical distinction between "productive" and "unproductive" labour, on which a great deal of the present prejudice against service production is based. But other definitions, such as in Hill (1977), are difficult to operationalize!
The "proximity" and "relational" aspects of service production and service use may explain the downward bias in the measurement of output, and the upward bias in the measurement of inflation. These biases represent a real difficulty for all analyses of low productivity and high inflation in the tertiary.
The difficulty of seizing the quality of the service, and therefore to measure product innovation, and identify new products, determines a serious obstacle to distinguishing between production costs and con-

sumers' welfare, and to using productivity indicators (output per man-hour) as measure of efficiency and effectiveness.

I will draw two examples in order to illustrate the complexity of the issues involved and their relevance for the analysis of the data.

If - as Grubel clearly points out - changing social and institutional conditions determine a transfer of certain activities from household production to the market, the increase in consumers' services may be fictitious; it would in fact be essentially produced by the fact that current accounting conventions do not fully account for household production.

A second illustration may be derived from the double deflation procedure. In Italy we do not have production price statistics for the service sector; therefore we use consumer prices. This introduces a downward bias in the measurement of service output (and productivity). If Statistics Canada did a better job at deflating current price output, this might contribute to explain why quantity indicators in Canada increased more than value indicators (current sales); contrary to what happened in Italy and other countries.

Measurement and conceptual issues become of paramount importance and relevance in international comparisons, particularly considering the increasing trend of internationalization of trade in services. Statisticians at the international level are engaged in providing standards and define best methods for the production of comparable basic statistics. However much remains to be done in this field. On the whole, the production of service statistics in industrial countries does not match the growing relative importance of this sector. It amounts in fact on average only to 1/3 of total production of statistics.

We need more statistical work and more economic analysis of service statistics, including their conceptual and theoretical basis.

Neverthless measurement difficulties and lack of data cannot become a pretext for not trying to analyze the service sector or denying legitimacy to economic analysis.

Grubel's paper is a very good example of what should be done to make progress in this tricky and intriguing area. Economists need to get their hands dirty developing ad-hoc indicators, even if they may sometimes appear approximate or even faulty, and may be in some cases largely based on an article of faith - as Grubel himself at one point honestly confesses - rather than simply leave these questions to a footnote - as most economists do - and in the hands of official statisticians alone.

In all instances it pays to develop an awareness, and possibly also a sensitivity analysis, of the impact of statistical concepts and measurement on the economic analysis and interpretation of the service sector.

References

Becattini G., (1987), ed., *Mercato e Forze Locali: il Distretto Industriale*, Il Mulino, Bologna.

Brusco S. and Garonna P., (1984), "Segmentation du Marchè du Travail et Relations Sociales en Italie", in Greffe X. (ed.), *Les Petites et Moyennes Enterprises: Crèent Elles des Emplois*?, Economica, Paris.

Garonna P., (1993), "Choisir l'Emploi", in B. Bruhnes (ed.), *Choisir l'Emploi*, Groupe de Preparation du XI Plan, Commissariat General du Plan, Paris, La Documentation Francaise, January 1993, 1-182, JEL 820.

Hill P.T., (1977), "On Goods and Services", *Review of Income and Wealth*, December.

2

Externalities and the Linkages Between Trade Sector and Manufacturing

Ernesto Felli
University of Molise

Giovanni Tria
University of Rome "La Sapienza"

1. Introduction

The trade sector, as well as the other service sectors, plays a complex role in determining economic growth.

A full evaluation of this role requires highlighting output and productivity linkages across sectors. Actually, modern economies exhibit in a pervasive way positive and negative spillovers and positive and negative strategic complementarities, producing complicated interactions between different sectors of the economy that can't be described by an input-output matrix.

Working out our previous work in the field (Felli and Tria, 1986, Felli, 1992), this paper investigates a conceivable explanation of the linkages between the trade sector and the manufacturing sector. If, as hypothesized in theoretical models and verified in empirical researches, the manufacturing sector enjoys aggregate increasing returns, a possible source of this phenomenon can be a trading externality. In this case, the trade sector, whatever its technology or market structure is, provides the transmission mechanism through which spillovers and externalities operate. The kind of effect we have in mind is the so-called "thick market externality" (Diamond, 1982). When many sellers crowd the market, when many customers visit the shops, the probability of a fast and successful match between agents increases making convenient an increase of manufacturing output. This formulation raises some conceptual difficulties that we try to minimize in the first part of the paper, but provides a sort of *reduced form* of these cross-sector linkages, useful to identify the possible alternative explanations. One alternative hypothesis which is often advocated in the literature is that of Marshallian externalities coming from intermediate goods linkages which hinge either on the greater specialization (Romer, 1986), or on the input-output transmission of the technological progress (Rosemberg, 1982). Of course, it is not necessary that the two effects - trading externalities and intermediate goods linkages - are alternative. Nothing prevents them from being present (absent) simultaneously; but it is important that they can be insulated. The econometric model which we present here makes this identification possible. Actually, the approach we have followed allows us to detect three kinds of interactions: inside a single branch (*internal returns to scale*), between the individual branch and all other branches of the same sector (*sectoral economies of scale*), and between each branch of any sector and the trade sector (*trading externalities*). Moreover, the estimation model is based on a specification that allows us to insulate the long run relationships from the short run dynamics that tend to be superimposed on these by cyclical variations.

This feature distinguishes our methodology from that adopted for instance by Caballero and Lyons (1991). To the aim of identifying and measuring external economies, Caballero and Lyons follow the Hall's approach inspired to the classical work of Solow (1957) and based on estimates of the rates of growth of output and total factor productivity.

Our estimates were performed for the manufacturing branches of a six country sample (France, Germany, Italy, Japan, UK, USA), using the sectoral data banks of OECD and Eurostat.

The remainder of the paper is arranged as follows. We develop in the second section the theoretical concern with the aid of a simple formal model in which the role of externalities is assessed. Section 3 describes the data sample features. In section 4 we outline the dynamic specification of the model. Because this postulates a cointegrated relation to estimate, we present the evidence in support of this hypothesis. Estimation and results are presented in the subsequent sections. The usual sections dedicated to conclusions and references end the paper.

2. A Model of Externalities

The idea that externalities play a crucial role in determining increasing returns is as old as Marshall, at least. More recently, it received new emphasis in growth literature, industrial organization studies and new Keynesian macroeconomics that pointed out spillovers and strategic complementarities across sectors as sources of multiple equilibria.

Taxonomy ranges from positive externalities in R&D, to the "learning by others" phenomena working through channels as labour mobility or inverse engineering, to network externalities analyzed in the recent works of Farrell and Saloner (1986) and Katz and Shapiro (1985), to participation externalities (Chatterjee, 1987), to trading externalities highlighted by Diamond.

In general the role of external economies and diseconomies linking manufacturing and trade sector has been little investigated.

The current debate focuses mainly on pecuniary externalities working through the input-output matrix: an increase (decrease) of trading service cost shifts upward (downward) the cost curve of producing goods firms, entering the cost function both directly as intermediate good or indirectly affecting the level of final consumer prices and the nominal wages. The result of this is a fall (an increase) of firms' equilibrium output and a change in marginal and average productivity depending on the technology underlying the production function. From this point of view, the price of trading service, determining trading mark-up, is important. For this reason research focused on dynamics of productivity and market power affecting this price.

Our paper, instead, investigates whether or not an increase of trading sector activity generates external economies or diseconomies for the manufacturing firms, producing as a result a positive (negative) correlation between manufacturing and trading output. The kind of externalities we consider is basically the trading externalities, *à la* Diamond, arising from the specific role played by the trading sector.
In modern economies where firms produce for exchange, seeking trading partners requires a specific activity that, as the productive one, absorbs real resources and obtains uncertain results. Defining costs faced by the firms for the trading process as "transaction costs", we can imagine, following Diamond, that the probability of finding a trading partner depends on the number of agents seeking to trade and on the amount of resources firms dedicate to this aim. Diamond's intuition is that, if the probability of finding a trading partner is an increasing function of the number of the agents seeking to trade, also the expected payoff to each firm from producing will be an increasing function of the number of the potential traders and this will induce each firm to increase production.
As Cooper and John (1988) pointed out, the externality of Diamond's model can be interpreted both as participation externality or, alternatively, as a complementarity in production or demand. This because a thick market can be viewed as a factor reducing transaction costs, for a given demand curve, or as a shift parameter for the firm's demand curve, for a given level of transaction costs.
Analyzing intersectoral effects of an increase in the trade sector output, we can imagine that manufacturing industries will benefit by a trading externality.
The existence of a trade sector implies that its trading technology is more efficient than the technology available for a single manufacturing firm. Therefore, a growing wholesale and retailing sector makes the market thicker and more efficient for the individual firm producing goods because it can meet a greater number of customers for given transaction costs. The externality arises when the market fails to fully evaluate this positive effect on the payoff of manufacturing firms.
We can view this externality, as above pointed out, alternatively as a production or demand externality. We prefer the latter interpretation

because it clarifies the difference from Marshallian externalities, that in this paper explain the positive correlation between output of each manufacturing branch and aggregate manufacturing output.
The workings of externalities whose existence we attempt to estimate in this paper can be shown by means of a simple model describing the static equilibrium of a firm of a manufacturing branch facing the inverse demand curve:

$$P_i(Q_i,Q_r) \qquad (1.1)$$

with $P_1 < 0$ and $P_2 > 0$

where P_i and Q_i are respectively the i-th firm's price and output and Q_r is the output of trading sector. The condition $P_1 < 0$ implies a downward sloping demand curve and condition $P_2 > 0$ the existence of a trading externality.
Because we assume a firm subject to external marshallian economies, the cost function can be written as

$$C = C\,(Q_i,Q_m,\tau) \qquad (1.2)$$

with $C_1 > 0$, $C_{11} > R''$ and $C_{12} < 0$,

where R'' is the second derivative of total revenue P_iQ_i, Q_m is the aggregate manufacturing sector output, and τ is a fixed transaction cost. The transaction cost appears this way in the cost function because trading externalities are considered on the demand side.
Condition $C_{12} < 0$, assuming a negative correlation between firm's marginal cost and manufacturing industry aggregate output, captures the strategic complementarity due to Marshallian external economies.

Taking Q_r and Q_m as given, the firm decides output that maximizes profit

$$Q_iP_i(Q_i;Q_r)\text{-}C(Q_i;Q_m)\text{-}\tau.$$

Usual first order condition for a maximum is

$$P_i(Q_i;Q_r)[1-1/\eta\,(.)] - C_1(Q_i;Q_m) = 0 \tag{1.3}$$

where η is the price elasticity of demand.

Considering equation (1.3) as an implicit function $G(\ )$, we find that the equilibrium value of Q_i positively depends on Q_r and Q_m, because

$$\frac{dQ_i}{dQ_r} = -\frac{G_{Q_r}}{G_{Q_i}} > 0 \tag{1.4}$$

$$\frac{dQ_i}{dQ_m} = -\frac{G_{Q_m}}{G_{Q_i}} > 0 \tag{1.5}$$

Derivative (1.4) is positive if $d\eta/dQ_r > 0$ and if second order condition for profit maximization holds. Also derivative (1.5) is positive because we assumed $C_{12}<0$.

Intersectoral linkages we wanted to highlight can be described through (1.3). An increase in trading sector production shifts upward the demand curve for the individual firm and this implies, given the marginal production cost curve, an increase in equilibrium output. Economies external to the firm but internal to the manufacturing industry are captured by the positive correlation between individual inputs productivity and aggregate industry output: when the aggregate output increases, marginal production costs of the individual firm decrease and this induces the firm to produce more.

3. Data Sample

Empirical analysis is based on an international sample including six countries: Italy (I), France (F), United Kingdom (UK), Germany (G), Unites States (USA) and Japan (J). Annual data for European countries come from Cronos-Sec2, the sectoral data-bank of

Eurostat. Data for Japan and USA are from International Sectoral Data Bank of OECD. The two sources, though not perfectly homogeneous, provide necessary data for the following variables: value added at current and constant prices, employment, capital stock, and employed workers' compensations. The available observations of this set are of the desirable length only for three countries - USA, Germany and Italy. For the last two countries, sample spans from 1960 to 1991; for the United States the covered period stops at 1987. For all other countries sample spans from 1970 to 1991 (1987 for Japan). Moreover, there are other minor limitations and inconsistency. For instance, in the case of Italy, necessary data do not cover the whole period for all thirteen branches of manufacturing sector (030 code in the Cronos classification): missing observations are relative to the following branches of Cronos nomenclature (the corresponding Nace-Clio codes are reported in parenthesis): 080 (19), 090 (21), 100 (23), 110 (25), 150 (47), 160 (49), 170 (48). We circumvented these obstacles, using the aggregate 640 of the first three branches, for whom data were available in the necessary length and disregarding the other branches, for whom also aggregate information before 1980 was absent. Because of this limitation, samples used for the other countries have been normalized in respect to Italy, even though, where possible, separate estimates for above mentioned branches have been performed.

4. Dynamic Specification and Cointegration

It seems difficult to formulate and estimate a dynamic structural model that fits the intersectoral linkages at level of outputs and is able to capture those externalities (spillovers and strategic complementarities), which, as seen in the first part of the paper, represent the reduced form of the complex interrelationships linking the single sectors. On the contrary, at a first look a VAR representation might seem more viable. For our sample, a spatial vector autoregressive model (SVARM) could have the following form:

$$Q_t = \begin{bmatrix} Q_{it} \\ \vdots \\ Q_{nt} \end{bmatrix} = A_0 + A_1 Q_t + A_2 Q_{t-1} + \cdots + A_p Q_{t-p} + \varepsilon_t \qquad (2.1)$$

where $\mathbf{Q_t} = (\mathbf{Q_{it}})$ is the stacked vector of outputs in the period t, $\mathbf{A_0}$ is a *nx1* of intercept terms, $\mathbf{A_1},\ldots,\mathbf{Ap}$ are *nxn* matrices of coefficients, with $\mathbf{A_1}$ measuring the instantaneous effect of externalities and thus having zeros along its diagonal, while other matrices incorporate their dynamics along diagonals and the lagged effects of externalities in the off-diagonal elements. ε_t is a *nx1* vector of disturbances subject to the usual assumptions. The strength and at the same time the weakness of this specification are represented by its generality. This specification is the most general possible since it allows that interactions operate between each sector and all others in a single country and between all other sectors in all other countries. Thus, even omitting some *interior* (i.e. domestic) linkages and suppressing in that way some r.h.s variables and choosing an (arbitrarily) small maximum lag (for instance $p < 3$), the parameters to be estimated would remain still too many. Thus, without appropriate parameters' restrictions, such a model could not be estimated even using a very large sample and this is not our case. Consequently, as first simplification we decided to neglect the *inter* countries' interactions, limiting our analysis to *intra*countries' linkages. Second, in the spirit of the first part we restricted the externality between sectors of a single country to that possibly linking the manufacturing sector and the other sectors. Third, we concentrated our analysis of externalities inside a sector of a single country to those of the manufacturing branches.

However a formulation like (2.1) presents other problems. If on the right side are present only lagged endogenous variables and if the r.h.s. variables are the same in each equation, *LS* provide consistent and efficient estimators. Nevertheless, this formulation does not allow to the separation of the possible *internal* scale economies (diseconomies) from externalities. This produces the risk that estimators could be biased in a direction determined by the form of internal returns to scale. To circumvent this problem we need a term in (2.1) that grasps the specific individual technology. However, because this term, whatever it is, could hardly be considered exogenous, and given the probable correlation between **Q's** and this term, estimating such a relation would require instrumental variables technique.

As shown in a different context by Caballero and Lyons (1990) an instrument exists that permits matching these questions. This instrumental variable, which we denote as X, for the i-th branch is given by:

$$X_i \equiv s_{ri} L_i + (1 - s_{ri}) K_i \tag{2.2}$$

where s_r = labour share on revenue basis = wL/PQ. w is per capita compensations of employed workers, L is total employment, K is capital stock at constant prices and P is output price. This variable was constructed for all the branches of sample using the value added as a proxy of output. This approach is reminiscent of the famous work of Solow (1957) and of the extensions made by Hall (1988)[1].

Substituting the **Q's** of the right side of (2.1) with this variable, for the i-th equation of the model we obtain:

$$Q_{it} = a_0 + \sum_{k=1}^{p} a_{1k} X_{i,t-k} + \sum_{k=1}^{p} a_{2,ik} \sum_{i=1}^{n} X^M_{i,t-k} + \sum_{k=1}^{p} a_{3,ik} \sum_{i=1}^{n} X^T_{i,t-k} + \varepsilon_{i,t} \tag{2.3}$$

where X^M and X^T grasp the interactions between the i-th branch and the other branches of the same sector and all other branches outside

1 Such a procedure is based on the neoclassical production function and assumes perfect competition and constant returns to scale. Decreasing marginal products determine factors' prices and equilibrium is where price equals real wage. Thus, implicitly (2.2) assumes that marginal cost is measured by market price (i.e. equilibrium price) of output that is an observable variable. A more attractive alternative is represented by the labour share on *cost* basis, where $s_c = (wL)/[wL+(r + d - \Delta p_k)p_k K]$. To compute user cost of capital, the price of new capital goods is needed. Attempts we made using the implicit price of fixed capital stock have produced discouraging results.

the sector, respectively. In other words, as we have seen in the first part, the former variable represents technological externalities and the latter trading externalities. Based on the restrictions we have introduced, X^M represents the interactions inside manufacturing sector and thus the summation is over all manufacturing branches. In the case of X^T, we want only to grasp the possible spill-over of the trade sector (the trading externality of bulk distribution and retailing) and thus the summation vanishes because no other non-manufacturing sector is considered.

As a final step, we have to model the dynamics of equation (2.3). To this aim we find the cointegration approach suggested by Engle and Granger (1987) a natural candidate. In the externalities we are discussing short and long run factors operate simultaneously making it difficult to distinguish between forces that are conceptually separable; thus the cointegration approach, allowing us to isolate long run externalities from those originating in the cycle, deserves our choice.

Of course, we have preliminarily to prove that a cointegrated relation to estimate exists for the variables of our model. Because a cointegrated relation is a stationary linear combination of processes that possess a unit root (i.e. are integrated of same order), we tested the presence of unit roots for the natural logarithms of $\boldsymbol{Q}$ and $\boldsymbol{X}$ variables[2].

The evidence in favor of this hypothesis is based on a LS estimation of an AR(1) model for each of 132 series of the sample and on the usual test statistics. Tables 1 through 6 report regression results together with those of the Augmented Dickey-Fuller Test.

The coefficient for q of the autoregressive process exhibits a mean of .889 (with a maximum value of 1.050 and a minimum value of .619); for x the mean is equal to .909 (the maximum value is 1.093, the minimum .630). As shown in the Tables relative to the six countries, the AR(1) coefficient is always highly significant. Based

---

[2] Using low-case letters to denote natural logarithms, for the variable X we have (suppressing indexes for ease of space): $x = s\,l + (1 - s)\,k$.

Because, for the presence of s, logarithmic transformation is not scale-invariant, we have first calculated first differences of s using a mean of the two adjacent years and then we have generated levels taking the initial year as basis.

on the results of the Augmented Dickey Fuller Test, null hypothesis is rejected only for some values of x, especially for the case of France and, on a very minor extent, of Italy. Never does rejection pertain to the aggregate manufacturing sector or the trade sector.
Clearly the sample narrowness casts a shadow over the robustness of these results. Though not pursued in this paper due to time constraints, an extension of the sample pooling time series and cross section data could significantly increase available information allowing to obtain more accurate estimates. Particularly, cointegration tests could be performed to produce more precise results than those very disappointing that we obtained using our short period sample. We feel that the approach of *random fields* as outlined by Quah (1990) can serve well to this aim[3].

5. Estimation

Based on the previous evidence that our variables are well characterized as first order integrated processes, we specified equation (2.3) following the method recently proposed by Phillips and Loretan (1991). Their procedure consists of estimating a non linear univariate version of the single equation error correction model (SEECM) of Hendry[4].
The equation to be estimated as cointegrated relation expresses output level of the i-th manufacturing branch as a function of level, of current and lagged rate of growth, and of leads of the inputs - weighted by labour share - belonging to the same branch, to the aggregate manufacturing sector and to the trade sector.

---

3 For a sample very similar to ours, Neusser (1993) uses the random field approach and obtains results supporting the hypothesis of a unit root.

4 See Hendry and Richard (1982) and Hendry (1987).

The equation is:

$$q_i = \alpha_i + \beta_i x_t^M + \delta_i x_t^T + \gamma_i x_{it} + \lambda_{1i}(q_{t-1} - \alpha_i - \beta_i x_{t-1}^M - \chi_i x_{t-1}^T - \gamma_i x_{t-1}) +$$
$$+ \mu_{11i}\Delta x_t^M + \mu_{12i}\Delta x_t^M + \mu_{13i}\Delta x_{it} + \mu_{21i}\Delta x_{t+1}^M + \mu_{22i}\Delta x_{t+1}^T + \mu_{23i}\Delta x_{it+1} +$$
$$+ \lambda_{2i}(q_{it-2} - \alpha_1 - \beta_i x_{it-2}^M - \chi_i x_{it-2}^T - \gamma_i x_{it-2}) + \mu_{31i}\Delta x_{t-1}^M + \mu_{32i}\Delta x_{t-1}^T +$$
$$+ \mu_{33i}\Delta x_{it-1} + \varepsilon_{it} \tag{2.4}$$

In respect to the Hendry model, the modifications introduced by Phillips and Loretan - a non linear specification augmented by leads and lags in the differences of regressors - make equation (2.4) fully efficient and asymptotically unbiased and let the hypotheses on the parameters valuable in the usual way. These properties come from, in the first place, the non linear specification of parameters. In other words, long run elasticities β, δ and γ enter the model in a non linear form through the explicit use of lagged equilibria between variables. Secondly, the inclusion of leads takes into account the fact that variables are not strictly exogenous specially when one looks at the complete system. And lastly, short-run dynamics relative to Δq e Δx are modeled separately from the cointegrated relation and including a lagged error correction mechanism apart from the lagged terms of difference variables. This allows, from one side, a more parsimonious representation than the inclusion of autoregressive terms (for their coefficients have not to decade with increasing lags) and, from the other side, to isolate the cyclical fluctuations (which may cause variations in the capacity utilization) from long run equilibrium over which they are ineffective.

Our specification insulates three long run parameters: γ represents the returns to scale internal to the i-th manufacturing branch, β the economies (diseconomies) of scale external to the branch but internal to the manufacturing sector, and δ the trading externalities (positive or negative) that (possibly) spill from trade over manufacturing. For the case of constant internal returns to scale γ = 1, and the model can be reformulated in terms of total factor productivity (*TFP*): $q_i - x_i = TFP$. In this case, the parameters to estimate are reduced. Clearly, in a world of generalized convex technology, the complete model could be reformulated in terms of *TFP*. However, we find it difficult to fit this vision to the analysis of the previous sections. Our attempt is mainly devoted to discover possible different effects and links, separating externalities from increasing returns. If we impose a priori the restriction $\gamma = 1$, the other elasticities and above all the β coefficient might result biased (upward or downward according to whether returns to scale are increasing or decreasing and not constant).

Beyond these long run elasticities, the model provides estimates for the short run effects through the μ's coefficients.

The specification in levels that characterizes this approach brings the potential risk of overfitting (e.g. a downward bias in the estimated residual sum of squares). Thus, interpretation of the usual statistics requires care.

One can estimate equation (2.4) singularly for each manufacturing branch of each country of our sample using LS. We used the more efficient technique of iterative seemingly unrelated equations (SURE - I), estimating simultaneously all the equations for each country. This procedure allows us to increase the degree of freedom and to take into account the cross-equations correlations of the disturbances.

In any case, the model as it is requires estimating a number of parameters that is still too large in respect to the sample wideness (especially for some countries); then we considered a more restricted version of the equation (2.4). In practice we suppressed the last four terms: the lagged error correction mechanism and the lagged differences.

Though generally not rejected by usual tests performed (*Wald Test* and *Likelihood Ratio Test*), these restrictions might invalidate the method we used. As a partial justification we checked that the restricted model did not appreciably modify the relevant parameters obtained estimating the single equations of the unrestricted model.

6. Results

The results obtained are summarized for each country by the estimated aggregate unrestricted equation that is reported in Table 7 and by SURE-I estimates reported in Table 8. Before commenting on these results, we want to stress that they are very tentative and still incomplete.

In interpreting these estimates, it is useful to remember that in the non restricted model relative to each manufacturing aggregate one estimator vanishes (the parameter for the external returns to scale) reducing by four the number of estimating parameters, but of course an important loss of information emerges. Thus, in the subsequent discussion we mainly refer to the single manufacturing branches estimates (Table 8).

In respect to the long-run relationships we may draw the following conclusions:

- with the remarkable exception of France, a sound evidence emerges supporting a *positive* trading externality (the δ parameter). Its influence varies from country to country - it is stronger in Germany, UK and Italy and weaker in Japan and US - and from branch to branch in the manufacturing sector, but it seems to be a dominant feature of the linkages here analyzed. We interpret this kind of linkage as proof that an important portion of the manufacturing productivity increase is due to a (positive) spill over which trade sector "transfers" to the manufacturing activities. Of course one can not exclude that this sort of relationship goes in both the directions and thus the existence of important feedbacks cannot be discarded. After doing reverse regressions in order to check for these possible feedbacks, we found that the effect going from the manufacturing sector to the trade sector is present but is weaker than that going in the reverse direction. Formal causality tests performed confirmed this result.
- The fact that in the long run such a mechanism was in effect is confirmed, in our view, by the inspection of the results relative to the other model parameters, β and γ. Either the evidence for internal economies, which seems to confine their importance to some branches of some countries (France and Japan especially), or that for sectoral economies, is more controversial. Surely, as pointed out in the theoretical and empirical literature in the field, the interactions operating inside manufacturing are very intricate,

due to the multiplicity of the sources and channels of transmission. This might be the cause of the quite implausible negative sign sometimes assumed by the coefficient γ. It seems to us, however, that another explanation of these results is possible and is that, in accordance with the findings of Caballero and Lyons, internal increasing returns play a minor role and probably have been over evaluated.

- Coming to the short-run dynamics, separately modeled by these long-run relations, the results we obtained outline a complex picture. This kind of interactions is generally not instantaneous as one may expect. Probably a specific analysis devoted only to study the short-run dynamics might provide more precise information.

A methodological remark to conclude this section. We see either the growth oriented externality *a là* Romer, or the trading externality *a là* Diamond as *long run* phenomena that are shaded by dynamics originating in business cycles. If the latter is not insulated and one estimates contemporaneous relations, and which happens even if one uses rates of growth or differences of logarithms, all that one is examining is "short run" because this approach does not permit to obtain a long run solution. In this case it is meaningless to speak about short run and long run externalities as instead do for instance Caballero, Lyons and Bartelsman (1991).

7. Conclusions

To evaluate the role played by service sectors in economic growth it is crucial to investigate how strongly and through which channels they affect the growth rate of output and productivity of the other productive sectors.

More specifically, the purpose of this paper was to verify a general intuition about the existence of external economies or diseconomies linking the performances of the manufacturing firms to the growth of the trade sector. The hypothesis we explored was that the manufacturing firms benefit from trading externalities arising from the growth of the trade sector activity and that these externalities could explain part of their productivity dynamics.

Accordingly, an econometric model has been estimated which makes possible to disentangle the effects of the trading externalities on output of a given manufacturing branch from internal economies of scale and from economies that are external to the branch but internal to the manufacturing sector.

Our results based on a sample of six countries (Italy, Germany, France, United Kingdom, United States and Japan) confirm, to a large extent, the hypothesis that the trade sector generates a positive externality of which the manufacturing firms benefit and show that this effect is far from negligible. The evidence is particularly significative in the case of Italy.

References

Bartelsman E., Caballero R., Lyons R., (1991), "Short and Long Run Externalities", NBER Working Paper no.3810.

Caballero R., Lyons R., (1990), "Internal vs. External Economies in European Industry", *European Economic Review*, 34, 805-26.

Chatterjee S., (1987), "Coordination Failures in a Competitive Model", University of Iowa, mimeo.

Cooper R., John A., (1988), "Coordinating Coordination Failures in Keynesian Models", *Quarterly Journal of Economics*, 103, 441-63.

Diamond P., (1982), "Aggregate-Demand Management in Search Equilibrium", *Journal of Political Economy*, 90, 881-94.

Engle R., Granger C., (1987), "Cointegration and Error Correction: Representation, Estimation, and Testing", *Econometrica*, 55, 251-76.

Farrell J., Saloner G., (1986), "Installed Base and Compatibility: Innovation, Product Preannouncement and Predation", *American Economic Review*, 76, 940-55.

Felli E., (1992), "Consumers, Producers, and Traders", Università del Molise, mimeo.

Felli E., Tria G., (1986), "Optimal Price and Quality Policies under Economies of Scale", in Pellegrini L. and Reddy S.K. (eds.), *Distributive Trades: An International Perspective*, F.Angeli, Milano.

Hall R., (1988), "The Relation between Price and Marginal Cost in U.S. Industry", *Journal of Political Economy*, 96, 921-47.

Hendry D., (1987), "Econometric Methodology: A Personal Perspective", in Bewley T. (ed.), *Advances in Econometrics*, vol. 2, Cambridge University Press, Cambridge.

Hendry D., Richard J., (1982), "On the Formulation of Empirical Models in Dynamic Econometrics", *Journal of Econometrics*, 20, 3-33.

Katz M., Shapiro C., (1985), "Network Externalities, Competition, and Compatibility", *American Economic Review*, 75, 424-40.

Neusser K., (1993), "Dynamics of Total Factor Productivities", *Revue Économique*.

Phillips P., Loretan M., (1991), "Estimating Long-Run Economic Equilibria", *Review of Economic Studies*, 58, 407-36.

Romer P., (1986), "Increasing Returns, Specialization, and External Economies: Growth as Described by Allyn Young", Rochester Center for Economic Research, WP no.64.

Rosemberg N., (1982), *Inside the Black Box: Technology and Economics*, Cambridge University Press, New York.

Solow R., (1957), "Technical Change and the Aggregate Production Function", *Review of Economic and Statistics*, 39, 312-20.

Table 1 Unit root tests for *q* and *x*. Italy
Equation: $z = b + c\, z_{t-1} + u_t$

Branch	c		T-statistic		Augmented Dickey-Fuller Test	
	q	x	q	x	q	x
03	.954	.858	60.8	21.4	-2.4539	-6.9161
05	.788	.845	11.9	19.7	-2.4539	-4.7848
06	.938	.789	36.7	22.3	-2.6109	-7.2455
07	.973	.857	109.7	17.2	-2.3731	-4.9941
64	.966	.899	50.1	20.4	-1.3627	-2.1454
12	.890	.886	23.3	22.0	-2.5793	-3.0831
13	.935	.802	60.3	17.5	-4.1373	-15.8889
14	.942	.633	56.9	10.7	-2.9453	-2.7190
20	.964	.993	72.5	45.7	-2.3650	-0.7925
22	.947	.985	57.25	34.7	-2.6757	-1.8023
MacKinnon Critical Values: 1%			-3.6661; 5%		-2.9627; 10%	-

Table 2 Unit root tests for *q* and *x*. Germany
Equation: $z = b + c\, z_{t-1} + u_t$

Branch	c		T-statistic		Augmented Dickey-Fuller Test	
	q	x	q	x	q	x
03	.934	.861	34.6	23.5	-2.2766	-2.8572
05	.837	1.007	12.2	21.1	-2.0468	0.6832
06	.876	.829	17.6	17.3	-2.3544	-2.6201
07	.934	.899	36.6	51.7	-2.7831	-4.7220
64	.944	.899	30.1	18.9	-1.4123	-1.3495
08	.904	.804	14.6	7.3	-1.3713	-1.2885
09	.859	.859	15.5	15.7	-2.0374	-1.6525
10	.953	.926	41.9	43.3	-1.9766	-1.3618
11	.965	.919	50.7	23.1	-1.5446	-0.7925
12	.948	.947	37.6	44.9	-2.1265	-2.2186
13	.834	.872	17.4	68.3	-3.4582	-9.0543
14	.992	1.028	17.3	55.7	-0.0348	0.2628
15	.949	.967	29.0	20.9	-1.6864	-0.5714
16	.941	.933	35.8	37.9	-2.4757	-2.3561
17	.859	.900	16.3	13.0	-2.5217	-1.5678
22	.947	.985	57.25	34.7	-2.6757	-1.8023
MacKinnon Critical Values: 1%: -3.6661; 5%: -2.9627; 10%: -2.6200						

Table 3 Unit root tests for *q* and *x*. USA
Equation: $z = b + c\, z_{t-1} + u_t$.

Branch	c		T-statistic		Augmented Dickey-Fuller Test	
	q	x	q	x	q	x
03	.945	.926	22.1	21.5	-1.6792	-2.3053
06	.858	.849	11.1	10.9	-2.1245	-2.3423
65	.961	.913	21.5	18.4	-1.2412	-2.2885
61	.953	.951	33.2	51.6	-1.7619	-3.2328
13	.950	.994	28.5	46.6	-1.7249	-0.7709
14	.912	.947	29.7	9.9	-2.4144	-0.5958
15	.947	1.000	25.5	45.7	-1.5391	-0.1184
56	.822	.977	6.7	11.9	-1.5268	-0.3684
17	.855	.866	9.5	12.2	-1.7057	-2.3515
22	.985	1.022	39.3	108.6	-1.2489	1.8297-
MacKinnon Critical Values: 1%			-3.7076; 5%		-2.9798; 10%	-2.6290

Table 4 Unit root tests for *q* and *x*. UK
Equation: $z = b + c\, z_{t-1} + u_t$.

Branch	c		T-statistic		Augmented Dickey-Fuller Test	
	q	x	q	x	q	x
03	.910	.944	6.2	14.7	-0.6430	-0.9078
05	.692	1.001	4.5	27.4	-.1538	0.2516
06	.799	.877	5.7	10.1	-1.3274	-1.4194
07	.932	.832	10.6	6.7	-0.8341	-1.2127
64	.893	.936	6.0	13.6	-0.7086	-0.9582
08	.845	.969	8.2	17.2	-1.2956	-0.6268
09	.869	.929	8.6	13.3	-1.0880	-0.9143
10	1.049	.843	24.8	5.2	1.0457	-0.8363
11	.936	.871	11.0	8.4	-0.8885	-1.2729
12	.895	.975	7.8	27.6	-0.9347	-0.7129
13	.915	.868	13.0	18.3	-1.4466	-2.6024
14	.893	.973	8.0	22.4	-1.0545	-0.6445
15	.972	.826	6.4	5.9	0-.2319	-0.9509
16	.943	.897	9.4	7.7	-0.6521	-0.8743
17	.845	.918	6.6	9.0	-1.1871	-0.7917
22	1.04	1.023	13.5	13.3	0.7769	-0.2140
MacKinnon Critical Values: 1%			-3.8304; 5%		-3.0294; 10%	-2.6552

Table 5 Unit root tests for *q* and *x*. France
Equation: $z = b + c\, z_{t-1} + u_t$.

Branch	c		T-statistic		Augmented Dickey-Fuller Test	
	q	x	q	x	q	x
03	.858	.938	15.0	10.3	-1.9204	-2.3744
05	.706	.767	4.0	36.8	-1.7852	-10.6499
06	.619	.847	4.4	40.6	-2.8136	-6.1743
07	.955	.920	19.8	34.7	-7.5080	-1.4673
64	.886	.928	19.5	73.5	-2.0380	-4.5892
08	.705	.905	4.7	44.1	-1.7322	-3.4362
09	.659	.858	5.7	46.4	-2.9394	-6.7465
10	.922	.953	26.8	61.6	-2.0672	-2.2191
11	.919	.946	37.5	198.9	-2.8593	-9.9517
12	.698	.985	7.7	42.1	-2.7603	-0.2008
13	.858	.919	11.7	27.0	-1.4074	-9.4727
14	1.06	.983	12.3	383	0.6129	-1.0789
15	.965	1.093	10.8	37.1	-0.1838	3.6933
16	.813	.898	8.0	19.6	-1.7627	-0.7866
17	.680	.916	8.7	81.0	-2.7272	-7.6819
22	.898	9.231	30.6	34.6	-2.0729	-74933
MacKinnon Critical Values: 1% -3.8067; 5% -3.0199; 10% -2.6502						

Table 6 Unit root tests for *q* and *x*. Japan
Equation: $z = b + c\, z_{t-1} + u_t$.

Branch	c		T-statistic		Augmented Dickey-Fuller Test	
	q	x	q	x	q	x
03	.949	.882	36.0	40.0	-1.3189	-4.2293
06	.704	.737	9.4	10.2	-3.1560	-3.6661
65	.969	.977	33.7	20.3	-0.6630	-0.1332
61	.902	.867	18.2	15.1	-1.6331	-2.1830
13	.801	.970	10.6	24.8	-2.5422	-0.2041
14	.794	1.010	9.5	16.3	-2.3727	-0.2989
15	.867	.911	19.2	14.8	-2.0786	-1.4627
56	.816	.787	12.6	32.0	-2.8760	-6.0288
17	.944	.781	19.3	10.9	-0.4186	-2.7567
22	.920	.925	41.3	47.3	-2.9339	-10.169
MacKinnon Critical Values: 1% -3.8067; 5% -3.0199; 10% -2.6502						

Table 7 SEECM ESTIMATES. Aggregate Equation

Italy

$$q^M = -10.809 + 1.096x_t^M + 1.245x_t^T + .413(Nlecm)_{t-1} + 1.110Dx_t^M - .780Dx_t^T +$$

(11.8) (1.736) (.194) (.103) (.229) (.601) (.492)

$$+ 1.052Dx_{t+1}^M + .347Dx_{t+1}^T + .104(Nlecm)_{t-2} - 1.111Dx_{t-1}^M - .742Dx_{t-1}^T$$

(.441) (.500) (.181) (.572) (.476)

N°Obs=29; R2 Adjusted=.996; S.E:R:=.025490; D.W.=2.237; F=744.2809,

where $Nlecm = q^M - \alpha - \beta x^M - \delta x^T - \gamma x^M$.
Mean value for the dependent variable is shown in parenthesis; standard errors in parentheses.

Germany

$$q^M = -3.445 + .010x_t^M + 1.616x_t^T + .473(Nlecm)_{t-1} + 1.185Dx_t^M - 1.470Dx_t^T +$$

(13.0) (1.654) (.312) (.203) (.087) (.375) (.411)

$$+ .464Dx_{t+1}^M - .042Dx_{t+1}^T + .016(Nlecm)_{t-2} + .116Dx_{t-1}^M - .141Dx_{t-1}^T$$

(.324) (.439) (.047) (.110) (.148)

N°Obs=29; R2 Adjusted=.984; S.E:R:=.025844; F=744.2721,

USA

$$q^M = .803 + .466x_t^M + .665x_t^T + .796(Nlecm)_{t-1} + .621Dx_t^M + .663Dx_t^T +$$

(13.1) (1.993) (.254) (.115) (.078) (.287) (.470)

$$+ .040Dx_{t+1}^M + .887Dx_{t+1}^T - .101(Nlecm)_{t-2} - .028Dx_{t-1}^M - .518Dx_{t-1}^T$$

(.185) (.402) (.046) (.070) (.149)

N° Obs.=26;Adjusted R^2 =.992; S.E.R.=.019429; D.W:=1.688; F=314.3533

France

$$q^M = -50.459 + 10.677x_t^M - 4.749x_t^T + .397(Nlecm)_{t-1} + 6.462Dx_t^M + .050Dx_t^T +$$

(13.8) (10.293) (1.759) (.837) (.165) (2.851) (3.002)

$$+ 3.614Dx_{t+1}^M - 7.819Dx_{t+1}^T - 0.105(Nlecm)_{t-2} - 10.112Dx_{t-1}^M + 2.013Dx_{t-1}^T$$

(1.638) (2.298) (.080) (2.291) (1.689)

N° Obs.=19; Adjusted R^2 = .980; S.E.R.= .010721; D.W.=2.188; F= 91.010721

where $Nlecm = q^M - \alpha - \beta x^M - \delta x^T - \gamma x^M$.
Mean value for the dependent variable is shown in parenthesis; standard errors in parentheses.

UK

$$q^M = -4.166 + .640x_t^M + 1.011x_t^T + .653(Nlecm)_{t-1} + .148Dx_t^M - .383Dx_t^T +$$

(11.3) (9.084) (.408) (.573) (.372) (.644) (.625)

$$+ 1.137Dx_{t+1}^M + .672Dx_{t+1}^T - .197(Nlecm)_{t-2} - .213Dx_{t-1}^M + .471Dx_{t-1}^T$$

(.354) (.343) (.312) (.435) (.458)

N° Obs.= 18; Adjusted R^2 =.906; S.E.R.=.022756;D.W.=1.610;F=17.44655.

Japan

$$q^M = -8.916 + 1.383x_t^M + .635x_t^T + .412(Nlecm)_{t-1} + 1.491Dx_t^M - 1.703Dx_t^T +$$

(17.9) (1.677) (.228) (.244) (.250) (.478) (.439)

$$+ 1.086Dx_{t+1}^M - .037Dx_{t+1}^T - .058(Nlecm)_{t-2} - .310Dx_{t-1}^M + .297Dx_{t-1}^T$$

(.310) (.515) (.117) (.497) (.789)

N° Obs.= 18; Adjusted R^2 = .997; S.E.R.=.018293; D.W.=1.896; F.=518.8744.

Table 8 SUR - Iterative Estimates: Italy

Branch	α	β	δ	γ	λ	μ_{11}	μ_{12}	μ_{13}	μ_{21}	μ_{22}	μ_{23}	Ser
05	15.496	1.367	-1.447	-.851	.642	-.173	.203	-.461	1.831	-1.700	-3.138	.05566
	(1.4)	(.6)	(-2.3)	(-.8)	(6.8)	(-.1)	(.2)	(-.5)	(1.8)	(-1.7)	(-4.0)	
06	-25.801	1.552	1.144	1.040	.749	-.817	-.657	-1.191	2.509	.375	.799	.04872
	(-4.5)	(1.9)	(4.5)	(.9)	(7.3)	(-.8)	(-1.0)	(-1.2)	(3.8)	(.5)	(2.2)	
07	-25.311	1.224	2.984	-.760	.389	-1.558	-2.331	.399	3.523	.353	-1.215	.02101
	(-11.7)	(3.1)	(68.3)	(-3.2)	(5.4)	(-3.3)	(-8.1)	(1.2)	(8.6)	(1.0)	(-6.1)	
64	-35.276	.820	1.776	5.021	.563	1.446	.003	-5.144	1.902	-.243	-1.655	.04579
	(-8.3)	(2.2)	(13.8)	(3.6)	(8.7)	(2.3)	(0.0)	(-3.7)	(3.0)	(-.3)	(-1.7)	
12	-16.802	2.242	1.228	-1.140	.537	-1.496	-1.540	1.736	1.410	2.135	.331	.06624
	(-1.6)	(1.4)	(4.5)	(-1.4)	(3.4)	(-1.0)	(-1.3)	(2.1)	(1.0)	(1.3)	(0.6)	
13	-11.544	.917	.948	.334	.174	.090	-.862	.482	.681	.625	.270	.02631
	(-8.5)	(5.5)	(23.1)	(2.2)	(1.2)	(.2)	(-2.1)	(1.1)	(1.6)	(1.5)	(.6)	
14	-11.726	1.391	1.158	-.399	.630	.037	-.052	.045	1.824	1.124	-.442	.02383
	(-3.3)	(8.0)	(10.2)	(-1.0)	(6.4)	(.1)	(-.1)	(.1)	(5.3)	(2.7)	(-2.8)	

Table 9 SUR - Iterative Estimates: Germany

Branch	α	β	δ	γ	λ	μ_{11}	μ_{12}	μ_{13}	μ_{21}	μ_{22}	μ_{23}	Ser
05	.653	-2.194	2.586	.770	.337	1.419	0.001	-.889	1.182	-1.649	1.045	.03294
	(.2)	(-1.6)	(2.7)	(3.1)	(2.0)	(1.4)	(0.0)	(-2.2)	(1.5)	(-1.9)	(2.9)	
06	-3.870	-1.013	1.572	1.098	.183	.812	-.832	-.897	-.742	1.733	2.402	.02789
	(-1.6)	(-1.2)	(3.4)	(3.5)	(.8)	(1.0)	(-1.2)	(-1.2)	(-1.0)	(1.9)	(4.4)	
07	-6.546	-2.485	2.783	1.783	.102	2.908	-2.113	-.420	.509	-.027	-.587	.06228
	(-2.1)	(-5.0)	(6.0)	(3.8)	(1.0)	(3.2)	(-1.7)	(-.9)	(0.6)	(-.0)	(-1.1)	
64	-3.130	-1.010	1.804	.842	.426	1.422	-1.554	.202	-.316	.198	.345	.02552
	(-2.1)	(-3.2)	(9.9)	(4.2)	(5.2)	(2.9)	(-3.8)	(.7)	(-.8)	(.4)	(1.8)	
12	-3.815	-1.319	2.033	1.005	.118	.329	-1.183	1.029	-1.885	.855	.885	.04795
	(-2.0)	(-3.1)	(4.9)	(9.6)	(1.2)	(.5)	(-1.5)	(5.3)	(-2.9)	(1.1)	(4.1)	
13	-.095	-.736	1.809	.194	.696	.530	-1.057	-.078	.454	-.266	-.951	.02554
	(-.0)	(-.3)	(.7)	(1.1)	(4.0)	(.2)	(-.5)	(-.1)	(.8)	(-.3)	(-.8)	
14	-4.007	-.258	1.056	.801	.248	-.002	-.446	.652	-.665	.471	.741	.02201
	(-3.3)	(-.5)	(2.5)	(10.5)	(2.1)	(-.0)	(-1.1)	(3.2)	(-1.8)	(1.0)	(4.1)	
15	-3.278	-.484	1.620	.302	.424	1.673	-1.778	-.254	1.020	.157	-.107	.02727
	(-1.7)	(-1.1)	(3.5)	(1.4)	(3.4)	(3.4)	(-3.6)	(-1.4)	(2.5)	(.3)	(-.7)	

Table 10 SUR - Iterative Estimates: USA

Branch	α	β	δ	γ	λ	μ_{11}	μ_{12}	μ_{13}	μ_{21}	μ_{22}	μ_{23}	Ser
06	4.302	-1.404	.727	1.691	.596	.849	-.100	.203	-.816	1.145	.650	.02637
	(1.9)	(-2.5)	(4.6)	(3.9)	(6.7)	(1.5)	(-.1)	(.4)	(-2.5)	(1.6)	(3.0)	
61	-6.001	.674	.592	.343	.451	-.894	.630	1.402	1.081	1.153	-1.362	.03386
	(-2.0)	(1.2)	(3.3)	(.8)	(3.8)	(-1.5)	(.8)	(1.9)	(1.8)	(1.6)	(-2.0)	
65	10.068	-2.973	.975	2.477	.525	2.796	.817	-1.271	.157	1.140	-.017	.01800
	(6.7)	(-8.6)	(13.8)	(10.5)	(12.1)	(6.8)	(1.9)	(-5.0)	(.6)	(2.9)	(-.1)	
13	6.070	1.164	.633	-1.579	.344	.196	-1.250	-1.490	.359	.690	-.900	.03256
	(1.1)	(3.6)	(2.8)	(-1.3)	(3.1)	(.5)	(-1.5)	(-1.4)	(1.0)	(1.0)	(-1.0)	
14	-6.593	1.867	-.036	-.396	.485	-.378	-1.285	.589	1.064	1.188	-.568	.02774
	(-4.5)	(4.3)	(-.2)	(-1.4)	(3.8)	(-.7)	(-1.9)	(2.0)	(2.6)	(1.9)	(-2.2)	

Table 11 SUR - Iterative Estimates: UK

Branch	α	β	δ	γ	λ	μ_{11}	μ_{12}	μ_{13}	μ_{21}	μ_{22}	μ_{23}	Ser
05	-7.956	2.930	-.946	-.716	-.277	-.135	-.601	.646	1.115	-.268	.556	.04987
	(-2.4)	(10.7)	(-3.4)	(-8.6)	(-2.1).	(-.2)	(-1.4)	(3.7)	(2.0)	(-.5)	(3.0)	
07	-9.829	-.073	2.055	.122	-.148	1.276	-.646	-.642	-1.040	1.403	2.808	.02355
	(-3.9)	(-.4)	(9.6)	(.6)	(-1.3)	(3.0)	(-2.0)	(-1.1)	(-2.4)	(6.1)	(5.8)	
08	7.179	.305	-.444	.310	.380	-.326	1.311	.379	.526	.511	.750	.03044
	(.4)	(.1)	(-.7)	(.2)	(1.9)	(-.1)	(2.2)	(.3)	(.4)	(1.1)	(1.0)	
09	-14.350	5.491	-.151	-3.871	.549	-4.107	.419	3.486	.800	.213	-.648	.03942
	(-.8)	(1.5)	(-.1)	(-1.2)	(2.0)	(-1.2)	(.4)	(1.3)	(.9)	(.4)	(-.9)	
10	-14.717	-2.509	3.953	1.973	.450	2.701	-2.131	-.676	-.256	2.631	.130	.04970
	(-.6)	(2.3)	(4.1)	(.7)	(1.3)	(1.4)	(-1.6)	(-.5)	(-.3)	(3.6)	(.1)	
11	20.741	-4.077	-.019	3.998	.746	3.249	.726	-2.734	-.427	.197	.943	.02924
	(.3)	(-.5)	(.0)	(.6)	(1.7)	(.5)	(.2)	(-.4)	(-.3)	(.5)	(1.0)	
12	23.041	-.464	-1.012	-.017	.698	-.542	1.961	1.494	-1.252	.283	1.058	.03650
	(.3)	(-0)	(-.4)	(-0)	(1.5)	(-.1)	(.9)	(.4)	(-.6)	(.4)	(.8)	
15	-9.597	.065	.718	1.604	-.346	-.027	.210	1.295	-.241	.525	1.906	.01469
	(-6.2)	(.7)	(5.9)	(10.5)	(-1.6)	(-.1)	(.8)	(2.2)	(-.7)	(2.2)	(5.8)	

Table 12 SUR - Iterative Estimates: Japan

Branch	α	β	δ	γ	λ	μ_{11}	μ_{12}	μ_{13}	μ_{21}	μ_{22}	μ_{23}	Ser
06	.420	-2.106	-1.595	5.775	.625	6.780	-2.682	-5.736	3.180	1.512	.411	.05580
	(.1)	(-.6)	(-.5)	(.7)	(1.5)	(1.3)	(-1.7)	(-.7)	(1.1)	(.8)	(.6)	
65	-25.963	1.097	1.596	.683	.213	2.551	-3.027	.712	2.317	.224	-.798	.02160
	(-11.7)	(2.4)	(8.8)	(2.5)	(8.6)	(8.2)	(-6.8)	(6.0)	(7.1)	(.4)	(-5.2)	
13	9.441	.132	1.338	-.860	-1.889	1.518	-5.319	-2.519	-2.193	-4.624	-2.033	.01366
	(3.6)	(.4)	(3.9)	(-4.7)	(-8.8)	(1.1)	(-1.5)	(-7.3)	(-1.4)	(-1.3)	(-7.2)	.016798

Legend:

Estimated equation is (2.4) of the text, with the following restrictions imposed: $\lambda_2 = \mu_{31} = \mu_{32} = \mu_{33} = 0$.

T statistics in parenthesis.

05 = Ferrous and non ferrous ores and metals, other than radioactive (Nace-clio 13);

06 = Non-metallic minerals and mineral products (Nace-Clio 15); 07 = Chemical products (Nace-Clio 17);

64 = 08+09+10+11= Metal products, except machinery and transport equipment,agricultural and industrial machinery,office and data processing machines, precision and optical instruments, electrical goods (Nace-Clio 19+21+23+25);

12 = Transport equipment (Nace-Clio 28);13 = Food,beverages, tobacco (Nace-Clio 36);

14 = Textiles and clothing,leather and footwear (Nace-Clio 42); 15 = Paper and printing products (Nace-Clio 47)

61=07+16= Chemical products, Rubber and plastic products (Nace-Clio 17+49)

65=64+12 (Nace-Clio 19+21+23+25+28).

3

Industrial Prices, Service Prices and Unemployment in Italy and Germany

Paola Manzini
University of Rome "Tor Vergata"

Massimo Tivegna
University of Rome "Tor Vergata"

1. Introduction

After a phase of inflation control from 1980 to 1987 prices started rising again in Italy during the period 1990-91. Although far from the values of early eighties -in terms of both dynamics and differential with respect to the other countries adhering to the Exchange Rate Mechanism (ERM) agreement. In spite of the fact that it has not yet manifested all its effects in terms of consumer prices, inflation in Italy is still a major source of concern, especially following the devaluation of the Lira in 1992 and because of the consequences that higher inflation rates can breed in terms of domestic interest rates and budget deficit.

The pick-up of inflation in Italy in the early nineties has been ascribed to short term factors and, more important, to structural elements, such as the inefficiency of the service sector and the North-South differences in the labour market (De Nardis-Micossi, 1991, Barca-Visco, 1991, Bodo-Sestito, 1989). On the other hand, structural explanations to inflation in Italy date back to the seventies with the debate over "productive" and "rent" sectors (see for instance Guiso, 1985 and Visco, 1990).

The acceleration of inflation in Italy until the end of last year and its "anomalous" slowing down after the devaluation of the exchange rate matches with an increase in unemployment. All this describes a situation of recession that is common to all the major European economies, where high unemployment rates go together with a slow down of prices and economic activity.

In this paper we will examine the role of the service sector as an amplifier of inflationary pushes of various origin, looking at aggregate variables and with a focus on the Italian situation in a European framework. Besides this inflation magnifying feature, it might well be that the service sector plays an important role in absorbing unemployment, even more than its capacity would allow to, because of its being a sheltered sector, at least if compared to the manufacturing sector.

The purpose of our analysis is to test the above hypotheses on the service sector as an inflationary shocks amplifier and employment stabilizer, with reference to the Italian and German economies.

It is well known (see for example Barca-Visco, 1991, page 44) that higher inflation (due to inefficiency or protectionism) of consumer prices with respect to producer prices determines in a static framework higher costs for the manufacturing sector and for the other productive sectors in the economy, while dynamically it constitutes a powerful propagating mechanism of inflation originated elsewhere.

The comparison between the Italian case and other European economies is self explanatory. Table 1 reports average values of changes in industrial and consumer prices together with the prices of imported inputs and of inputs from the manufacturing to the service sector and viceversa. By looking at these data it is possible to detect the mechanism through which inflationary impulses are transmitted to the economic system.

During the seventies industrial prices rose more than consumer prices (Table 1, first and second row) due to the continues shocks from foreign prices-exchange ratios, in 1973-75, and devaluation of the Lira, 1976-79 (third row), while from the beginning of the eighties consumer prices grew more than industrial prices.

The same pattern applies to input prices from manufacturing to services, in the seventies, and from services to manufacturing in the eighties (lines four and five).

From Table 2 it is clear that the comparison with industrial and consumer prices in Germany is unfavourable to Italy. Besides 1973-75 and 1980-82 - with high increases of imported inputs prices - where industrial prices tend to grow more rapidly than industrial prices, in all other periods consumer prices' dynamics is stronger than for industrial prices in other countries as well, although less than what experienced in Italy.

The comparison between consumer and industrial prices (represented by manufacturing and service sector deflators) shows that unlike other countries, where periods of high growth of industrial prices alternate with periods of higher growth of consumer prices, in Italy consumer prices have always been above industrial prices, especially in the eighties.

Empirical evidence shows that the service sector contributed everywhere -Italy, Germany, France and United Kingdom - in absorbing unemployment, analogously to what happened outside Europe, i.e. in the US. This has affected, however, productivity in the service sector (proxied by real value added per worker), affecting France and the United Kingdom before Italy.

On the other hand, in Germany labour productivity has always been higher in the service sector than in the manufacturing sector, especially in the last few years.

All the above leads to investigating how inflation propagates to the sectors in the economy in response to input price shocks and how this affects employment at the industry and national level.

In this paper we focus on Italy and on one of its major trade partners, Germany, which also plays an important role in the ERM. The exchange rate agreement prescribes the convergence - at least in the medium run - of member countries inflation rates to a common level, which is an even more important objective after the devaluation of the Lira, which dropped out ERM.

Table 1 % variations of input and output prices in the manufacturing and service sectors in Italy

	72I-72IV	73-75	76-79	80-82	83-85	86-87	88-91IV	72-91III
Increase in industrial prices	5.0	16.9	16.1	16.3	9.0	2.4	3.7	10.9
Increase in consumer prices	5.8	15.7	15.1	18.5	11.6	5.3	6.0	12.0
Increase in industrial imported input prices	2.4	24.8	15.9	17.4	8.6	-3.9	2.8	11.2
Increase in the price of inputs from services to manufact.	7.9	15.3	12.5	18.2	12.2	5.3	7.0	11.7
Increase in the price of inputs from manufact. to services	3.6	19.6	15.0	15.7	8.9	3.4	3.9	11.0

SOURCE: Banca d'Italia

Table 2 % variation of consumer prices, industrial prices and of imported input prices in Italy, Germany and the United Kingdom

	71-72[1]	73-75	76-79	80-82	83-85	86-87	88-91[2]	71-91[3]
ITALY:								
Increase in ind. prices	5.8	15.7	15.1	18.5	11.6	5.3	6.0	12.0
Increase in cons. prices	5.0	16.9	16.1	16.3	9.0	2.4	3.7	10.9
Increase in imported input prices	2.4	24.8	15.9	17.4	8.6	-3.9	2.8	11.2
GERMANY								
Increase in ind. prices	5.4	6.3	3.8	5.7	2.6	0.1	2.5	3.9
Increase in con. prices	2.4	9.8	3.0	7.3	2.5	-3.1	1.7	3.6
Increase in imported input prices	-2.1	19.6	3.9	14.6	2.0	-14.3	1.2	4.6
UNITED KINGDOM:								
Increase in ind. prices	8.3	16.4	13.6	12.7	5.2	3.8	7.0	10.0
Increase in con. prices	7.1	20.3	13.8	10.4	5.7	4.1	5.3	9.9
Increase in imported input prices	4.1	39.8	13.8	5.8	5.5	-1.1	1.9	10.6

(1) For Italy 1972I-1972IV. (2) For Italy 1988I-1991III. (3) For Italy 1972I-1991III.

SOURCE: Italy: ISTAT for the consumer price index, Banca d'Italia for other prices;
Germany and the United Kingdom: OECD, "Main Economic Indicators".

In this paper we study the effects produced by various shocks to the relative dynamics of industrial and consumer prices by means of small quarterly aggregate econometric models (estimated over the period 1970-1991) of a two sector system (manufacturing and service sector) in which we consider the prices-wages-unemployment links for Germany and Italy.
Due to both structural differences and availability of data, the two models are different, although similar, for the two countries. For the case of Germany the data base was built on a combination of domestic and international sources; for the Italian model we used national account statistics and the series produced by Banca d'Italia (see Rubino, 1991) of output prices for the manufacturing sector and of input prices of imported goods and goods produced domestically in the manufacturing and service sectors.
Because of a greater availability of data the model for Italy is a bit more detailed than the one for Germany, although it shares the same common structure.
In the following section we introduce a two sector (manufacturing-service) model that works as a theoretical framework for our empirical analysis. In section three we briefly describe the econometric techniques used and the estimates obtained; in section four we show the results of some simulation experiments. Concluding remarks and the main findings of this exercise are reported in section five.

2. The Theoretical Model

We consider a simple two sector model of the economy (see Gordon, 1987), and assume that in both sectors the level of wages and employment are determined as the outcome of a bargaining between unions and firms.
The two sectors differ in market structure; we assume that one is perfectly competitive, while in the other sector firms are price setters. Therefore we could use this framework to describe the relationship between the manufacturing sector, exposed to challenges by foreign firms, and the service sector, whose firms are sheltered with respect to international competition, and can therefore enjoy a negatively sloped

demand schedule; however they cannot avoid domestic competition, so that extra-normal profits will vanish in the long run.
Output y_i produced in one sector is used as an input from the other one, so that a link arises between production prices in the two compartments of the economy. Moreover, in both sectors firms use an imported input, whose price is exogenously determined (i.e. energy inputs, etc.). Each firm will want to maximize its profits

$$\Pi_i = p_i \cdot y_i - L_i \cdot w_i - p_j \cdot IN_i - p_3 \cdot IN_{i3} \quad \text{with} \quad i, j = 1,2 \tag{1}$$

with

$$y_i = f_i(L_i, IN_{ij}, IN_{i3}) \quad , \quad \text{i=1,2} \quad \text{with} \begin{cases} f'_{iL_i} \rangle 0 \\ f'_{iIN_{ij}} \rangle 0 \\ f'_{iIN_{i3}} \rangle 0 \end{cases} \tag{2}$$

In (2)' all first derivative are positive. p_i is the price of output produced in sector i and used as an input in sector j; w_i and L_i are wages and employment in sector i, while IN_{i3} is the level of foreign inputs that firms in sector i require at price p_3.
Unions will maximize their payoff from reaching an agreement with employers; therefore if we let U_i be the utility of the union in sector i from agreeing and U_{i0} the fallback position in case of disagreement, the payoff to union in sector i is going to be:

$$U_i - U_{i0} = w_i L_i + \overline{w}(\overline{L}_i - L_i) - \overline{w}_i \overline{L}_i \tag{3}$$

where $\overline{L_i}$ is union membership and w is unemployment benefits.
Equilibrium wages and employment will be determined by maximizing the Nash product:

$$\begin{aligned} MAX\Omega &= \Pi^{1/2}(U_i\_U_{i0})^{1/2} = L_i, w_i \\ &= [p_i f(L_i, IN_i) - w_i L_i - p_j IN_i]^{1/2}[(w_i - \overline{w})L_i]^{1/2} \end{aligned} \tag{4}$$

If we let subscript 1 indicate the perfectly competitive sector (where firms are price taker) and subscript 2 the "sheltered sector" (where firms are price setters) then first order condition yield for sector 1:

$$\frac{\partial \Omega_1}{\partial L_1} = (p_1 f'_{1L} - w_1)L_1 + [p_1 y_1 - w_1 L_1 - p_2 IN_{12} - p_3 IN_{13}] = 0 \quad (5)$$

$$\frac{\partial \Omega_1}{\partial L_1} = p_1 y_1 - w_1 L_1 - p_2 IN_{12} - p_3 IN_{13} - L_1(w_1 - \overline{w}) = 0 \quad (6)$$

In order to completely characterize sector 1 we can just add the price rule that imposes perfect competition on foreign markets and the demand function for output produced by sector 1:

$$p_1 = p_3 \quad (7)$$

$$y_1 = g_1(p_1) \quad g'_1 \rangle 0 \quad (8)$$

Analogously, for sector two first order condition for the maximization of the Nash product together with the demand function and price schedule yield:

$$\frac{\partial \Omega_2}{\partial L_2} = (p_2 f'_{2L} - w_2)L_2 + [p_2 y_2 - w_2 L_2 - p_1 IN_{21} - p_3 IN_{23}] = 0 \quad (9)$$

$$\frac{\partial \Omega_2}{\partial L_2} = p_2 y_2 - w_2 L_2 - p_1 IN_{21} - p_3 IN_{23} - L_2(w_2 - \overline{w}) = 0 \quad (10)$$

$$p_2 = p(p_1, p_3, p_{w_2}) \qquad p'_{2p_1} \rangle 0, \mathrm{p}'_{2\mathrm{p}_3} > 0, p'_{2w_2} > 0 \quad (11)$$

$$y_2 = g_2(\mathrm{p}_2) \qquad \mathrm{g}'_2 > 0 \quad (12)$$

It is therefore possible to use the above framework to work out the effects on prices, wages, output and employment of an exogenous shock to foreign input prices. All the considered variables change in the same direction as the administered shock, although the magnitude of the reaction of a given variable varies across sectors. Comparative statics details are reported in the appendix; however we can summarize the results of an increase in foreign input prices as follows:

- **employment:** it increases more in the sheltered sector as long as either of the two following conditions is satisfied:
  a) output prices in the sheltered sector are more elastic to own prices than to foreign prices;
  b) output price in the sheltered sector is higher than in the competitive sector;
  c) productivity is higher in the sheltered sector than in the competitive sector.
- **prices:** service sector prices will grow higher than manufacturing prices only if the price level in the service sector is already high. If we match this result with the one above it is possible to explain the stylized facts observed for Germany and Italy (higher productivity and lower prices in the service sector for the German case when compared to Italy: therefore this explains why in Italy the service sector works as an amplifier of inflationary shocks and as an employment absorber).
- **wages:** they will be higher in the sheltered sector when compared to the competitive sector the higher is output price elasticity to input prices.
- **output:** as above, output will be greater in the sheltered sector than in the other sector if output price elasticity to input prices is sufficiently high.

3. Structure and Equations of the Estimated Models

In order to give homogeneous evaluations on the economic systems analyzed, the basic structure of the estimated models for Italy and Germany is similar, although not identical due to different availability of data.

We therefore consider two price equations - industrial prices and CPI - two wage and labour demand equations for each of the sectors examined - manufacturing and service sector - and a set of identities that "close" the model; prices of imported inputs, output (proxied by real value added) and labour force are left as exogenous explanatory variables, as well as other less relevant technical coefficients.
The two models - estimated on quarterly data from 1970 to 1991 - are in Tables 3 and 4, while Tables 5 and 6 report sources and description of the series employed. It has often been necessary to use dummy variables to take into account well known domestic and foreign inflationary short term cycle, like those occurred in 1973, 1975, 1976, 1978, 1980, 1981, 1986.
One of the main features of the models is to use industrial prices as one of the variables explaining the behaviour of CPI and viceversa, in order to capture the reciprocal inflationary pushes between the manufacturing and the service sector.
Wage equations all conform to the inflation augmented Phillips curve, while labour demand schedules are positively related to output and negatively related to unit labour cost.

4. Model Simulation

The models have been simulated using Gauss-Seidel method, with the impulse response function technique, often used for VARs. We imposed shock of the size of one standard error to the perturbed variables between 1984 and 1990 and then analyzed the response of endogenous variables to such shocks (Sims, 1980).
Impulse responses from the perturbed simulation have to be compared to the values obtained from the base simulation (whose values are obtained by simulating the models using actual values of the exogenous variables).
We considered three shocks:

1. A one standard error increase in industrial input prices (0.0202 for the Italian model, 0.0359 for the German model).
2. An increase in the intercept of the industrial price equation of size equal to one standard error of the implicit add factors generated for

that equation by dynamic simulation of the model (0.0051 for Italy, 0.0038); this shock is to mimic a temporary increase of the markup or a temporary rise in indirect taxes.
3. An increase in the intercept of the consumer price equation of size equal to one standard error of the implicit add factors generated for that equation by dynamic simulation of the model (0.0046 for Italy, 0.0042), to be interpreted as exercise 2 above.

The main objective of this exercises is to determine a hierarchy of inflationary responses of industrial prices as opposed to consumer prices and to examine the consequences on wage behaviour and on employment in the manufacturing and service sector.
The three exercises show that responses are qualitatively similar, although they differ in intensity. This is quite reasonable, since all experiments consider inflationary shocks; we could have obtained more visible reactions by delivering stronger shocks for longer time spells, but we preferred to conform to a more traditional approach (Sims, 1980).
Consumer price responses *vis à vis* industrial prices differ among countries: Italian consumer prices tend to grow more rapidly than German consumer prices in response to shocks. On the other hand Italian industrial prices increase less than in Germany. In general, employment in both sectors responds more positively in Italy, while in Germany employment in the service sector falls.

5. Concluding Remarks

The results of this study show:
- the Italian service sector amplifies inflation generated by various inflationary shocks more than the German service sector;
- employment in services is more "resistant" in Italy than in Germany;
- industrial wages response to shocks is stronger in Italy than in Germany;
- the response of service sector wage rates to inflationary shocks is similar in the two countries;
- total employment increases more in Italy than in Germany.

Our results depict a "two speed Europe": on one side Germany, that often (though not always) exhibits a weaker reaction in terms of wages and prices to inflationary shocks, with little if any consequences on employment or the unemployment rate. On the other hand inflationary shocks are more effective in Italy, but this is matched by a more consistent increase of employment levels.

Simulations show that for Italy consumer prices grow more than industrial prices, but also employment grows more in the service sector than in the manufacturing sector.

Table 3 Italy

EQUATION 1: dep. variable:DLPOUTR
QUARTERLY data for 82 periods from 1971Q2 to 1991Q3

dlpoutr

= 0.12775 * log(cltri.1/cltri.2)
(5.07939)

+ 0.09329 * log(cltri.1/cltri.2)[-1] + 0.31342 * dlpintre
(3.38526) (12.3394)

+ 0.43141 * log(cpi/cpi.1) - 0.00297 + Dummies
(5.86346) (1.76274)

Sum Sq 0.0030 Std Err 0.0063 LHS Mean 0.0245
R Sq 0.9134 R Bar Sq 0.9053 F 7, 74 111.564
D.W.(1) 1.7135 D.W.(4) 1.9004

EQUATION 2: dep. variable:DLCPI
QUARTERLY data for 77 periods from 1971Q4 to 1991Q4

dlcpi

= 0.38731 * log(poutr.1/poutr.2) + 0.42357 * log(clsdv/clsdv.1)
(7.48589) (6.02268)

+ 0.00487 + Dummies
(2.49877)

Sum Sq 0.0033 Std Err 0.0068 LHS Mean 0.0284
R Sq 0.7907 R Bar Sq 0.7791 F 4, 72 68.0030
D.W.(1) 1.7185 D.W.(4) 1.3966

(Table 3)

EQUATION 3: dep.variable DLOTTRI
QUARTERLY data for 82 periods from 1971Q3 to 1991Q4

dlottri

$$= 0.52557 * \log(ottri.1/ottri.2) \quad (6.31725)$$

$$+ 0.02649 * \log(paitrx.1/paitrx.2) + 0.10380 * dlvatrix - 0.00203$$
$$(2.28941) \qquad (3.70242) \qquad (2.71168)$$

Sum Sq 0.0029 Std Err 0.0061 LHS Mean -0.0015
R Sq 0.4818 R Bar Sq 0.4618 F 3, 78 24.1717
D.W.(1) 2.1248 D.W.(4) 2.0042

EQUATION 4: dep.variable:DLOTSDW
QUARTERLY data for 86 periods from 1970Q3 to 1991Q4

dlotsdv

$$= 0.39211 * \log(otsdv.1/otsdv.2) - 0.07659 * \log(clsdv/clsdv.1)$$
$$(4.66326) \qquad (2.17456)$$

$$+ 0.13811 * \log(vasdv/vasdv.1) + 0.00111 + Dummies$$
$$(3.87949) \qquad (0.96681)$$

Sum Sq 0.0010 Std Err 0.0036 LHS Mean 0.0066
R Sq 0.6344 R Bar Sq 0.6016 F 7, 78 19.3336
D.W.(1) 1.7706 D.W.(4) 1.9007

(Table 3)

EQUATION 5: dep. variable: DLWTRI
QUARTERLY data for 87 periods from 1970Q2 to 1991Q4

dlwtri

= - 0.01779 * log(ur) + 0.69178 * log(cpi/cpi.1)
(1.72712) (3.45980)

+ 0.05262 + Dummies
(2.16344)

Sum Sq	0.0524	Std Err	0.0251	LHS Mean	0.0349
R Sq	0.3752	R Bar Sq	0.3526	F 3, 83	16.6116
D.W.(1)	2.4468	D.W.(4)	2.1039		

EQUATION 6: dep.variable:DLWSDV
QUARTERLY data for 87 periods from 1970Q2 to 1991Q4

dlwsdv

= - 0.01199 * log(ur) + 0.59085 * log(cpi/cpi.1)
(2.88584) (7.36646)

+ 0.04032 + Dummies
(4.05888)

Sum Sq	0.0077	Std Err	0.0098	LHS Mean	0.0322
R Sq	0.6520	R Bar Sq	0.6306	F 5, 81	30.3567
D.W.(1)	1.6204	D.W.(4)	2.1087		

Identities Table 3

CLTRI = WTRI + OSTRI ;

CLSDV = WSDV + OSSDV ;

POUTR = EXP(DLPOUTR)*POUTR.1 ;

CPI = EXP(DLCPI)*CPI.1 ;

DVASDV = QDVASDV * CPI ;

OTTRI = EXP(DLOTTRI)*OTTRI.1 ;

OTSDV = EXP(DLOTSDV)*OTSDV.1 ;

OTAL = QOTAL * (OTTRI + OTSDV) ;

FL = EXP(DLFL) * FL.1 ;

UR = (1 - ((OTTRI + OTSDV + OTAL) / FL)) * 100 ;

WSDV = EXP(DLWSDV)*WSDV.1 ;

WTRI = EXP(DLWTRI)*WTRI.1 ;

VATRIX = EXP(DLVATRIX) * VATRIX.1 ;

VASDVX = EXP(DLVASDVX) * VASDVX.1 ;

VASDV = VASDVX * DVASDV ;

DVATRI = QDVATRI * POUTR ;

PAITRX = ((DVATRI * VATRIX) - RLTRI) / POUTR ;

RLTRI = CLTRI * ODTRI ;

ODTRI = QODTRI * OTTRI ;

Table 4 Germany

EQUATION 1:dep. variable:DLGFPOU
QUARTERLY data for 82 periods from 1971Q3 to 1991Q4

dlgfpou

= 0.10163 * log(gfw.5/gfw.6) + 0.17174 * dlgfq[-1]
(1.46503) (3.63564)

+ 0.25220 * dlgfpin + 0.47892 * log(gfcpi.1/gfcpi.2)
(14.0856) (3.45585)

- 0.00088 + Dummies
(0.51348)

Sum Sq 0.0034 Std Err 0.0068 LHS Mean 0.0085
R Sq 0.8460 R Bar Sq 0.8314 F 7, 74 58.0556
D.W.(1) 1.6876 D.W.(4) 1.8860

EQUATION 2: dep.variable: DLGFCPI
QUARTERLY data for 87 periods from 1970Q2 to 1991Q4

dlgfcpi

= 0.17916 * log(gfpou/gfpou.1) + 0.14538 * log(gfcls/gfcls.1)
(5.32029) (3.40412)

+ 0.00624 + Dummies
(7.07461)

Sum Sq 0.0019 Std Err 0.0048 LHS Mean 0.0094
R Sq 0.4987 R Bar Sq 0.4806 F 3, 83 27.5268
D.W.(1) 1.6099 D.W.(4) 1.3096

(Table 4)

EQUATION 3: dep. variable:DLGFOD
QUARTERLY data for 86 periods from 1970Q3 to 1991Q

---

dlgfod

= 0.82181 * log(gfod.1/gfod.2) - 0.06463 * log(gfw/gfw.1)
(19.5329) (2.63090)

+ 0.09826 * dlgfq - 0.00001 + Dummies
(5.68557) (0.01125)

Sum Sq 0.0006 Std Err 0.0026 LHS Mean -0.0018
R Sq 0.8584 R Bar Sq 0.8514 F 4, 81 122.796
D.W.(1) 2.2832 D.W.(4) 1.9654

EQUATION 4: dep.variable: DLGFODS
QUARTERLY data for 82 periods from 1970Q4 to 1991Q1

---

dlgfods

= 0.43956 * log(gfods.1/gfods.2) - 0.02110 * log(gfcls/gfcls.1)
(3.97338) (0.60527)

+ 0.02683 * log(gfrs.2/gfrs.3) + 0.00269 + Dummies
(1.58624) (3.49218)

Sum Sq 0.0011 Std Err 0.0038 LHS Mean 0.0045
R Sq 0.2255 R Bar Sq 0.1853 F 4, 77 5.6046
D.W.(1) 2.1228 D.W.(4) 1.2819

(Table 4)

EQUATION 5: dep. variable: DLGFWS
QUARTERLY data for 85 periods from 1970Q4 to 1991Q4

---

dlgfws

= - 0.00810 * log(gfur) + 0.09142 * log(gfcpi.2/gfcpi.3)
(7.50706) (0.76406)

+ 0.02629 + Dummies
(10.6691)

Sum Sq 0.0036 Std Err 0.0066 LHS Mean 0.0147
R Sq 0.7439 R Bar Sq 0.7344 F 3, 81 78.4143
D.W.(1) 2.2031 D.W.(4) 1.6517

EQUATION 6: dep.variable:DLGFW
QUARTERLY data for 84 periods from 1971Q1 to 1991Q4

---

dlgfw

= - 0.00462 * log(gfur) + 0.34329 * log(gfcpi.3/gfcpi.4)
(3.95586) (2.48292)

+ 0.01848 + Dummies
(7.11955)

Sum Sq 0.0034 Std Err 0.0067 LHS Mean 0.0142
R Sq 0.4803 R Bar Sq 0.4398 F 6, 77 11.8598
D.W.(1) 1.9325 D.W.(4) 2.2925

Identities Table 4

GFCLS = GFWS + GFOSS ;

GFPOU = EXP(DLGFPOU)*GFPOU.1 ;

GFCPI = EXP(DLGFCPI)*GFCPI.1 ;

GFDRS = QGFDRS * GFCPI ;

GFRSX = EXP(DLGFRSX) * GFRSX.1 ;

GFRS = GFRSX * GFDRS ;

GFOD = EXP(DLGFOD)*GFOD.1 ;

GFODS = EXP(DLGFODS)*GFODS.1 ;

GFODAL = QGFODAL * (GFOD + GFODS) ;

GFODT = GFODAL + GFOD + GFODS ;

GFFL = EXP(DLGFFL) * GFFL.1 ;

GFUR = (1 - ((GFOD + GFODS + GFODAL) / GFFL)) * 100 ;

GFWS = EXP(DLGFWS)*GFWS.1 ;

GFW = EXP(DLGFW)*GFW.1 ;

GFQ = EXP(DLGFQ) * GFQ.1 ;

Table 5 Variables and Sources: Italy

CLSDV	endogenous: Labour Costs in Services ISTAT
CLTRI	endogenous: Labour Costs in Manufacturing ISTAT
CPI	endogenous: Consumer Price Index ISTAT
DLPINTRE	exogenous: Variation of Manufacturing Input Prices Bank of Italy
DLVASDVX	exogenous: Variation of Real Value Added in Services ISTAT
DLVATRIX	exogenous: Variation of Real Value Added in Manufacturing ISTAT
DVASDV	endogenous: Services Value Added Deflator ISTAT
DVATRI	endogenous: Manufacturing Value Added Deflator ISTAT
FL	endogenous: Labour Force ISTAT
ODTR	endogenous: Employment in Manufacturing, Wage and Salaries ISTAT
OSSDV	exogenous: Social Security Rate, Services ISTAT
OSTRI	exogenous: Social Security Rate, Manufacturing ISTAT
OTAL	endogenous: Employment in Agriculture and other Sectors ISTAT
OTSDV	endogenous: Employment in Services, Total ISTAT
OTTRI	endogenous: Employment in Manufacturing, Total ISTAT
PAITRX	endogenous: Real Profits in Manufacturing ISTAT
POUTR	endogenous: Price of Output in Manufacturing Bank of Italy
QDVASDV	exogenous: Technical Ratio

(Table 5)

QDVASDV	exogenous: Technical Ratio ISTAT
QDVATRI	exogenous: Technical Ratio ISTAT
QODTRI	exogenous: Technical Ratio ISTAT
QOTAL	exogenous: Technical Ratio ISTAT
RLTRI	endogenous: Labour Cost in Manufacturing ISTAT
UR	endogenous: Unemployment Rate ISTAT
VASDV	endogenous: Nominal Value Added, Services ISTAT
VASDVX	endogenous: Real Value Added, Services ISTAT
VATRIX	endogenous: Real Value Added, Manufacturing ISTAT
WSDV	endogenous: Wages, Services ISTAT
WTRI	endogenous: Wages, Manufacturing ISTAT

Table 6 Variables And Sources: Germany

DLGFFL	exogenous: Variation of Labour Force EUROSTAT
DLGFPIN	exogenous: Variation of Manufacturing Input Prices OECD
DLGFQ	exogenous: Variation of Industrial Production OECD
DLGFRSX	exogenous: Variation of Retail Sales (Volume) OECD
GFCLS	endogenous: Labour Cost in Services EUROSTAT
GFCPI	endogenous: Consumer Price Index OECD
GFDRS	endogenous: Retail Sales (Value) OECD
GFFL	endogenous: Labour Force OECD
GFOD	endogenous: Employment in Manufacturing, Wage and Salaries OECD
GFODAL	endogenous: Employment in Agriculture and Other Sectors EUROSTAT
GFODS	endogenous: Employment in Services EUROSTAT
GFODT	endogenous: Employment in Manufacturing, Total EUROSTAT
GFOSS	exogenous: Social Security Rate, Services EUROSTAT
GFPOU	endogenous: Price of Output in Manufacturing OECD
GFQ	endogenous: Industrial Production OECD
GFRS	endogenous: Retail Sales (Value) OECD

(Table 6)

GFRSX	endogenous: Retail Sales (Volume) OECD
GFUR	endogenous: Unemployment Rate OECD
GFW	endogenous: Wages, Manufacturing OECD
GFWS	endogenous: Wages, Services EUROSTAT
QGFDRS	exogenous:Technical Ratio OECD
QGFODAL	exogenous: Technical Ratio EUROSTAT

APPENDIX

Totally differentiating equations (5) to (12) and rearranging them in matrix form we get:

$$\begin{bmatrix} a & 0 & -2L_1 & 0 & b & -IN_{12} & 0 & 0 \\ 0 & d & 0 & -2L_2 & -IN_{12} & e & 0 & 0 \\ c & 0 & -2L_1 & 0 & y_1 & -IN_{12} & 0 & 0 \\ 0 & h & 0 & -2L_2 & -IN_{21} & y_2 & 0 & 0 \\ 0 & 0 & 0 & 0 & 1 & 0 & 0 & 0 \\ 0 & 0 & 0 & -p'_{w_2} & -p'_{p_1} & 1 & 0 & 0 \\ 0 & 0 & 0 & 0 & -g'_1 & 0 & 1 & 0 \\ 0 & 0 & 0 & 0 & 0 & -g'_2 & 0 & 1 \end{bmatrix} \cdot \begin{bmatrix} dL_1 \\ dL_2 \\ dw_1 \\ dw_2 \\ dp_1 \\ dp_2 \\ dy_1 \\ dy_2 \end{bmatrix} = \begin{bmatrix} IN_{13} \\ IN_{23} \\ IN_{13} \\ IN_{23} \\ 1 \\ p'_{p_3} \\ 0 \\ 0 \end{bmatrix} \cdot [dp_3]$$

where:

$a = p_1 f''_{1L_1} L_1 + 2(p_1 f'_{1L_1} - w_1)$ (>0 from second order conditions)

$b = f'_{1L_1} L_1 + y_1$

$c = p_1 f'_{1L_1} L_1 + 2w_1 - \overline{w}$

$d = p_2 f''_{2L_2} L_2 + 2(p_2 f'_{2L_2} - w_2)$

$e = f'_{2L_2} L_2 + y_2$

$h = p_2 f'_{2L_2} L_2 + 2w_2 - \overline{w}$

Here b>0, e>0, while both c and h are less than zero, since from the bargaining it turns out that:

$$\begin{cases} \overline{w} = p_1 f'_{1L_1} \Rightarrow c = 2(\overline{w} - w_1) < 0 \\ \overline{w} = p_2 f'_{2L_2} \Rightarrow h = 2(\overline{w} - w_2) < 0 \end{cases}$$

Comparative static results yield:

$$\frac{dL_1}{dp_3} = \frac{(b - y_1)[(dy_2 - eh)p'_{2w_2} - 2(d-h)L_2]L_1}{\Delta}$$

$$\frac{dL_2}{dp_3} = \frac{(c-a)(y_2 - e)[(IN_{21} + IN_{23})p'_{2w_2} - 2(p'_{2p_1} + p'_{2p_3})L_2]L_1}{\Delta}$$

$$\frac{dw_1}{dp_3} = \frac{(dy_2 - eh)[(a-c)IN_{13} + (bc-a)y_1]p'_{2w_2} + (d-h)[(a-c)(IN_{21} + IN_{23})IN_{12}p'_{2w_2} +}{2\Delta}$$

$$\frac{2(a-c)(d-h)(IN_{13} + IN_{12}p'_{2p_1} + IN_{12}p'_{2p_3})L_2}{2\Delta}$$

$$\frac{dw_2}{dp_3} = \frac{(c-a)[(d-h)(IN_{21}+IN_{23})-(dy_2-eh)(p'_{2p_1}+p'_{2p_3})]L_1}{\Delta}$$

$$\frac{dp_1}{dp_3} = \frac{(c-a)[(dy_2-eh)p'_{2w_2}-2(d-h)L_2]L_1}{\Delta}$$

$$\frac{dp_2}{dp_3} = \frac{(c-a)(d-h)[(IN_{21}+IN_{23})p'_{2w_2}-2(p'_{2p_1}+p'_{2p_3})L_2]L_1}{\Delta}$$

$$\frac{dy_1}{dp_3} = \frac{(c-a)g'_1[(dy_2-eh)p'_{2w_2}-2(d-h)L_2]L_1}{\Delta}$$

$$\frac{dy_2}{dp_3} = \frac{(c-a)(d-h)g'_2[(IN_{21}+IN_{23})p'_{2w_2}-2(p'_{2p_1}+p'_{2p_3})]L_1}{\Delta}$$

It is not possible to determine univocally the sign of the numerator and of the denominator of the above expressions: however it is possible to show that they will share the same sign, so that all the above turn out to be positive. In order to ascertain under which conditions the increase of a variable (employment, wages, prices and output) will be greater in one sector when compared to the other it will suffice to look at differences.

References

Banca d'Italia, (1986), "Modello Econometrico Trimestrale dell'Economia Italiana", *Temi di Discussione, Banca d'Italia*, no. 80, December.

Barca F., Visco I., (1991), "L'Economia Italiana nella Prospettiva Europea", presented at a Seminar on "La Posizione Esterna dell'Italia - Incontro di Studio in Memoria di Stefano Vona", Rome, 6-7 December 1991.

Bean, C.R., Layard P.R.G.,. Nickell S.J., (eds. 1987), *The Rise in Unemployment*, Basil Blackwell, Oxford.

Blanchard O., Dornbush R., Dreze J.H., Giersch H., Layard P.R.G., Monti M., (1985) "Employment and Growth in Europe: a Two Handed Approach", *CEPS Paper 21*, Brussels.

Bodo G., Sestito P., (1989), "Disoccupazione e Dualismo Territoriale", *Temi di Discussione, Banca d'Italia*, no.123.

Bruno M., Sachs J., (1987), *Economics of Worldwide Stagflation*, Basil Blackwell, Oxford.

D.G. Blanchflower, Oswald A.J., (1990), "The Wage Curve", in B. Holmlund, K.G. Lofgren (eds.), *Unemployment and Wage Determination in Europe*, Blackwell, 1990.

De Nardis S., Micossi S., (1991), "Disinflation and Re-Inflation in Italy and the Implications for Transition to Monetary Union", Banca Nazionale del Lavoro, *Quarterly Review.*

Dreze, J.H., Bean C.R., (19..), *Europe's Unemployment Problem*, MIT Press, Cambridge, Mass., 1991.

Gordon R.J., (1987), "Productivity, Wages, and Prices Inside and Outside of Manufacturing in the US, Japan and Europe", *European Economic Review.*

Guiso L., (1985), "Il Dibattito sull'Inflazione Italiana negli Ultimi Quindici Anni", *Contributi all'Analisi Economica del Servizio Studi della Banca d'Italia*, March.

McDonald I. M.,. Solow R. M., (1981), "Wage Bargaining and Employment", *American Economic Review*, 71.

Blanchard O., Summers L., (1986), "Hysteresis and the European Unemployment Problem".

Phelps, E.S., (1992), "A Review of Unemployment", *Journal of Economic Literarure.*

Rubino P., (1991), "Indicatori dei Prezzi Input-Output", *Banca d'Italia, Supplementi al Bollettino Statistico*, Year I, no. 8.

Sims C.A., (1980), "Macroeconomics and Reality", *Econometrica*, 48.

Visco I., (1990), "L'Economia Italiana dal 1975 al 1989", mimeo (for the Enciclopedia Italiana), October.

Comment

Giovanni Piersanti
University of Teramo

The Manzini and Tivegna study appears as another important contribution in the research area on the structural causes of Italian inflation vis a vis that of other European countries. The analysis is perfomed with a two sector model emboding the relationships between the industrial and the service sector, and aims at the target to examine and test a thesis widely spread and deeply rooted in the Italian literature on this subject, i.e. that of the service as a sector which amplifies the inflationary shocks but stabilizes employment. The model is applied to the four major European countries and, indeed, the results do not reject that view, especially for Italy. Moreover, if we look at the results as a whole, we cannot reject another view equally spread and rooted even at the level of public opinion: that of a Europe with two speeds. Thus, we have countries as France and Germany, classified as "virtuous" countries, which, to an exogenous shock on different kind of prices, show a low inflationary reaction and negligible effects on employment, and countries as Italy and the United Kingdom, classified as "vicious" countries, which show to the same kind of shocks greater effects on both inflation and employment.

Now, avoiding, as far as possible, to focus attention on too many details or, worse, to continue in a useless summary of the results and simulations performed, I shall concentrate on some general issues that concern either the theoretical or the empirical investigation.

Let me begin from the theoretical model. The first point regards the subdivision of the economy in two sectors: the industrial sector, which is governed by perfect competition, and the service sector in which prevails monopolistic competition. Here I have immediately to reveal my dissatisfaction and the numerous perplexities which prevent me from accepting this model as appropriate. These perplexities arise not only from the simple evidence that in reality things are not like that (an issue that is of little significance at the teoretical level) as for the belief that this approach is not very useful to study the relationship between the two sectors. After all, if we neglect that strand of thought known as New Classical Macroeconomics, which explains the behaviour of economic agents within the private sector by models *à la* Arrow-Debreu, more or less modified to take account of the different kind of rigidities and frictions existing in the real world (a research program that is not without any difficulty and inconsistency at the pure theoretical level), then it is rather difficult to find a support so evident and conclusive to this approach in the modern literature. Indeed, it is going to spread more and more another strand of thought, known as New Keynesian Economics, which thinks as more appropriate the opposite view of a world of imperfect competition to study the behaviour of the private sector, including the tradable sector.

Thus if we consider, for example, a market opened to international competition in which the prices are set at a world level, then, according to this new approach, it is possible to describe the behaviour of the firm with a demand curve that at the world price is no longer perfectly elastic but kinked. Such demand curve, in fact, shows at the world price a segment that is horizontal until the firm's share of the market and then has a negative slope (see Carlin and Soskice, 1990).

Moreover, it must be stressed that some attempts to apply the above mentioned two sector model to the Italian economy, with the aim to test the hypothesis that in the tradable sector the price dynamic is entirely determined by the world price, has not produced the expected results and the hypothesis has been rejected at the empirical level (see Bodo, 1979 and Zandano, 1982). At any rate, the dissatisfaction with this approach is by now unquestionable and such to stimulate the research and employment of other explanatory schemes as, for example, models that focus their attention on the different kind of product supplied by the two sectors (Felli-Piersanti, 1985) or on the particular kind of externalities and relationships existing between them (Felli and Tria, 1993).

Now let me go to the second point. It concerns the wage equation and the role of the unions. In their model Manzini and Tivegna assume the existence, in both sectors, of unions which bargain with the firms both the wages and the level of employment benefit. From the first order condition they obtain, then, the equilibrium level for wages and employment that, in the industrial sector, are higher than that of the service sector and this situation persists also in the long run, given the degree of competition and the elasticity of demand in both sectors.

This long run property of the model is rather unusual and Manzini and Tivegna don't offer any explanation for it. Nevertheless, this condition is very difficult to understand. Indeed, I have not been able to find any reason which could explain why in the non - competitive sector either the union should accept a wage that is permanently lower than that of the competitive sector or the workers don't go towards the sector with higher wages. If this could happen and if the wage gap should persist in the long run, as Manzini and Tivegna model suggests, then the likely result would be very paradoxical: a zero level of employment in the service sector. However, this little attractive property of the model derives from the fact that the alternative wage is given only by the unemployment benefit and should disappear if we introduce the wage of the other sector in the utility function.

Now I come to the empirical section. Here Manzini and Tivegna employ VAR models to examine the impulse response to exogenous shocks (or innovations) that hit either the consumer or the output prices. As stressed above, I don't dwell now on the numerous results obtained by those simulations though I have found them very interesting. On the contrary, what I like to discuss are some aspects of the econometric investigation by which I have been particularly impressed and that left me rather perplexed. The first thing concerns the lack of any attempt to find the cointegrating relations among the relevant variables, though the model and the purpose of the analysis seem to demand such investigation. This is very surprising, especially if we think that the job could have been done, very simply, by enlarging the base model to VAR models with error correction and testing, with one of the available method, for the presence of cointegrating vectors among the variables of the model (see, for example, Engle-Granger, 1987, Johansen, 1988, Stock-Watson, 1988). This would have increased not only the output of empirical results but also supplied some information on the existence of long run equilibrium solutions among the variables of the model.

The second point concerns the lack of some important diagnostic tests on normality, independence and homoscedasticity of the residuals that represent a crucial aspect in the analysis of this kind of models.

Finally, the third point regards the arguments produced to justify the second kind of shock in the simulations of empirical models. Indeed, if we accept the logic of the theoretical model and take into account that the firms in the industrial sector are not able to set the price, then it is very difficult to understand what means an exogenous increase in the margins of industrial firms.

References

Bodo G., (1979), "Il Modello Scandinavo di Inflazione: Una Applicazione al Caso Italiano", *Banca d'Italia*, typewritten.

Carlin W. and D. Soskice, (1990), *Macroeconomics and the Wage Bargain. A Modern Approach to Employment, Inflation, and the Exchange Rate*, Oxford University Press, Oxford.

Engel R.F. and C.W.J. Granger, (1987), "Co-Integration and Error Correction: Representation, Estimation, and Testing", *Econometrica* 55, 251-76.

Felli E. and Piersanti G., (1985), "Salari, Prezzi e Produttività nel Commercio", *Studi Economici*, no. 27, 141-76.

Felli E. and. Tria G.,(1993), "Manufacturing Industry, Service Sector and Externalities", tipewritten; now in this book as chapter 2.

Johansen S.,(1988), "Statistical Analysis of Cointegration Vectors", *Journal of Economic Dynamics and Control*,_12, 231-54.

Stock j. M. and M. W. Watson, (1988), "Variable Trends in Economic Time Series", *Journal of Economic Perspectives*, 2, 147-74.

Zandano G., (1982), *Un Modello Econometrico a Due Settori per l'Economia Italiana*, ASEA, Torino.

4

The Growth of Market Service Sector in Italy

Roberto Monducci
ISTAT Rome

Stefano Pisani
ISTAT Rome

1. Structural Evolution of the Service Sector over the Last 20 Years

1.1 Growth Patterns in the Service and Industrial Sectors

During the past 20 years the significant expansion of the service sector has been noteworthy both in terms of employment and real product growth. From 1970 to 1992 the share of the market service sector value added (excluding housing) in total market value added, grew from 41.4% to 57.7% at current prices and from 46.5% to 53.4% at constant prices (fig. 1). A closer examination of this general trend in the manufacturing and market service sector shows significant aspects of the expansion of the service sector, namely a "relative" acceleration of the real growth in the service sector during the 1980's. Indeed we found greater average growth of real value added in manufacturing in the 1970's (5.8%, as opposed to 4.5% for the service sector) while, from 1980 to 1992, the trend is reversed: average growth of the industrial sector (2%) is 1% less growth in the service sector (2.9%).

As may be noted in fig.1, during the 1970's there was an increase of the share (measured at constant prices) of both the service and manufacturing sectors. The 1980's saw the growth of the service sector and the contraction of the industrial sector. This development would seem to partly contradict the "traditional" economic literature which viewed the relative expansion of the service sector as limited to quantities expressed in employment and nominal terms. Considering the employment, the increase of the market service share is more relevant than for (real and nominal) production, with an increase in employment of approximately 20% over the last 20 years. As a result of this dynamic we may note that in 1992 more than half the total employment in the market sector was in service activities.

This increase in employment levels determined a modest tendential growth in labour productivity (average increases: 0.4%/year) which is well below the increase observed for the preceding period (1.8%). Evidence is also noted in the manufacturing sector of the weak dynamic in labour productivity (fig. 2a, 2b) despite the significant reduction of employed personnel in the industrial sector (-1.8%/year).

In any case, between the 1970's and the 1980's, the mean growth differential of productivity in the industrial and in the service sector increased from 2.9% to 3.5%.

A comparison of the "levels" of real productivity between the service and manufacturing sectors shows that in 1980 real product per labour unit in industry was 21% lower than real product per labour unit in the service sector. Between 1980 and 1992, however, the upward trend of industrial productivity determined recovery, and in fact the positive differential was estimated in 1992, for industrial transformation, at 19%. Despite this, in 1992, distinctly higher productivity levels for labour were noted for the service sectors in transportation, communication, credit and insurance as compared to industry.

Comparing productivity levels of "traditional" manufacturing industries (branch 4) - characterized by relative smallness of the firms in question vis-a-vis the mean for the industrial sector - with productivity levels for the service sector, significant differences were not observed. For example, the textile, clothing and footwear branch (one of Italy's strongholds in the export market), exhibits lower productivity than that of the retail and wholesale sector and of household services.

The aggregate dynamics of labour productivity in the service and industrial sectors are deduced from the direct effect of levels and evolution of the productivity in each branch, and of changes in the composition of the employment profile of macro-sectors. Calculation of mean productivity in the service sector through application of quantification related to the structure of employment during a "base" year permits us to carry out a preliminary assessment of the aggregate effect of sector employment dynamics for 9 areas of activity.

According to this simple scheme, aggregate productivity of the service sector obtained on the basis of the composition of personnel employed in 1970 is less than "observed" during the 1970-86 period. This indicates that, during the years considered, the employment structure of the service sector favoured sectors with higher levels of labour productivity.

During the following period (1987-92) this tendency reversed: employment trends favoured areas of activity with lower productivity levels. In general, "observed" productivity increased during the 1970-1992 period at a rate of 1.0%, compared with 1.1% "standardized" productivity. We may note instances of employment recomposition in the service sector - even if they do not significantly alter the tendential growth of the two productivity indicators - does in fact determine significant differentiation between the 1970's and the 1980's. Consideration of effects on employment from sector to sector in industry assessed on the basis of the employment structure in 15 areas of activity does not reveal significant differences between the two types of measurement adopted.

The application of quantities regarding composition of the employed population in 1980 confirms evidence of a progressive reallocation of employment toward the service sectors characterized by lower productivity levels over the last decade.

This analysis was repeated by assessing the differences between "observed" and "standardized" productivity related to industry and the service sector considered together. The results of such examination permit us to verify that aggregate "standardized" productivity is lower than "observed" productivity over the 1970-1984 period. Until

1984, modifications to the structure of the employed population in regard to industry and services, and the favouring of the latter, contributed to increased mean productivity in the two sectors. From 1985 on employment reallocation depressed the mean real product.
The intensity of employment recomposition with regard to industry and the service sector during the 1980's, together with the effects of a persistent differential of mean "observed" productivity growth between the two sectors, thus determined a mean "observed" rate of growth in productivity (i.e.: for 1970-1992, 2.3%; as opposed to a "standardized" value of 2.5%).
Greater service sector expansion in real terms with regard to the manufacturing sector is therefore associated with a strengthening of the potential impact of the productivity differential on changes of relative prices.
Observation of the trend of output prices (fig. 2a, 2b) shows that, in the 1970's, the inflationary differential favouring the service sector was less than 1% per year (mean value). In the 1970's no greater inflationary trend was noted in the service sector as compared to that of industry. During the 1980's there was an evident modification of the exchange ratio, and industrial prices rose by 6.6% while service sector prices rose by 10%.
If, instead of output prices, we consider the deflator of value added, we see greater persistence over the last 20 years of an inflationary differential benefiting the service sector. This differential in the 2 sub-periods considered is 2.5% (mean annual value) during the 1970's and 3.3% over the 1980-1992 period.
However, we should note that the deterioration of the ratio of prices for industry, vis-à-vis services, was less than the relative increase in productivity. Examination of a synthetic indicator of the dynamics of productivity and implicit prices[1] permits us to verify how productivity gains accumulated in the industrial sector, as compared to those in the service sector where losses were satisfactorily compensated for in term of prices.

---

[1] The index of relative profitability (RPI) is given by the following expression: RPI = (RPs/RPi) * (PDs/PDi) * 100; where: RP = deflator, PD = productivity, i= manufacturing industry, and s = service sector.

Fig. 1 Share of branches in total market activities (in %)

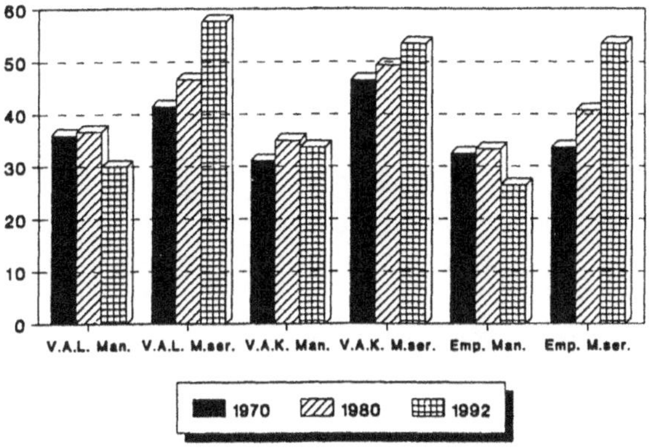

Fig. 2a Average annual growth rate (in %) - 1970-1980

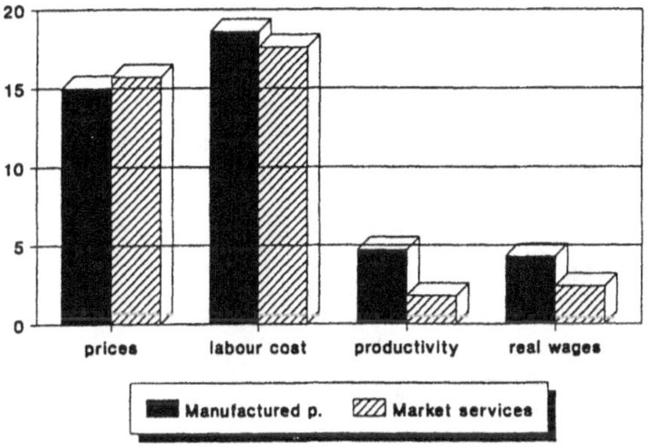

Fig. 2b Average annual growth rate (in %) - 1980-1992

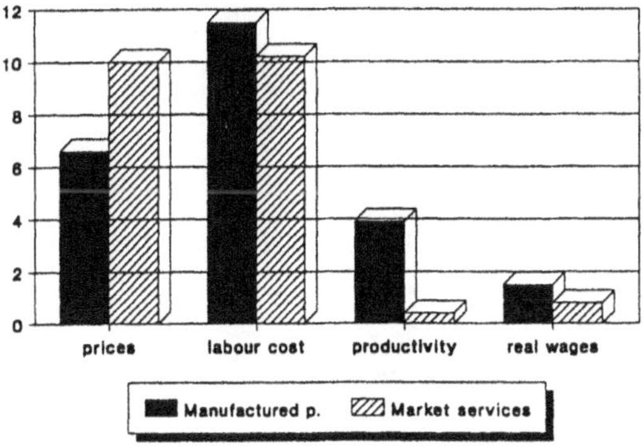

Fig. 3 Difference between market services and manufacturing

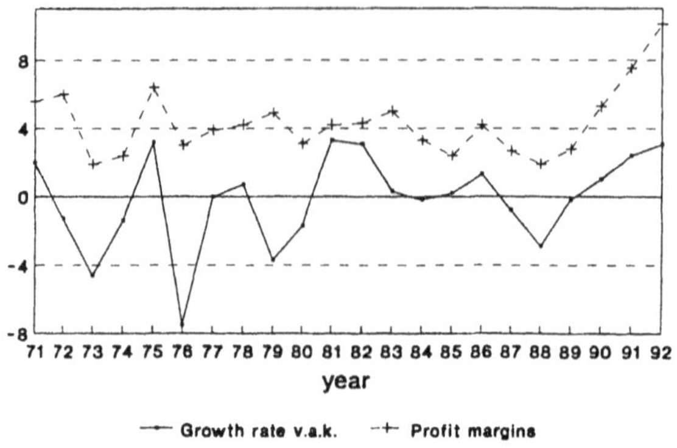

Fig. 4 Share of wage and salary earners in occupied population (in %) - 1990

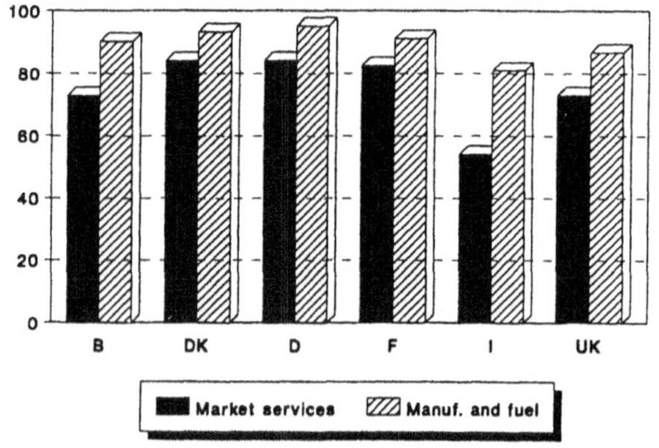

Fig. 5a Share of market services employees in occupied population (in %)

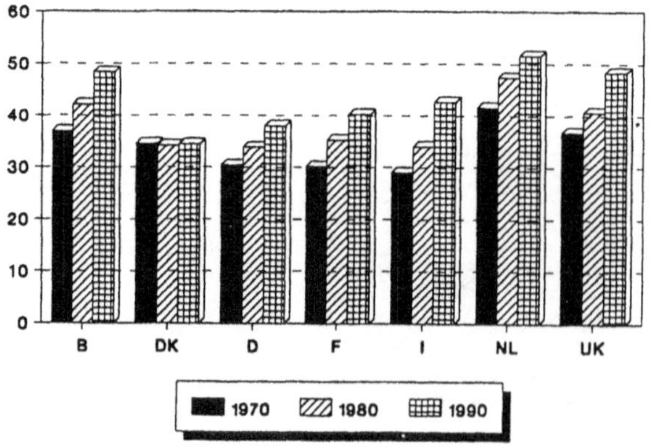

The indicator in fact exhibits an approx. 7% reduction in the 1970's and a further 5% fall over the following 13 years, despite evident recovery during 1990-92.
The effects on sector-to-sector distribution of these trends depend on the evolution of pay and changes in composition of employed population with regard to autonomous and employed work force. Holding to the hypothesis of homogeneity of pay trends between industry and the service sector, and the relatively greater growth in productivity observed in the industrial sector, with regard to loss of exchange ratio, should have determined a favourable impact on industry in terms of profit. The fact that this did not occur may be quantified in terms of greater growth of labour cost in industrial transformation (1.0% per year mean value during the 1970's; 1.3% during the 1980-92 period. In 1970 labour costs per employee in the service sector was approx. 20% more than in the sector of industrial transformation. From the mid-1980's on the relative advantage of employees in the service sector had been practically completely eliminated. These diverging pay dynamics therefore permit a differential of profit margins which benefits the service sector. Irrespective of tendential trends, the dynamic of relative profit margins in the service sector appears to be consistent with the differential of growth of real industrial output (fig. 3); this may supply a preliminary indication of a sensitivity to the relative profitability of the areas of service sectors to "product" cycle.

1.2 Relative Prices, Demand Pressure and Persistence in Differences in Profit Margins

The identification of a demand-factor in the dynamic of relative prices between industry and the service sector may provide useful indications for an assessment of the degree of sector-to-sector competitiveness[2]. With the aim of verifying the existence of a component in the dynamic of relative prices, which may be ascribed to the

[2] In a report of the Centro Europa Ricerche (CER) of 1991, we may note anticyclical progress of relative prices between the private service sector and industry. This is explained in terms of convergence among service sector firms in periods of a slowing up of the economy and a policy of more "competitive" pricing during periods of more sustained growth.

effect of the various pressures on demand addressed to the sectors, we estimated an equation for the total of service industries which associates the differential of growth of output prices (OP), with regard to the manufacturing sector, to the differential in total unit labour costs (LC) and input prices (IP)[3].
Furthermore, an indicator of the relative pressure of real demand is introduced (VA), and this is given as the ratio between the value of production at constant prices for services and the value of the manufacturing industry. All variables are expressed as annual percentage variations. The equation is as follows:

$$OP = \alpha + \beta_1.LC + \beta_2.IP + \beta_3.VA + e \qquad (1)$$

based on annual data for 1971-1992. Here, we give the results of OLS estimates.

α	β_1.	β_2.	β_3.	R^2AD	DW	STDER
0.09	0.45	0.64	0.44	0.80	1.71	1.10
(0.3)	(5.3)	(7.4)	(3.9)			

Student's T test values are given in brackets.

The results of the estimate of the equation (1) indicate that inflation, regarding supply of services not "explained" in terms of differential of increase in costs, is positively correlated to the dynamic of real demand. This evidence appears to contradict some verification hypotheses, regarding the weakness of the disciplining power of the market in the service sector through comparison between the progress of relative prices, and the progress of the economic cycle. According to such hypotheses, service sector firms tend to act in collusion during periods of cyclical deceleration, contrasting with more competitive price behaviour during moments of acceleration of demand.

[3] The total labour costs per unit of production is given by the cost of (employee + autonomous) labour related to the value of production at constant prices.

As a further analysis of the structural aspects of sector-to-sector dynamics, an attempt was made to "qualify" the evidence of a gap in profit margins observed between industry and the service sector with verification of persistence, if and when present, of differentials of profitability between the various areas of the service sector. The data used here condition the analysis in at least two ways: the level of aggregation of data and available profit indicators.

Turning our attention to the former we can indicate, given the level of aggregation of available data, that the analysis proposed does not take into consideration convergence processes "within" the sectors, which represent the traditional terrain of empirical verification on the degree of market competitiveness[4]. This theme is to be seen in the light of various observations proposed by economic theory in order to explain the emergence and persistence over long periods of time of differentials in the profit margins of a single firm in regard to the mean for the sector in question[5].

According to a neoclassic approach, the absence of a convergence of profits toward a single market level should be considered as a significant indicator of the presence of inefficiency with regard to allocation and deviation from competition[6]. Various alternative approaches indicate an entrepreneurial logic in an environment characterized by dynamic competition as an innate feature of systematic opposition to a scaling down of super profits[7]. In particular, firms may be adopting strategic behaviour patterns through investment which aim at creating barriers which cause profits to remain above mean values[8]. Persistence is therefore endogenously determined, as opposed to the "traditional" theory which associates barriers with exogenous factors giving an advantage to all firms in the sector where impact is related to the relative size of the firms in question[9]. If this constitutes a brief summary of the theoretic picture, then the

---

[4] Cubbin and Geroski (1987).

[5] For a broad overview see Guelpa (1990)

[6] G.J. Stigler (1963)

[7] Williamson (1975), Caves and Porter (1977), Hay and Vickers (1987), Kamien and Schwartz (1982).

[8] Caves and Porter (1977).

[9] Bain (1951), Sylos-Labini (1967).

data gathered permit only preliminary inspection of persistence of differences in profitability within the service sector. This may in any case be consistent with the hypothesized presence of "exogenous" barriers in regard to entire sectors. As has been pointed out, this situation emerges as a consequence of the situation characterized by oligopoly power where there is a strong resistance to incoming firms and competition among those already in existence, not only "... in sectors commonly referred to as 'underdeveloped', but also in the industrial sector, often considered 'advanced'"[10].

Turning our attention to limitations relating to the available data, it is clear that such data - since it does not permit assessment of profit differentials in terms of ROI or ROE, but only gross profit margins on value added (or on production value) - in fact comparison conditions, in terms of level, between sectors characterized by capital intensity vary significantly[11]. Beginning with these premises we have a priori reasons to imagine the persistence of even greater differences if we calculate these on the basis of margins in regard to ROI and ROE profit rates[12]. While it is necessary to continually bear in mind the complexity of the problem, we may affirm that the identification of possible persistence of profit differentials between various areas of the service sector will in any case be significant even when assessed on the basis of margins.

With this in mind, we can limit ourselves to a simple task: estimation of an equation which - for each branch of the market service sector - should verify if, on the appearance of sector-to-sector profit differentials, adjusting mechanisms arise which tend to re-absorb such differences within a short period. The differential observed

---

[10] Spaventa (1973), p. 313.

[11] ROI is the rate of operating profitability (gross operating income / net invested capital) and ROE is the rate of global profitability (net income / equity capital).

[12] ...margins converge less rapidly than rates since they are correlated to capital intensity and, with regard to their margins including tax, also with leverage. Indeed, we have: MOL/F = (MOL/K)*(K/F) ... Businesses characterized by high capital intensity will structurally have, as with ROI, high operative margins. The same applies to gross margins ... "Technical factors are also present. Inflation generates effects of distortion which are more sensitive with regard to stock than to flows, and therefore indices which have invested capital as denominator exhibit upward distortion ... since the denominator is undervalued and furthermore in a tendentially growing manner in time ... the serial correlation of profit rates is thus less than that of relation of the margins", Guelpa, (1990), 229-232.

each year between the profit share of value added for a sector, and the mean for the service sector is:

$$D_t = P_t - E(P_t)$$

In the hypothesis that the mechanism of re-absorption may be represented through a first order autoregressive process, we obtain:

$$D_t = \beta_0 + \beta_1 D_{t-1} \qquad 0 < \beta_1 < 1 \qquad (2)$$

Coefficient β_0 expresses the long-term profit gap and β_1 measures "persistence". A coefficient β_1 of near-1 value describes a mechanism of adjustment over the short period gap toward β_0, this shows slow movement. A value of β_1 close to zero, instead, indicates that the process of reduction of the short-term gap is immediate.
Equation (2) was estimated in relation to wholesale and retail trade, lodging and catering enterprises, business and household services. The "mean" share of profits is compared with that of each sector, and is therefore made up of the share pertaining to the total area of activity considered. Below, we see the results of OLS estimates carried out on annual data over the period 1970-1992.

Sectors of economic activity	β_0.	β_1	R^2AD	DW	h stat.
Wholesale and retail trade	-0.39 (-1.0)	0.87 (6.6)	0.67	2.07	-0.21
Lodging and catering services	2.62 (1.5)	0.77 (5.3)	0.56	2.06	-0.21
Business services	-1.74 (-2.5)	0.74 (6.7)	0.68	2.12	-0.32
Household services	0.72 (1.1)	0.98 (10.9)	0.85	2.29	-0.75

Student's T test values are given in brackets.

As we see, trade sector and household services show problems related to significance of β_0. coefficients, while Durbin's h statistics indicate the presence of auto-correlation of residuals in the equation pertaining to household services. With the results obtained we may assess how lodging and catering firms exhibit long-term positive profit differentials (approx. 2.6%); business services exhibit a lower rate of return (lower than the mean by 2%). Within this range we find household services with profits of 0.7% above the mean, and commerce, of which the negative gap amounts to approx. 0.5%.

On the other hand, applying model (2) to differentials pertaining to branches of the manufacturing sector in regard to the mean of industrial transformation, we find β_0 coefficients which are notably high also for industry.

If model (2) is estimated through comparison with each branch of the manufacturing sector, using the mean value of the "sector" in question, it is possible to obtain β_0. coefficients which are in all cases less than 1. In industry, it would appear that a more correct identification of reference "markets" would determine considerable reduction of long-term gaps in profit margins.

Comparison of the profitability gaps existing between the various areas of industrial activity and of the service sector should therefore be carried out given the impossibility of further "disaggregating" the service sector, through aggregation of the branch of industry in the various areas of activity. Such verification has shown up long-term profitability differentials between the branch of industrial manufacturing, which are significantly less marked, than for the service sector.

According to the hypothesis that, in terms of capital intensity, comparisons reflect a more correct identification of the sector-to-sector aggregations, both for industry and the service sector, this higher degree of "compactness" within the manufacturing sector may be associated with at least two explanations (which can be considered separately or together): 1) the manufacturing sector is significantly more homogeneous in terms of capital intensity compared to the service sector[13]; 2) in industry, profit differentials assessed on the

---

[13] An examination of the capital intensity in the various sectors of the economy based on recent data published in Annunziato, Manfroni and Rosa (1992) in fact confirms a variability of the relation between capital/labour within the three industrial branches which is much lower than that to be found in the various service sectors, even excluding Transportation and Communication.

basis of margins are less dissimilar than those calculated on rates in the service sector.
The estimates of the coefficients β_1 , which are highly significant for all sectors of the service sector considered, show a slow profit differential absorption. In fact β_1 values are all above 2/3, and the convergence of profits toward their long run values can only be reached after several years.
Considering the effects of the process of convergence toward the long-term gap according to the estimated β_1 coefficients, we may in fact calculate that - after three years following an initial shock - the sector of the lodging and catering services sector will have absorbed 44% of the gap. This percentage falls to 41% for business services and to 34% for distributive services. Personal services exhibit an even slower convergence.

1.3 The Expansion of the Service Sector in Italy and Europe

A deeper comparative study on an international level has permitted us to shed some light on the main differences between the service sector in Italy and that of other EEC countries. The main feature that emerges is the high level of fragmentation of the supply of services. This feature becomes clear if we consider the distribution of employment between employees and employers (fig. 4). From fig. 4 we note that the share of employees (54.1%) in Italy is much lower than for that of other European countries. In particular, within the market service sector, the commercial sector shows more differences than for the rest of Europe.
High levels of fragmentation of the commercial distribution system is more pronounced if we examine national accounts data together with the density of customers per sales outlet (56 in Italy, a figure which is much lower than for the main EEC countries: Great Britain, Germany, Denmark and France have the following densities, 165, 148, 101 and 91 respectively). Equally clear is the sign of a change in commercial structure, as over 1988-1990 there was a considerable increase in the number of supermarkets (20.6%) and shopping centres (75.0%). The growth rate in Italy of this segment of the market is well above the rate for France and Germany. The picture is con-

firmed also by national account data, which show an increase in the share of employees in the commercial sector during 1984-1990.

The fragmentary nature of the structure of commercial services in Italy, as compared to other EEC countries, also poses considerable problems regarding the measurement of economic aggregates characterizing this area of activity. The dynamic of this sector appears to be bound mainly to the progress of small firms rather than to the economic progress of a well-defined group of larger firms (the only ones being regularly surveyed). This creates problems of a strictly statistical nature such as those involved in updating and managing archives on firms concerns. Furthermore, this segment of the market is found to be the least accessible to fiscal and administrative control, and we may therefore find it plausible that this sector is the least inclined to supply statistical information.

As we already pointed out above (see 2.1), during the 1980's we witnessed a notable increase in employment share in the service sector as to that of total employment. If we compare the national situation with that prevailing in the EEC in 1980 (fig. 5a, b) we may note that total employment in market services in Italy (34.0%) was among the lowest in Europe and was significantly higher only to that of Portugal (23.8%). During the 1980's, we witnessed a change in regard to Italy's relative position: in 1990, the share (42.6%) in the European context is only lower than that of Holland (51.5%), Great Britain and Belgium (48.3%). Empirical evidence shows that the service sector in Italy absorbed more employment over the last decade than in other EEC countries.

In 2.1 we have already seen growth in employment in Italy followed a different pattern during the 1970's than it did in the 1980's. During the 70's, there was an increase in the share of employees in the commercial service sector together with an increase of employees in the industrial sector. Over the last decade, we witnessed an acceleration in terms of employment of the process of expansion in the service sector that was concurrent with mass dismissals of labour from the manufacturing sector. This development differs from EEC data (fig. 5a, 5b). Indeed, during the 1970's in the EEC, the relative fall in manufacturing employment figures was already evident, while the contraction over the 1980's was less dramatic than in Italy (the only exception being the United Kingdom, in which the contraction of industrial employment is greater than in Italy).

As we have already noted, the growth in employment during the 1980's is associated with moderate growth in the quantity of market services supplied. This increase (on average 3.0% per year) corresponds with other European figures (lower than the UK, 4.0%, Germany and France, 3.4%, but higher than Denmark, 2.6%, Belgium and Greece 2.5%, Holland, 2.3%, and Spain, 1.5%). Again, the specifically Italian situation emerges if we also consider the 1970's. During the twenty-year period 1970-1990, the quantitative increase of supply in Italy was dominated by the growth of the manufactured product sector with an annual mean growth rate of 4.1%. Therefore, in this period, market services, although developing at a mean annual rate of 3.7%, which is lower than that found in France and Greece (4.0%), do not exhibit positive growth differentials in regard to manufacturing. For the main European countries, on the contrary, the growth differential in favour of market services persists over the entire period, leading to a more advanced "service economy" than Italy.

If, instead, we focus our attention on the last decade, we may conclude that the industrial sector in Italy dismissed more workers than for the European average, and the service sector has guaranteed employment absorption to a greater extent than for that of other EEC countries. At the same time, the quantitative development of services corresponds with that noted throughout the continent, and labour productivity, measured in terms of value added at constant prices per worker, is lower than for all other European countries (fig. 6a, 6b); yet, during 1985-90 (table 2), the picture changes significantly, as the productivity growth differential *vis-à-vis* the main European competitors narrows and the mean growth rate is higher than those found in Belgium, Denmark and Germany.

During 1980-1990 it was seen throughout Europe that the increase of the implicit deflator in the service sector exceeded the increase of the GDP deflator, the only exception to this rule being Germany. From Table 1 we learn that, in this context, the Italian situation does not appear to be anomalous, since a lower differential between the two rates of increase is observed than in France and Belgium, and is on a par with the UK. Things change notably when we compare the price trends of services with the prices in the manufacturing sector. In this case Italy exhibits the greatest differential in the EEC. This underlines the fact that Italy, compared to other countries of the European community, has to deal with the inflationary impulses arising out of other areas of activity, such as nonmarket services and energy.

If we limit our observations to the period 1985-1990 (Table 2), we may note that Italy's relative position within the Community does not show change breaks. From a disaggregate analysis of the service sector, it is clear that the branch "lodging and catering services" systematically exhibits price increases which are higher than the mean in the service sector.

This fact may be rather difficult to interpret since, within the context of the market service sector, lodging and catering services should be a sector among those most open to international competition. It should be remembered that this area is characterized by many small enterprises which feel the impact, not only of tourist flow, but also of behavioural changes and the spending capacity of the resident population.

Various comparative studies carried out using business data reveal an efficiency gap between some "network" services in Italy and Europe. This is true of sectors in which public intervention prevails, such as in the rail and postal services. Such inefficiency may adversely affect Italian businesses in terms of costs since they face fewer possibilities than their foreign competitors. Both macroeconomic data and business data confirm that, as in Italy the most dynamic area of activity within the service sector is telecommunications (Table 2).

In this sector expansion is to be found all over Europe, and in Italy the efficiency gap is not as dramatic as it is for other sectors which includes public intervention. In this case problems arise in regard to the difference between tariffs in Italy and mean EEC values.

From comparative studies carried out up to the present, we may conclude that there are signs of a change in Italy with regard to the development model during the 1970's and 1980's. In particular, the expansion of the service sector only appears in definitive form over the last decade.

Fig. 5b Share of manufactured products employees in occupied population (in %)

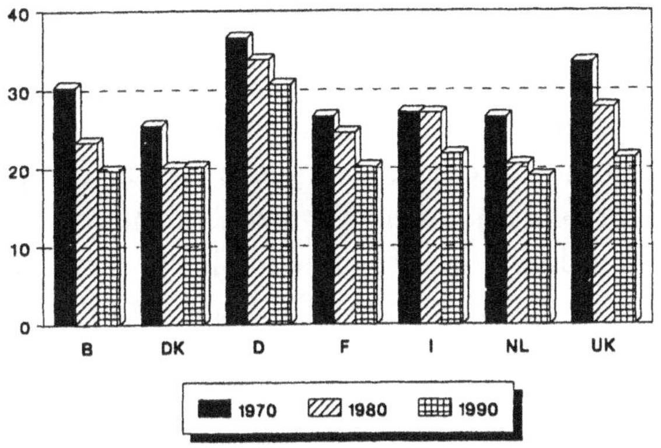

Fig. 6a Average annual growth rate of apparent productivity of labour (%) in the market services

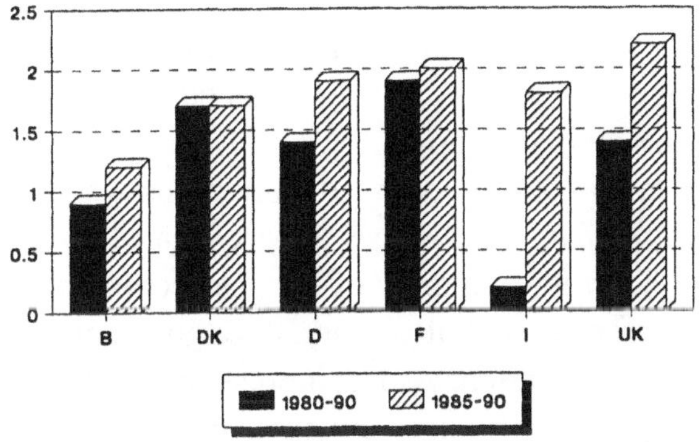

Fig. 6b Average annual growth rate of apparent productivity of labour (%) in manufactured products

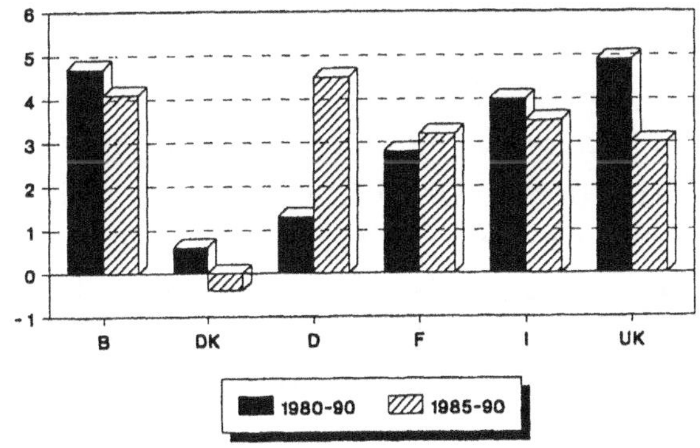

In regard to the main European competitors this dynamic was already evident during the 1970's. Furthermore signs of structural change became evident in the Italian market service sector during the second half of the 1980's. In this context even though problems of "inefficiency" persist (generally quantifiable in terms of low productivity), signs of development route convergence are emerging in the Italian service sector and in other European countries. This clearly does not mean that dissimilarities are completely eliminated but it does indicate a tendential reduction of the distance between players.

2. The Role of Demand Factors

2.1 Expenditure on Services in Household Consumption

Given expansion of the service sector in the context of national supply a dramatic change has taken place in demand for services directed both at businesses and households.

With reference to this latter aspect, demand conditions generally associated with expansion of the service sector are related to high income elasticity, and rigidity to own price of services consumption. The demand factors therefore essentially work through income effect: the resources freed by a tendency to compression of share of expenditure dedicated to grocery products and primary needs may be addressed to the acquisition of services. However, the empirical evidence in Italy shows substantial stability over the last 20 years in regard to the share of expenditure on services in the aggregate of household consumption expressed in terms of constant prices (Tables 3 and 4).

Over the same twenty-year period this share, if we calculate it in nominal terms, is seen to have grown considerably. If we limit ourselves to the specific time period, 1980-1992, the scenario is somewhat different. In this period we see a relative increase in the quantity of services demanded by households as compared to goods, this is concurrent with an above-mean growth of the deflator implicit in services. In particular, a more evident inflationary trend in regard to service prices, as compared to non-grocery product prices, is noted only in the 1980's (11.4% as opposed to 8.4%) while, during the preceding decade, the trend of relative prices was mainly unfavourable to the service sector for durable goods (Table 5).

A more detailed examination of spending for services (Table 5) shows that there is spending in supply of services in regard to real demand trends and relative prices. Services for the home, domestic services, recreational spending, spending for education, spending for hair and body care, and other services n. e. c. reveal, in the 1980's, a real trend greater than that of total expenditure together with a significant increase of relative prices. The only items of service consumption which have produced notable performance in real terms, together with a moderately inflationary dynamic, are those related to communication and financial services. The remaining items (rents, medical expenses, private and public transport, hotels and restaurants) show less real growth than total expenditure accompanied by highly inflationary trends.

To be more specific, real growth rates for the 1980-1992 period for services for the home (2.8%), domestic services (3.5%), recreational services (3.2%) and body care (4.8%), are above those pertaining to non or semi-durable, and non-grocery products (approx. 2.7%), while the spending trend for communication (6.8%), education (5.7%), financial services (11.0%) and services not classified here (5.6%), is higher than that to be found for durable goods (4.8%). As we have noted, such trends are observed within a context of particular change in trends in regard to relative prices.

The complexity emerging from changes in consumer behaviour over the last 20 years may be represented by an estimate of a demand equations system in order to measure the income and relative prices effect on the allocation of total spending between goods and services, and see if in Italy we can verify the "traditional" hypotheses concerning a significant income effect, which considered together with rigidity to relative price would dominate the evolution of service consumption.

The evidence of relative stability of the share of services on total expenditure may in fact be associated with both unit income elasticity and relative rigidity to prices, and also to a more than unitary income elasticity and significant elasticity to relative prices. High elasticity of income implies a change in the "tendencies" of the structure of consumers spending in favour of service consumption; significant price elasticity indicates conditions of demand which do not exclude substitution of goods with services and therefore may determine a relative competitive pressure on supply.

To measure the effect of income and the relative prices on the allocation of total expenditure between goods and services, we estimated a small "Almost Ideal" (A.I.) model[14] for the years 1970 to 1992. The system groups consumption into three broad categories and shows a value of income elasticity of 0.27 for expenditure on food (GR), 1.29 for non-food expenses (not including durable goods and health expenses), NGR. The services group (SER) not including health spending has an income elasticity of 1.38[15].

Own-price elasticity for service expenditure is significant and equal to -0.45, this is less (in absolute value) than that for non-food consumption (-0.67), but greater than that for food consumption (-0.28). Once the income effect is eliminated examination of compensated food consumption price elasticities shows considerable rigidity of services consumption. For the n items of spending considered, the A.I. system may be represented as follows [16]:

$$\mathbf{W} = \mathbf{A} + \Phi\,(\log \mathbf{P}) + \mathrm{B}\,(y/p_0) + \mathrm{U} \tag{3}$$

$$\log p_0 = \alpha_0 + \mathbf{A}'(\log \mathrm{P}) + 1/2\,(\log \mathbf{P})'\ \Phi\,(\log \mathbf{P}) \tag{4}$$

where: $\mathbf{W}$ = vector (nx1) of shares on total expenditure for the n goods; $\mathbf{P}$ = vector (nx1) of prices of same goods; y = a scalar, is total expenditure; p_o is also a scalar defined by (4); **A** and **B** (vectors nx1), Φ (nxn matrix) and α_0 are parameters; U = vector of stochastic

[14] Deaton and Muellbauer (1980).

[15] Elimination of durable goods depends on the one hand on the fact that a significant part of spending is not financed by current income, and on the other hand, prices do not fully reflect relative costs for the use of various goods. As regards spending for health services, the fact that this has not been included is connected to growing public spending for health care over the period in question.

[16] The exposition of the model is derived from Rossi (1983).

terms. Total per capita expenditure is calculated through the annual series of the average resident population. Elasticities were calculated relative to year 1980. Estimates were carried out placing restrictions only on Φ coefficients. The results of the constrained OLS estimates are given below:

Aggregates	A	B	Φ_1	Φ_2	Φ_3	R^2AD	DW	STDER
GR	.308 (121)	-.228 (-25.2)	.156 (9.0)	-.079 (-3.9)	-.077 (-7.5)	0.997	1.58	0.003
NGR	.345 (124)	.110 (11.1)	-.034 (-1.8)	.166 (7.5)	-.132 (-11.8)	0.982	1.65	0.003
SER	.347 (82)	.118 (7.9)	-.121 (-4.3)	-.088 (-2.6)	.209 (12.3)	0.982	1.36	0.005

Student's T test values are given in brackets.

Total expenditure (Ei) and own-price elasticities (Ep^1: compensated Ep^2: uncompensated)

Aggregates	Ei	Ep^1	Ep^2
GR	0.27	-0.28	-0.20
NGR	1.29	-0.67	-0.18
SER	1.38	-0.45	-0.02

The results given refer to an estimate of model (3) (4) imposing the homogeneity condition, so that autocorrelation of residuals arise. Statistical tests carried out from further unconstrained estimates (according to which absence of autocorrelation of residuals is verified) show that homogeneity is rejected for expenditure on food and services.

Considering this group, the positive sum of Φ coefficients indicates that a proportional increase in prices and total expenditure will increase expenditure on services. This is accompanied by a significant difference, between the elasticity to total real expenditure, as we move from restricted to unrestricted estimates.

In this case, the estimated value is only slightly higher than 1 with a clear weakening of the explanatory performance of the model. This suggests that understanding of the spending trends for services requires a more complex interpretative scheme than that incorporated in the model used.

The failure of homogeneity is a result which is common to many econometric studies, and it may be explained by the relative inflexibility of certain items of spending in the short term, by the omission of expectations on prices, or by problems of aggregation across various consumer types[17].

These results suggest that a more careful examination of explanatory factors for the trend of spending share on services must be conducted by means of greater disaggregation of spending categories, by considering the existence of pre-allocated spending, and by a better specification of the dynamic aspects. All these elements converge to delineate a future line of research based on the use of quarterly data.

Using sample-survey data on a cross-section of Italian households in 1989, an estimate of income elasticity in service spending was derived which was still above unit, (1.11), but below the one obtained with time-series data (constrained). The estimates carried out also reveal an elasticity of 0.57 for food consumption and of 1.22 for non-food consumption. The elasticity calculated for services not including housing is instead 1.42. The parametrization of the "income effect" alone was carried out through the Engel's curve that follows:

$$W = \alpha + \beta \log (Y) + e \qquad (5)$$

where W = the share of each item of consumption on total "observed" spending, and Y "current" spending per unit of consumption[18].

For each household current spending was deduced by comparing total expenditure and income class declared. If total spending was

---

[17] Deaton and Muellbauer (1980), p. 320. Rossi (1983), p. 58.
[18] Working (1943).

above the upper limit of the income class, it was corrected assigning 1/24 of expenditure on durable goods above a minimum amount.
Although the problem of "demographic effects" is far more complex, in order to reduce effects of distortion induced by the varying size of family units, a scale of equivalence was adopted which in each household gives value 1 to the head of the family, 0.7 to other adults, and 0.5 to other members aged less than 16[19]. Thus expenditure in the larger households is divided by a number of "units of consumption", which is lower than the number of real components. With reference to the composition of households in the population (as inferred through the sample) that correction determines a 30% increase of per capita spending. Equation (5) may represent the cross-section of the A.I. system of demand represented by (3) and (4). This "aggregates perfectly over consumers without invoking parallel and linear Engel's curves; it has a functional form which is consistent with known household-budget data"[20].
The method used is weighted LS. The weight is the size of each observation in terms of population. The estimates were based on approx. 500 observations derived from the aggregation of individual data in 50 classes of current per capita spending and 10 household types[21]. The households in the survey were classified according to the age of the members of the household. The typologies of children were allocated on the basis of their age. For family units without children the typologies were related to the age of the members[22]. The ten family typologies selected are: young person alone, adult alone, young couple, couple with infants, adult couple, couple with youngsters, couple with adult offspring, old couple, old person alone, other family units. Elasticity was calculated at the "mean" current spending per unit of consumption (= 752,000 Liras/month).
Comparison of the estimated income elasticities of expenditure on services for each of the selected family types allows us to remark

---

[19] Insee (1960).
[20] Deaton and Muellbauer (1980). p. 312.
[21] Criteria of selection of family typologies applied to study of Italian family spending in 1989 reflect to a great extent the criteria proposed by Carlucci-Levrero (1989).
[22] Infants: aged below 4; young children: aged 4-15; youngsters: 16-34 years old; adults: 35-64 years old; the old: more than 64 years old.

relatively low values for the young living alone, adult couples, and old couples. Levels are higher for the old living alone. Considering couples, we may note a progressive fall of the elasticity of expenditure on services with the age of the couple, once housing is eliminated. Elasticity in fact falls from 1.564 for young couples to 1.409 for couples with infants, falling yet further as the children grow up (1.376 for couples with youngsters and 1.351 for couples with adult offspring). The elasticity increases in the final stages of the life-cycle (1.506 for old couples and 1.679 for old people living alone). This evidence indicates that the propensity to acquire services in correspondence with varying income levels is significantly affected by family typology. On the basis of this observation, extrapolation of the results carried out in a dynamic sense suggests that, over the past decades, modification of the demographic structure may have had significant effects on the division of aggregate spending.

Lastly, comparison made between the results of estimates carried out on the basis of time-series data and cross-section data may be interpreted as an indication of an overestimation (in time-series) of the income elasticity of spending for services, induced by the exclusion of durable goods from the expenditure system. This implies that the introduction of new durable goods within the market may have determined substitution of services with goods.

2.2 The Demand for Services by Firms

Analyses of demand pressure on the service sector must consider the development of demand share coming from businesses. This type of analysis is conducted using input-output tables (hereafter referred to as TEI) produced by ISTAT in the 1980's. Therefore, contrary to the analysis conducted on data pertaining to demand for consumption by households, we have to accept a degree of approximation due to the level of disaggregation with which data are produced on the supply side[23].

[23] For the matrices for 1982 and 1985, see ISTAT (1987) and (1989). As regards sector-to-sector flow for supply of services, many bibliographic references are available. Among these, see Momigliano & Siniscalco (1982 and 1986), Pellegrini (1988), Uno (1989) and Lunghini and Rampa (1992).

Fig. 7 Share of intermediate inputs at current prices in total intermediate inputs (in %) - total economy

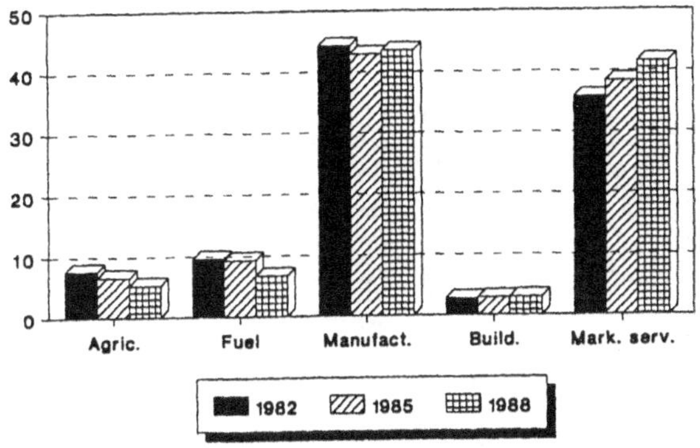

Fig. 8a Share of intermediate inputs at constant prices in total intermediate inputs (in %) - total economy

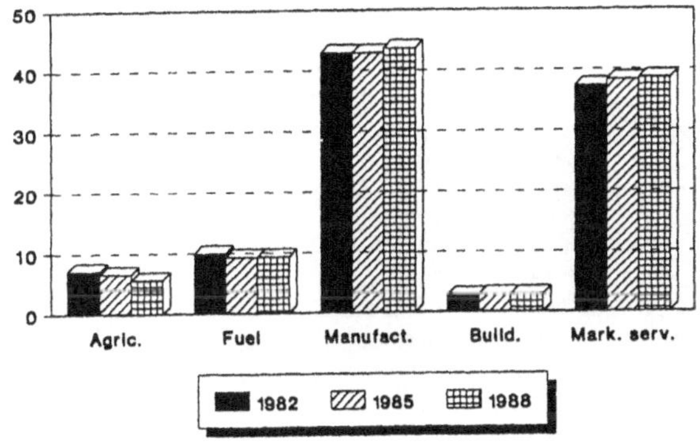

Fig. 8b Share of intermediate inputs at constant prices in total intermediate inputs (in %) - manufactured prod.

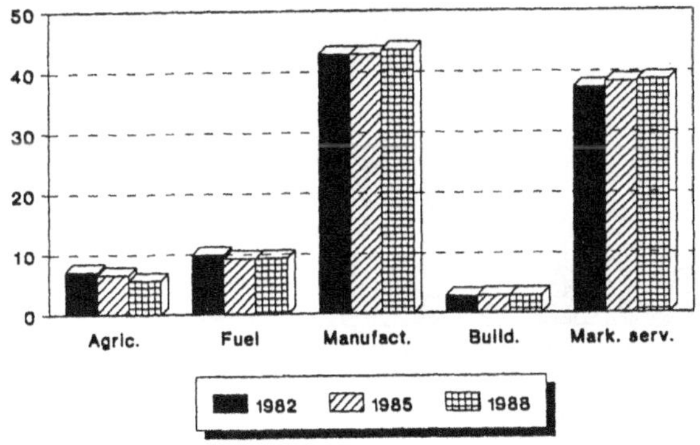

Fig. 8c Share of intermediate inputs at constant prices in total intermediate inputs (in %) - market services

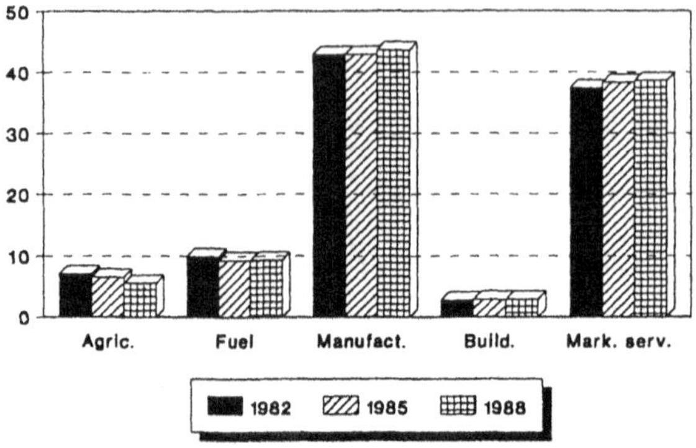

Fig. 9a Average annual growth rate of the gross value added at 1985 constant prices (in %)

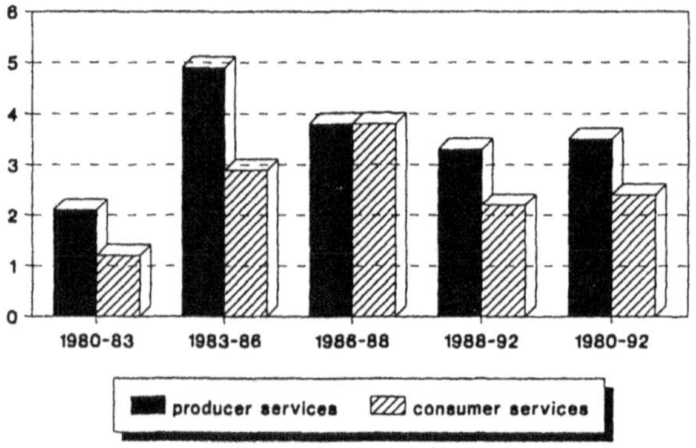

Fig. 9b Average annual growth rate of implicit prices of gross value added at market prices (in %)

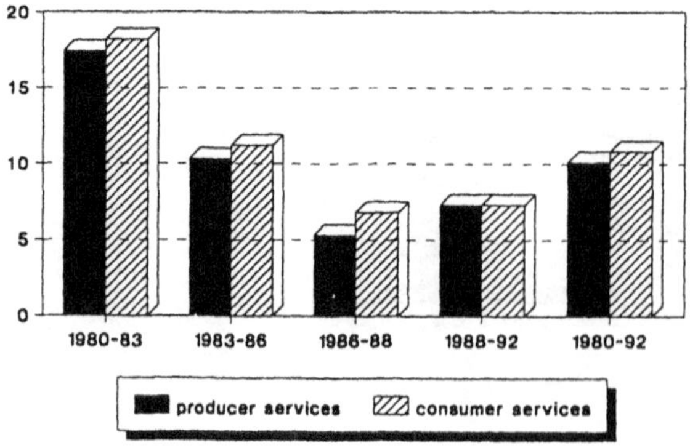

Through observation of the TEI for the years 1982, 1985 and 1988 it is noted that there has been a significant increase of the incidence of costs for the acquisition of market services on nominal costs for the whole national productive system. Indeed, for the total of intermediate domestic costs, the percentage of market services increases from 35.7% in 1982 to 41.5% in 1988 (fig. 7). This development contributes to an explanation of the development of the market service sector at current prices through increased demand by businesses, confirming progressively greater inter-dependence between processes of industrial restructuring, and the development of so-called "producer services". Turning our attention to this development we observe that the most active component is business services which, during the period observed have grown from 6.2% to 9.0% of costs. This is also explained by the fact that in this branch we have a greater concentration of so-called "advanced" service activities. We also observe that the share of the branch comprising more traditional activities, such as the commercial sector and lodging and catering has remained constant over time.

Apart from dynamic aspects, it is appropriate to stress the fact that the commercial intermediation sector is an important part of intermediate costs. Cost consideration of internal origin pertaining to industrial transformation, showed the commercial sector was above 12%. Furthermore, we may note a growing demand for services from businesses operating in the same sector, which increase the use of services from 64.9% in 1982 to 66.5% in 1988. Growing internal integration within the areas of activity has not been linear, since the greatest development is to be found for 1985-1988. Expansion of the service sector has been fastest in the following branches: credit and insurance, supply of business services, and distributive sectors with shares of 97.3%, 57.2% and 60.5%.

To examine the dynamic of intersectoral net flows of the component due to the differential in price increases, costs of internal origin were deflated by the index of production prices[24]. Taking constant prices for the economy as a whole, from 1982 to 1988, we confirm that

[24] Deflation was carried out at the level of disaggregation of 44 branches assigning to each line of costs the corresponding price estimated per branch.

integration increased with regard to service activities, the shares of which, in relation to intermediate costs, went from 37.4% in 1982 to 38.6% in 1988 (fig. 8a, b, c). Clearly, that increase looks very small if we compare it with the increase in nominal terms, given the greater inflationary trend exhibited by the market service sector as compared to other productive sectors. Here too, the most active component is business services. Commenting on the relative growth of demand for services we should also consider the fact that a part is due to a process of externalization of service activities previously included in the productive processes of the other sectors.

Similar evidence emerges when we consider manufacturing, inside of which the share of expenditure on services increases from 25.3% in 1982 to 26.3% in 1988. In this case, however, the trend is not uniform within the period considered, as growth is concentrated in the 1982-1985 period, after which it was basically stable up until 1988.

In the commercial service sector progress was dissimilar in that the quantity of services demanded within the sector appears to fall during the period in question.

The trend observed, furthermore, is verified over the entire period for which we note shares of 64.8%, 63.8% and 62.8% for 1982, 1985 and 1988 respectively. Therefore, from the analysis of cost flows in constant liras, we may note growing integration of the service sector with the economic system and the manufacturing products sector. However, growing activity of the service sector is not noted within branches producing services.

A further point concerns the targeting of supply for each service sector. On this basis we may attempt a subdivision of these activities according to whether their production is aimed prevalently at intermediate uses (producer services), or final use (consumer services). Using 1988 data (Table 6) in the first category we have: credit and insurance (91.5%), business services (83.1%), and communication (61.4%). A share higher than 50% is also noted for the transportation sector. This is mainly due to the prevalence of road transport of goods.

To increase over time series information on the development of "consumer services" and "producer services", our proposal is quite simply to reclassify the activities which make up the area of market services. By doing so, on the basis of shares of destination of the product deduced from the TEI Tables for 1985, added value was reallocated at current and constant prices for each branch, according to whether they were directed at final consumption or intermediate use, thereby leading us to total supply of services for producers and consumers, both in nominal and real terms (fig. 9a, 9b)[25].

Given the methodology adopted for the construction of the aggregates just mentioned, the operation exclusively considers the effects of composition verified from sector to sector of economic activity, which thus appear to be classified differently.

The empirical evidence shows that at the beginning of the 1980's "consumer services" were the prevalent element in the market service sector exhibiting a share of 58.5% of total of value added at constant prices. During the 1980's, greater relative growth of "producer services" was noted, and thus in 1990 the real share of consumer services on the total went down to 55.3%.

The growth of "producer services" occurred during the first half of the 1980's and in particular during the period 1983 - 1986 (fig. 9a). From 1986 to 1988 we note a convergence between the two sectors produced mainly by an acceleration of "consumer services". Furthermore, the end of the 1980's and the beginning of the 1990's witnessed a new divergence between the sectors, since consumer services slowed down and producer services recovered.

From the stand point of inflationary trends, the most dynamic component was the consumer service sector which, over the entire 1980-1992 period, increased prices at a mean rate 0.7% greater than producer services. Analysis of sub-periods reveals systematically greater price increases in consumer services up to 1988. Toward the end of the period (1988-1992) stronger inflationary trends are noted for the supply of services for intermediate use, determining prices comparable to those observed for consumer services.

The final aspect which we shall consider is the growing role of services in terms of demand for investment goods. In this case, we

---

[25] We are dealing with a high degree of approximation the main causes of which may be identified in the level of disaggregation (44 branches) and in the non-availability of a distinct price system for producer and consumer services. A similar decomposition, using a different technique, was recently applied to the Canadian economy; see Grubel (1993).

follow a different track, since the demand we consider comes from the service sector and this induces a supply of both internal and external instrumental goods. Considering the volume of investment in machinery and instruments used in the manufacturing and private services, we may assess how the composition of demand from these two sectors has changed in the 1980's and as result there has been considerable relative growth in the flow of investment goods used by the service sector. Indeed, the share ascribed to the service sector increased from 34.2% in 1980 to 50% at the end of the decade. The relative growth (Table 7) is irrespective of the cyclical phase throughout the 1980's. This trend involves all branches of the service sector. Furthermore, growth of investment in machinery, tools and various products used in the service sector is associated with a significant increase, with respect to manufacturing, both in the accumulation rate and flow of investments per unit of labour. Exclusion of transportation, communication, credit and insurance from the sector does not modify the situation.

3. Acceleration of Service Sector Expansion During the 1980's

3.1 Sectoral Developments in Market Services

During 1980-1992, there is a lessening of the relative importance of commerce, hotels and catering as well as of the various branches of transportation in total value added at current prices (Table 8). Structural changes at constant prices only partly confirm this evidence, since internal transportation exhibits increased relative importance, while consumer services are decreasing. We note that the structure of value added, at constant prices of the service sector, has changed progressively in the sense that the sectors producing services mainly for business have grown (see 3.2).

Within this picture of recomposition of the supply of services we also find, as we have already noted, a generalized increase in labour units of both autonomous worker and employee. This tendency is associated with a progressive reduction in the growth rate of autonomous workers. This indicates the development of intense restructuring in the service sector.

Over the 1980-1992 period, the private service sector absorbed approx. 2,600,000 new jobs, together with a loss of employment totalling approx. 1,200,000 jobs through industrial transformation. In Table 9 we particularly note business service performance with 980,000 added jobs of which 660,000 are wage-earning. This sector differs from other service areas, given the growth in high wage earners (+8.5% per year on average), and the substantial change in the composition of employment favouring the said employment.

As we note from table 10, employment structure differs greatly from area to area. Taken together, the share of autonomous workers grew from 43.5% in 1980 to 44.9% in 1992, and this development was largely due to the notable growth in the intensity of autonomous work in services to families, lodging and catering as well as to inland transportation. At the same time, the commercial sector was substantially stable in terms of the share of autonomous workers (approx. 60%). There has been a sharp increase in wage-earners within the area of business services.

Assessment of trends in employment according to this typology show, for the private service sector taken as a whole, a mean annual growth rate of 2.5% for regular workers (2.1% for employees and 3.1% for autonomous workers), while for irregular workers the growth rate is 3.3% (5.1% for employees and 1.8% for autonomous workers). In the private service sector taken as a whole, the different evolution of employment determines a - 2% increase of the share of irregular jobs on total employment, growth of more than 5% of the relative share of wage-earners and a 3% fall in the share of autonomous workers (Table 11). This lesser incidence of irregular workers among autonomous workers is verified, except for inland transportation, in all branches of the service sector. An increase in irregular jobs is found commonly also in the commercial and transportation sectors. The share of irregular jobs is instead falling both for wage-earners and autonomous workers in services to firms and households.

These dynamics were characterized by a high turnover in business, from which we may deduce that the growing supply of entrepreneurship is associated both with significant selection by the market, and with a slight growth in the size of the business. In particular, between 1987 and 1990, we note how on average one job out of five in market services is created and destroyed every year and how, as opposed to industry, growth of employment is the result of the positive balance both in existing firms and in those "started" and "failed" during the year. Obviously the employment "turbulence" of the market service sector is particularly intense in the smallest firms where turnover is on average 75% (involving not less than half a million jobs every year). Sector data concerning aggregate dynamics show an annual change of 3 employees out of 10 in commerce, hotel and catering, and approx. 2 in services to firms and to households[26].

Examination over the 1980's of indicators of production, employment, inflation and distribution in the different areas of the market service sector allows us to make further distinctions within this area (Tables 12a, 12b).

Turning our attention to commercial distribution (Table 12a) we may note a much weaker trend in "prices" (input, output, deflator of value added) than for the service sector taken as a whole. These tendencies are associated with a relative fall, both of the mark-up and the share, of gross profit on value added while wage increases were on average 0.7% per year above that of the service sector taken as a whole. Furthermore, relative productivity grew modestly. Indeed, after the sharp fall in productivity of labour over the 1980-1983 period (-2.4% per year), there was an acceleration between the 1983-1988 (+0.7% in 1983-1986 and +3.2% in 1986-1988) followed by a slowing down to 1.3% over the last four years. As noted below, the productivity trend in the commercial sector was significantly greater during 1980's than that of areas in which the current debate is defined as more "advanced" (in that they are more sensitive to technological change and demand pressures from business).

The most acute phase of the employment restructuring in the distribution sector was seen in 1986-1988, this coincided with the period of fastest growth in productivity which in turn was associated with a fall in wage-earning jobs (-0.2%) as opposed to a 2.0% growth in

---

[26] Albisinni (1992), p. 26-28.

autonomous workers. Furthermore, in this period growth of final prices was greatly reduced (+4.8%) even if profits are higher than in the preceding period. Irrespective of residual components present in the employment dynamic of the commercial sector, it is common knowledge that the evolution of the distribution sector over the 1980's reflects above all the increased importance of commercial distribution as opposed to the production of goods[27]. The different quality of development of commercial distribution during the second half of the 1980's is evident and runs parallel to greater sensitivity on the part of public administration to the needs of large scale distribution (put into effect through automatic mechanisms for the granting of authorizations). This has meant an increased growth rate for shopping centres and supermarkets, as pointed out above (2.4)[28]. The evidence of greater market share as ascribed to large scale distribution is not the only result of modernization within the commercial sector during the second half of the 1980's. As opposed to grocery trade, modernization of the distribution of non-grocery goods does not necessarily require increased sales space per shop. In fact, "... The proliferation of products and the great number of variants within the same product reduce the importance of the main advantage of large department stores, i.e. their informative role, and gives greater weight to the rigidities of choice characteristic of these despecialized formulae"[29]. There has been a positive response in the commercial sector differentiation of industrial supply through a net increase of contractual integration (franchising)[30].

The restructuring of the commercial sector, from 1987 to 1990, exhibited intense numeric growth of non-grocery wholesale firms, especially in the Northern regions of the country. This may be an indicator of the convergence of relations between production and distribution at the expense of the intermediary phase[31]. On the retail side we see a contraction of traditional grocery shops and accelerated growth of small and medium-sized shops in the non-grocery sector.

---

[27] Zanderighi (1992).
[28] Cescom-Mondo Economico (1992).
[29] Zanderighi (1992), p. 16.
[30] Pellegrini L. (1986).
[31] Minisci and Negrini (1991).

Restructuring of the grocery sector appears to be considerably faster in Northern and Central Italy. In the South, the diffusion of more modern sales formulae proceeds with greater difficulty.

Within this general picture the distribution sector appears to be interested in a concentration of locally significant businesses. In the second report presented by the Antitrust Authority it was noted, in 1991, there were 15 concentrations deals in the commercial distribution sector for 24 markets. Many of the operations were horizontal and involved the same products in the same geographic area. Bearing in mind the growth of market shares of the 15 buyer companies (from 0.4% in 1990 to 6.7% in 1991) we may conclude that in the commercial sector significant concentration is taking place which must be carefully assessed[32].

In a recent report, the Antitrust Authority claims that "Just as we cannot support the view that the law should prevent the modernization of the sector, we must point out that the limits deriving from the rules in their present form and the low numbers of large retail firms in Italy do not in themselves imply that market competition is lacking in the retail distribution sector, above all if we consider the context, characterized by a high fragmentation of supply. It should be noted, however, that the existing barriers to market access and flexibility of supply have brought about distortions and limited the efficacy of market function thus inhibiting full competition defined as a stimulus for the adoption of more efficient production and localizations and also the spread of new technological and organizational developments in the commercial sector, to the benefit of consumers"[33].

In business services (Table 12b) relative prices (in regard to total supply of the market service sectors) shows a decrease in relative prices during the first half of the 1980's and evident recovery during the second half of the decade. The intense growth in this sector nevertheless is associated with a fall in mark-up and profit share in respect to the service sector as a whole. At the same time wage levels

---

[32] Giancane and Sechi (1992), p. 29.

[33] "Autorità Garante della Concorrenza e del Mercato" (Antitrust Authority) (1993, p. 17-19).

show less growth and a significant tendency toward lower labour productivity. The trend of this latter indicator (-1.6% per year in 1980-1992) brings with it significant problems regarding a correct interpretation of the situation. The fact that business services in the 1980's fared more badly than other services in terms of labour productivity, makes it difficult to associate the dramatic development of "advanced" activities (this area within the sector is growing in importance induced by the need for greater specialization, in a framework of growing inefficiency prompted by the trend of real product per employee).

An assessment of real product trends per labour unit as an indicator of gain or loss in sector efficiency is, in this case, conditioned by the view that the considerably expansive cycle of business services along with intense competition may determine gains in terms of efficiency, especially for the industrial sector, and for other segments of the market services sector. The productivity "missing" in the business services branch is found in other sectors which have increased demand for services. On the other hand, heterogeneity of the activities in this area (ranging from car-rental to professional, technical, computer, security and cleaning services) means that the problem is not typical of other services (such as distribution) which favour the identification of structural factors hindering significant progress in terms of efficiency. For example, the importance of professional activities within the business service sector does not permit us to make general statements as to the persistence of barriers to entry that determine the maintenance of rent positions.

The household services sector (Table 12b) is composed of recreational and cultural services, private teaching, research and health care, and is one of the most inflationary segments. The relative increase in price of output determines high growth both in mark-up and profit share given final demand which is particularly dynamic and sensitive to changes in services supplied. At the same time, we may note an evident fall in relative productivity associated with a wage trend equal to the service sector average. In this sector, as for business services, labour productivity tends to fall (-0.6% a year during 1980-1992). As already noted, the sector is also characterized by a growing presence of autonomous labour in regard to total employment.

In "hotel and catering" (Table 12a) we may note a considerable price inflation accompanied by a constant increase of relative profitability. These results are obtained irrespective of a negative trend of real product per unit of labour (-0.6%), even when the employment dynamic is relatively weak.

Lastly, relative price trends in domestic transportation (Table 12a) show notable gains during the first half of the 1980's followed by a tendency to fall. The significant increase in relative productivity accompanied by a wage dynamic slower than the average for the service sector permits stabilization of relative profitability margins in the decade.

3.2 Trends and Territory

The acceleration of the expansion of the service sector in the Italian economy during the 1980's followed different paths in the various regions of the country. As may be noted in Table 13, over 1980-1990, growth (both in nominal and real terms) of the private service sector in the South appears to be more rapid than in Northern and Central Italy and, concurrently, we may note a relatively quick development in autonomous workers.

Within each sector faster real growth in the South involves all areas of activity, with the exception of services n.e.c. (to firms and households) where, compared with an average annual growth of 3% in the South, firms in Central Italy and the North exhibit a growth of 3.9%. If we bear in mind the fact within the services n.e.c. we find most of the so-called "advanced" services, we may imagine that while Northern and Central Italy developed according to the international trend, the South was to a greater extent bound to more traditional models of development.

Changes in the composition of value added in the service sector appear to be less predominant in the South compared to Central and Northern Italy, where the commercial sector has shrunk approx. by 4.2% of services value added while in the South it has shrunk by approx. 1.3%.

At the same time, the share of value added of services n.e.c. has increased in Northern and Central Italy by 3%, while decreasing in the South by 1%. Taken as a whole, the faster growth of value added on employment in the South leads to a negative tendency in productivity (-0.1%) compared with a slight growth in the Northern and Central regions (+0.3%). This result is determined by the fact that in the South a substantially stationary situation is observed in distribution sector productivity, and a greater fall in the productivity of services n.e.c. A slower trend in labour costs in the Southern region determines the growth 10.2% in labour cost per unit of product in the South, as compared with 10.8% in the Central and Northern regions. During the 1980's we note a strengthening of margins in the service sector in the South. The differential between the South and Central-Northern areas (1.6% in 1980) becomes 2.3% in 1990.
These tendencies are to be considered within a structural framework which, still in 1990, displayed a share of real value added of the service on total private value added equal to 61.8% in the South compared to 54.4% in the Central and Northern areas. In 1980, these same shares were 56.3% and 51.9% respectively. Turning our attention to employment the association of greater growth rates for the service sector and higher dismissal rates for industry in the Southern regions has led to notable relative growth of service employment on total private sector employment (above 13% in the South compared to 10.6% in Central and Northern Italy). The employment share of the service sector in 1990 was 52.7% in the South and 51.8% in Central and Northern Italy.

3.3 Cyclical Phases

Considering the market service sector in general, the last decade may be divided up into 4 sub-periods (Table 14).
The first phase (1980-1983) seems to have been characterized by the reaction of the sector to a series of dramatic developments in terms of employment consequent both to the rapidity and intensity of industrial readjustment and to general weakness of real activity of the entire economic system.

During the second period (1983-1986) we may note a preliminary adjustment to the supply of services for quantitative and qualitative development in final demand. Over the first half of the 1980's the widening of the inflation differential to the benefit of the service sector appears to be associated with massive sector-to-sector redistribution of employment, to relative pressure on nominal income, and to changes occurring to the exchange regime.

The third phase (1986-1988), in consequence of the oil counter-shock, represents a time of "virtuous" development of the market service sector accompanied by deep internal restructuring as a response to exceptionally high demand. During this period, in fact, the contribution of services to the process of disinflation is significant.

Later (1988-1992), wage increases in the service sector, caused by improved conditions in the labour market, and by significant increases in productivity in the preceding years, determine a stronger pressure on final prices. Over the same period, therefore, there is a re-opening of the positive differential between to the growth of the prices of services and there of industrial transformation, since harsher exchange regime conditions induce greater disciplining of the prices of goods. Internationally speaking, as compared to the EEC mean, there is a more than 3% relative price rise differential of nationally produced industrial products.

References

Albisinni, M., (1992), "Struttura e Flussi dell'Occupazione nella Seconda Metà degli Anni Ottanta. Un Riscontro Quantitativo sulla Base dei Dati INPS", *Rassegna di Lavori dell'ISCO*, no.17.

Annunziato P., Manfroni P., Rosa G., (1992), "La Stima del Capitale per Settore e Area Geografica e Alcuni Indici di Produttività", *CSC Ricerche*, no.66.

Autorità Garante Della Concorrenza e Del Mercato, (1993), "Regolamentazione della Distribuzione Commerciale e Concorrenza", *Relazione al Presidente del Consiglio dei Ministri.*

Bain, J.S., (1951), "Relations of Profit Rate to Industry Concentration: American Manufacturing, 1936-40", *Quarterly Journal of Economics*, August.

Barca, F. e Visco, I., (1991), "L'Economia Italiana nella Prospettiva Europea: Terziario Protetto e Dinamica dei Redditi Nominali", *Temi di Discussione del Servizio Studi,* Banca d'Italia, 175.

Baumol W.J., Batey Blackman S.A., Wolff E.N., (1989), *Productivity and American Leadership. The Long View*, The MIT Press, Cambridge, Massachusetts.

Carlucci Levrero, M., (1989), "Una Proposta di Classificazione dei Consumi Secondo il Ciclo di Vita della Famiglia", *Saggi di Statistica Economica*, Università di Roma, Facoltà di Scienze Statistiche, Istituto di Statistica Economica.

Caves, R.E. and Porter, M.E., (1977), "From Entry Barriers to Mobility Barriers", *Quarterly Journal of Economics,* May.

CER, (1991), Centro Europa Ricerche, Report 5/1991.

CESCOM-Mondo Economico, (1992), "Rapporto sul Commercio", *Mondo Economico*, 10 October.

Cubbin, J. and Geroski, P., (1987), "The Convergence of Profits in the Long Run: Interfirm and Interindustry Comparisons", *Journal of Industrial Economics*, June.

D'Antonio, M., (1992), "Concorrenza, Sviluppo, Inflazione: Il Caso dei Servizi", *Economia Italiana,* no.3, Sept.-Dec. 1992.

Deaton, A. and Muellbauer, J., (1980), "An Almost Ideal Demand System", *American Economic Review*, 70.

Felli, E., (1989), "Il 'Puzzle' Produttività: Il Caso dei Servizi Distributivi e Turistici", *ISCOM, Quaderni di Politica Commerciale e Turistica,* year VII, no.3.

Fuà, G., (1993), *Crescita Economica. Le Insidie delle Cifre* , Il Mulino, Bologna.

Giancane, A. and Sechi, S., (1992), "La Regolamentazione della Concorrenza: Analisi della Struttura Istituzionale che Sovrasta i Servizi Pubblici e Privati", *OECT,* July.

Guelpa, F., (1990), "Persistenza dei Profitti e Dinamica della Concorrenza", *L'Industria,* April-June.

Grubel H., (1993) "Producer Services: Their Important Role in Growing Economies", paper presented at the meeting *The Service Sector: Productivity and Growth.* Rome, 27-28 May.

INSEE-CREDOC, (1960), "La Consommation des Menages Francais en 1956", *Consommation*, 7, 2.

ISTAT, (1987), "Tavola Intersettoriale dell'Economia Italiana, Anno 1982", *Collana d'Informazione*, no.22.

ISTAT, (1989), "Tavola Intersettoriale dell'Economia Italiana, Anno 1985", *Collana d'Informazione*, no.43.

ISTAT, (1991a) "Conti Economici delle Imprese con 20 Addetti e Oltre, Anno 1988", *Collana d'Informazione*, no.1.

ISTAT, (1991b), "Conti Economici delle Imprese con Addetti da 10 a 19, Anno 1988", *Collana d'Informazione*, no.17.

ISTAT, (1991c) "Conti Economici delle Imprese con Meno di 10 Addetti, Anni 1986 e 1988", *Collana d'Informazione*, no.17.

ISTAT, (1993) *Rapporto Annuale - La Situazione del Paese - 1992* , bozza.

Kamien, M.I. and Schwartz, N.L., (1982), *Market Structure and Innovation*, Cambridge University Press, Cambridge.

Lunghini G. and Rampa L., (1992), *Struttura, Interdipendenza e Tecnologia nell'Economia Italiana*, Milano.

Minisci, M. and Negrini, D., (1991), "L'Evoluzione più Recente dell'Offerta Commerciale: Un'Analisi dei Dati del Ministero dell'Industria", *OECT*, December.

Momigliano, F. and Siniscalco, D., (1982), "Note in Tema di Terziarizzazione e Deindustrializzazione", *Moneta e Credito.*

Momigliano, F. and Siniscalco, D., (1986), "Mutamenti nella Struttura del Sistema Produttivo e Integrazione fra Industria e Terziario", in *Mutamenti Strutturali del Sistema Produttivo. Integrazione tra Industria e Settore Terziario*, L.Pasinetti editor, Il Mulino, Bologna.

Pellegrini, G., (1988), "Integrazione dei Settori Produttivi e Sviluppo del Sistema Produttivo", *Contributi all'Analisi Economica*, Banca d'Italia, no.4.

Pellegrini, G., (1990), "La Produttività nei Servizi Destinabili alla Vendita: Nuove Evidenze per un Vecchio Problema", *Mimeo*, Banca d'Italia, April.

Pellegrini, L., (1986), "Evoluzione e Prospettive della Distribuzione in Italia", in *Secondo Rapporto CESCOM sulla Distribuzione Commerciale in Italia*, F.Angeli, Milano.

Rey G.M., (1992a), "I Mutamenti della Struttura Economica: Fattori Produttivi, Distribuzione del Reddito, Domanda", in *L'Italia Verso il 2000: Le Istituzioni, la Società, l'Economia*, SIPI, Collana Studi e Ricerche.

Rey G.M., (1992b), "I Servizi per le Imprese in Italia: Caratteri e Dimensioni" in *I Servizi alle Imprese in Italia*, Unioncamere, Maggioli Editore.

Rossi, N., (1983), "Sistemi di Domanda Condizionali e Non: Un Esperimento Disaggregato", in *Ricerche di Economia Applicata: Il Caso Italiano*, N. Rossi e P.Rovelli editors, F.Angeli, Milano.

Spaventa, L., (1973), "Note su Rendite e Profitti: l'Esperienza Italiana", *Moneta e Credito,* December.

Stigler, G.J., (1963), *Capital and Rates of Return in Manufacturing Industries*, Princeton University Press, Princeton, N.J.

Sylos Labini, P., (1967), *Oligopolio e Progresso Tecnico*, Einaudi, Torino.

Uno K., (1989), *Measurement of Services in an Input-Output Framework*, North-Holland.

Zanderighi, L., (1992), "Sviluppo Economico e Commercio. Gli Anni '80", *Note di Ricerca,* CESCOM, no.26, Milano.

Williamson, O.E., (1975), *Market and Hierarchies*, Free Press, New York.

Working, H., (1943), *Statistical Laws of Family Expenditure*, JASA, 38, 43.

Statistical appendix

Table 1 Average annual growth rate of implicit prices of value added at market prices by branch, in % - 1980-90

Branches	B	DK(1)	D	F	I	NL	P	UK
Agricultural products	3.3	1.7	-0.3	3.6	6.2	1.4	12.5	2.5
Fuel and power products	3.2	0.2	3.3	6.6	15.1	1.1	18.6	2.6
Manufactured products	2.6	6.3	3.1	6.3	7.9	2.8	17.2	4.8
Buildings and constructions	3.7	6.9	2.8	4.9	10.0	1.7	18.4	8.4
Market services	5.4	6.0	2.7	7.1	11.1	2.6	17.6	6.8
Non market services	3.8	6.2	2.7	6.5	13.1	1.2	18.6	8.6
Total of branches	4.3	5.7	2.8	6.5	10.4	1.8	17.3	6.4

Source: Eurostat

(1) These data relate to value added at factor cost and not at market prices.

Table 2 Average annual growth rate of: value added at 1985 constant prices (q), implicit prices (p) and apparent productivity of labour (pro) by branches, in % - 1985-90

	B			K			D(2)		
Branches	q	p	pro	q	p	pro(1)	q	p	pro
Manufactured prod.	3.6	2.9	4.1	-0.5	5.4	-0.4	2.0	4.6	-0.2
Market services	3.8	4.9	1.2	2.7	3.6	1.7	4.3	3.6	0.5
Trade services	0.9	8.2	-0.6	0.9	2.5	1.6	2.4	3.5	0.7
Lodging and cat.	3.4	5.7	3.4	-1.1	7.2	-2.6	-0.2	6.4	-1.9
Inland transport	6.4	3.3	6.6	0.6	6.7	-1.4	-	-	-
Maritime, air transp.	0.4	1.8	3.8	24.6	12.9	25.8	-	-	-
Auxiliary transp.	3.0	4.9	2.6	1.2	4.7	-1.3	-	-	-
Communications	5.1	3.4	5.7	3.7	3.6	1.9	6.3	0.6	5.1
Credit and insurance	6.4	0.2	4.6	2.5	3.1	0.5	5.4	-0.1	3.3.
Other services	4.8	4.4	-0.3	2.4	6.0	-0.1	5.2	4.6	-3.3.
Total of branches	3.2	4.0	1.8	1.7	4.1	1.3	3.0	4.1	0.7

	F			I			UK		
Branches	q	p	pro	q	p	pro	q	p	pro
Manufactured prod.	2.1	3.4	3.2	3.6	3.3	3.5	3.4	0.1	3.0
Market services	4.4	4.1	2.0	3.7	6.2	1.8	4.7	2.5	2.2
Trade services	2.6	4.2	1.8	3.4	4.8	2.5	4.2	2.6	3.4
Lodging and cat.	2.3	7.9	-1.4	1.7	7.2	1.0	3.9	2.9	-0.1
Inland transport	4.3	1.3	2.9	6.2	6.2	3.1	5.1	1.0	6.0
Maritime, air transp.	5.6	-3.5	4.5	3.3	5.1	4.4	7.3	-1.7	5.0
Auxiliary transp.	4.5	1.7	2.6	3.7	6.3	3.7	2.7	2.6	-1.3
Communications	6.9	-2.6	7.4	5.3	2.9	3.8	6.3	-1.4	5.5
Credit and insurance	2.4	5.5	2.4	4.8	4.8	3.2	7.6	1.8	3.3
Other services	5.8	4.5	1.0	3.4	8.1	-0.2	4.4	2.2	0.2
Total of branches	2.9	3.5	2.2	3.0	5.7	2.4	3.1	1.9	1.4

Source: Eurostat

(1) For transport services 1985-1988.(2) For Lodging and catering, communications and other market services is 1985 - 1989.

Table 3 Final consumption of households

Anni	(1)	(2)	(3)	(4)	(5)	(6)	(7)	(8)
1970	29.0	32.9	.	.	.	100.0	100.0	100.0
1971	29.7	33.1	4.8	7.3	2.5	102.3	102.4	102.0
1972	30.4	33.3	5.5	7.9	2.4	104.6	102.7	105.7
1973	29.9	32.6	13.5	14.5	1.0	105.6	103.0	106.7
1974	29.7	32.9	22.2	19.3	-2.9	103.0	103.7	101.3
1975	30.6	33.9	16.5	16.6	.1	103.1	103.3	101.6
1976	30.2	33.6	17.9	17.1	-.8	102.4	101.9	101.1
1977	29.9	33.4	17.9	17.0	-.9	101.6	101.0	100.1
1978	29.8	33.0	12.7	14.6	1.9	103.4	102.6	101.8
1979	29.4	32.3	14.2	15.4	1.2	104.5	103.4	102.5
1980	29.1	32.1	20.6	20.0	-.6	103.9	107.1	99.3
1981	30.4	32.8	17.1	20.4	3.3	106.9	110.7	101.8
1982	31.1	33.2	16.4	18.7	2.4	109.1	114.0	103.3
1983	32.1	33.3	13.5	18.0	4.5	113.4	121.2	105.9
1984	33.3	33.5	10.3	15.5	5.2	118.6	128.2	110.3
1985	33.3	33.3	8.6	9.7	1.1	119.8	129.6	111.3
1986	34.4	33.3	4.5	9.7	5.2	125.8	134.8	117.4
1987	34.8	33.1	4.5	7.0	2.5	128.8	138.9	119.8
1988	35.2	32.7	4.5	8.2	3.7	133.4	145.1	123.6
1989	35.3	32.5	5.7	7.7	2.0	135.9	147.3	126.1
1990	36.2	32.9	5.4	7.6	2.2	138.7	149.3	129.1
1991	36.7	32.9	6.0	8.4	2.4	141.9	151.8	132.4
1992	37.5	32.9	4.2	7.5	3.3	146.4	155.8	136.9

Columns:

(1) Share of services consumption in total final consumption (current prices);
(2) Share of services consumption in total final consumption (constant prices);
(3) Annual growth rate of implicit price of total final consumption;
(4) Annual growth rate of implicit price of services consumption;
(5) (4)-(3);
(6) Relative prices services/goods;
(7) Relative prices services/food;
(8) Relative prices service/non-food.

Table 4 Final consumption of households: share of purposes in total consumption; V: current prices Q: constant prices (1985)

	1970		1980		1992	
Purposes	V	Q	V	Q	V	Q
Goods	71.0	67.1	70.9	67.9	62.5	67.1
Food	35.8	31.3	26.4	24.1	18.5	19.5
Non-Food goods	35.2	35.8	44.5	43.8	44.0	47.6
Non-durable goods	12.5	12.3	13.2	14.0	13.3	14.1
Semi-durable goods	15.8	16.3	19.9	19.6	18.9	20.2
Durable goods	7.0	7.3	11.4	10.2	11.8	13.3
Services	29.0	32.9	29.1	32.1	37.5	32.9
Services (*)	20.2	23.0	19.7	21.9	25.8	23.1
Total	100.0	100.0	100.0	100.0	100.0	100.0

(*) Excluding house rent

Table 5 Final consumption of households: annual growth rate V: current prices Q: constant prices (1985) P: implicit prices

Purposes	1970-1980			1980-1992		
	V	Q	P	V	Q	P
House rent	20.4	4.8	14.9	14.2	2.1	11.8
Household operation	27.1	12.3	13.2	12.5	2.8	9.5
Domestic services	17.5	1.6	15.6	16.1	3.5	12.2
Medical care	22.5	9.7	11.6	16.0	1.8	13.9
Hospital care and cure	18.9	2.0	16.5	16.0	1.4	14.5
Personal transport services	17.4	0.3	17.1	11.6	1.9	9.5
Purchased transport	16.5	2.9	13.2	13.9	2.5	11.1
Communication	20.0	5.1	14.1	16.0	6.8	8.6
Entertainment, recreational and cultural services	15.6	2.1	13.2	13.9	3.2	10.4
Education	17.1	2.9	13.8	18.0	5.7	11.6
Personal care	17.9	2.4	15.2	16.1	4.8	10.8
Hotel, restaurant and cafés	21.1.	4.3	16.1	13.7	2.2	11.3
Financial services n.e.c.	15.8	1.7	13.8	20.0	11.0	8.2
Services n.e.c.	16.4	0.7	15.5	16.9	5.6	10.7
Total Services	19.6	4.1	14.9	14.5	2.7	11.4
Total Services (*)	19.3	3.8	14.9	14.6	3.0	11.3
Total Goods	19.6	4.5	14.4	10.9	2.4	8.3
Food	16.0	1.7	14.1	8.8	0.8	8.0
Non Food	22.4	6.5	15.0	12.0	3.3	8.5
Non durable goods	20.3	5.7	13.8	12.2	2.6	9.3
Semi-durable goods	22.4	6.3	15.1	11.6	2.8	8.6
Durable goods	25.6	7.9	16.4	12.5	4.8	7.3
Total final consumption	19.6	4.4	14.6	12.1	2.5	9.3

(*) Excluding house rent

Table 6 Share of intermediate and final uses in total resource

Branches	Intermediate demand	Final domestic demand	Export	Total
1982				
Agriculture	67.2	26.6	6.2	100.0
Fuel and power products	58.5	31.2	10.3	100.0
Manufactured products	43.7	35.6	20.7	100.0
Buildings and construction	14.7	85.3	0.0	100.0
Market services	40.6	53.8	5.6	100.0
Wholesale and retail trade(1)	32.0	63.2	4.8	100.0
Lodging and catering services	11.2	88.7	0.0	100.0
Transport services	52.5	27.7	19.8	100.0
Communications services	61.8	36.2	1.9	100.0
Services of credit and insurance	90.9	4.5	4.6	100.0
Business services	80.0	11.4	8.6	100.0
Other market services(2)	18.5	81.3	0.2	100.0
1988				
Agriculture	66.3	27.6	6.1	100.0
Fuel and power products	60.1	36.1	3.8	100.0
Manufactured products	44.6	35.7	19.6	100.0
Buildings and construction	18.2	81.8	0.0	100.0
Market services	41.9	53.3	4.8	100.0
Wholesale and retail trade(1)	32.1	63.0	4.8	100.0
Lodging and catering services	12.3	87.7	0.0	100.0
Transport services	53.8	28.6	17.7	100.0
Communications services	61.4	36.7	1.9	100.0
Services of credit and insurance	91.5	5.8	2.7	100.0
Business services	83.1	10.5	6.5	100.0
Other market services(2)	20.7	79.2	0.1	100.0

(1) Including recovery and repair services. (2) Including: gross rent, recreational and cultural services, health services, education and research.

Table 7 Gross capital formation by user branch: metal products and machinery (at 1985 prices). Annual growth rate

Branches	80-83	83-86	86-88	80-88
Market goods and services	-4.9	4.4	12.6	2.7
Agriculture	-8.3	.3	5.3	-1.8
Industry	-8.4	1.7	13.1	.4
Industry(1)	-8.1	2.2	13.4	.8
Manufactured products	-9.0	.7	16.4	.5
Branch 2 (2)	-8.9	.2	14.7	.0
Branch 3 (3)	-7.3	-.5	18.1	1.2
Branch 4 (4)	-10.7	2.3	16.0	.3
Buildings and construction	-11.0	-2.7	9.0	-3.2
Market services	3.7	9.7	13.6	8.4
Wholesale and retail trade	-.5	15.6	9.9	7.9
Lodging and catering services	-3.0	10.1	16.3	6.5
Transport services	3.0	22.5	4.4	10.3
Communications services	12.4	3.3	12.1	8.8
Services of credit and insurance	8.5	-1.5	9.2	4.8
Other market services	2.6	10.2	19.7	9.5
Non market services	8.2	12.5	8.6	9.9
Total	-4.5	4.8	12.4	3.0

(1) Excluding building and construction.

(2) Mining, processing of non energetic minerals and derivative products, chemicals.

(3) Metal manufacture and precision instruments.

(4) Food, drink, tobacco, textiles, leather, clothing, timber, wooden fourniture and other manufactures.

Table 8 Share of branches in total value added at factor cost of market services

	Current prices		Constant prices	
Branches	1980	1992	1980	1992
Wholesale and retail trade	41.1	35.6	40.3	37.3
Lodging and catering services	7.3	7.1	8.5	6.3
Inland transport	10.3	8.7	9.7	10.6
Maritime and air transport	1.2	1.6	1.3	1.7
Auxiliary transport services	3.5	2.7	3.3	2.6
Communications services	3.2	4.2	3.0	4.8
Services of credit and insurance	12.0	12.0	11.6	12.4
Business services	8.9	14.1	9.0	12.3
Other market services	12.0	14.5	13.1	12.2
Total market services	100.0	100.0	100.0	100.0

Table 9 Changes in labour units (1980-1992) - in thousands

Branches	Employed	Self employed	Total
Manufactured products	- 1131.1	-42.8	-1173.9
Market services	1317.2	1259.2	2576.4
Wholesale and retail trade	316.3	433.4	749.7
Lodging and catering services	27.4	83.6	111.0
Inland transport	107.7	91.0	198.7
Maritime and air transport	-5.3	.1	-5.2
Auxiliary transport services	-19.2	4.9	-14.3
Communications services	53.5	.0	53.5
Services of credit and insurance	92.0	.0	92.0
Business services	660.7	317.5	978.2
Other market services	84.1	328.7	412.8

Table 10 Share of self employed labour units in total sectoral

Branches	1980	1986	1992
Manufactured products	13.9	16.1	16.4
Market services	43.5	45.1	44.9
Wholesale and retail trade	59.9	60.3	59.5
Lodging and catering services	42.8	45.8	46.5
Inland transport	25.3	28.5	29.6
Maritime and air transport	0.9	1.1	1.1
Auxiliary transport services	20.0	23.5	24.6
Communication	0.2	0.2	0.2
Services of credit and insurance	0.7	0.6	0.6
Business services	45.5	39.0	37.9
Other market services	35.9	45.6	48.6

Table 11 Share of irregular units in total sectoral employment

	Employed		Self-employed		Total	
Branches	1980	1992	1980	1992	1980	1992
Manufactured products	8.3	15.2	28.9	29.3	11.1	17.4
Market services	16.4	21.7	29.2	26.2	22.0	23.7
Wholesale and retail trade	12.4	20.7	25.0	21.2	19.9	21.0
Lodging and catering services	52.8	47.1	33.5	27.1	44.5	38.0
Inland transport	17.7	45.4	33.9	50.8	21.8	47.0
Maritime and air transport	35.3	54.5	85.7	87.5	35.8	54.8
Auxiliary transport services	10.6	23.8	47.4	47.8	17.9	29.5
Communication	1.4	1.5	66.7	66.7	1.5	1.7
Services of credit and insurance	.0	.0	84.0	84.0	.6	.5
Business services	11.4	12.6	41.9	31.1	25.2	19.6
Other market services	12.5	15.5	31.7	27.0	19.4	20.8

Table 12a Market services branches. Annual growth rate of main economic indicators - 1980-1992

	Wholesale and retail trade	Lodging and catering	Inland Transport	Maritime and Air Transport	Auxiliary transport serv.
Value added at current prices(1)	11.9	12.9	11.6	10.1	10.9
Value added deflator(1)	9.4	12.4	7.7	8.5	9.9
Value added at constant prices(1)	2.3	0.4	3.7	1.5	0.9
Labour units (total)	1.7	1.0	2.0	-0.6	-0.7
Employed	1.8	0.5	1.5	-0.6	-1.2
Self employed	1.7	1.7	3.4	1.1	1.0
Labour productivity(2)	0.5	-0.6	1.6	2.1	1.6
Labour productivity(3)	10.0	11.8	9.5	10.7	11.7
Labour cost per employee	10.8	10.8	9.4	10.2	10.2
Wage per employee	10.9	10.4	9.5	10.1	10.2
Labour cost per employee(4)	1.3	-1.5	1.6	1.6	0.3
Wage per employee(5)	1.4	1.0	-0.2	0.7	0.8
Input prices(6)	8.4	9.6	10.4	9.7	9.9
Cost of labour per unit of output	11.4	7.7	8.0	8.5	10.3
Output prices(6)	9.2	11.1	10.2	9.6	9.9
Income share in value added					
Labour cost (employed l.u.)(7)	25.3	24.8	51.9	53.3	39.2
Labour cost (self employed l.u.)(7)	38.8	21.1	20.4	0.5	12.2
Gross profits(7)	35.9	54.0	27.7	46.2	48.6
Gross profits(8)	-0.1	1.1	1.2	2.3	2.5
Gross profits(9)	4.7	5.0	10.5	11.6	10.3

(1) At factor cost.
(2) At constant prices.
(3) At current prices.
(4) deflated by value added deflator.
(5) Deflated by final consumption deflator.
(6) At market prices.
(7) Average figures.
(8) Trend coefficients.
(9) (Standard deviation/mean)*100.

Table 12b Market services branches. Annual growth rate of main economic indicators - 1980-1992

	Commu-nication	Credit & insurance	Business services	Other services	Total market serv.
Value added at current prices(1)	15.9	13.2	17.7	15.1	13.
Value added deflator(1)	8.2	9.4	11.4	12.5	10.
Value added at constant prices(1)	7.1	3.5	5.6	2.3	2.
Labour units (total)	1.6	2.0	7.4	2.9	2.
Employed labour units	1.6	2.0	8.5	1.0	2.
Self employed labour units	0.0	0.0	5.8	5.5	2.
Labour productivity(2)	5.4	1.5	-1.6	-0.6	0.
Labour productivity(3)	14.0	11.0	9.6	11.8	10.
Labour cost per employee	9.6	9.6	10.0	11.0	10.
Wage per employee	9.3	10.8	9.4	10.7	10.
Labour cost per employee(4)	1.3	0.2	-1.3	-1.3	0.
Wage per employee(5)	0.0	1.3	0.1	1.2	0.
Input prices(6)	6.5	9.6	9.8	9.2	9.
Cost of labour per unit of output	4.0	7.9	11.8	11.7	9.
Output prices(6)	7.7	9.6	10.5	12.0	10.
Income share in value added					
Labour cost (employees l.u.)(7)	60.9	58.7	41.0	28.3	36.
Labour cost (self employees l.u.)(7)	0.1	0.4	26.8	20.7	24.
Gross profits(7)	39.0	40.9	32.2	51.1	39.
Gross profits(8)	6.7	0.2	0.0	4.6	0.
Gross profits(9)	24.0	8.1	4.1	16.9	4.

(1) At factor cost.
(2) At constant prices.
(3) At current prices.
(4) deflated by value added deflator.
(5) Deflated by final consumption deflator.
(6) At market prices.
(7) Average figures.
(8) Trend coefficients.
(9) (Standard deviation/mean)*100.

Table 13 Market services by geographical area. Annual growth rate of main economic indicators (1980-89)

	ITALY	Centre-North	South
Value added at current prices(1)	14.2	14.1	14.6
Value added at constant prices(1)	3.0	2.9	3.3
Labour units (total)	2.9	2.6	3.4
Employed labour units	2.4	2.4	2.6
Self employed labour units	3.4	3.0	4.3
Labour productivity	.2	.3	-.1
Labour cost per unit of labour	10.7	10.8	10.0
Labour cost per unit of output	10.5	10.5	10.3
Value added deflator	10.9	10.9	10.9
Labour cost per employee(2)	1.2	1.4	.8

(1) At factor cost.
(2) Deflated by value added deflator.

Table 14 Market services. Annual growth rate of main economic indicators

	80-83	83-86	86-88	88-92	80-92
Value added at current prices(1)	19.9	14.8	8.9	9.6	13.2
Value added deflator(1)	18.1	10.5	4.7	6.7	10.1
Value added at constant prices(1)	1.5	3.8	4.0	2.7	2.9
Labour units (total)	3.6	3.6	1.8	1.2	2.5
Employed labour units	2.2	4.0	1.2	1.6	2.3
Self employed labour units	5.4	3.2	2.4	.7	2.8
Labour productivity(2)	-2.1	.2	2.2	1.5	.4
Labour productivity(3)	15.7	10.8	7.0	8.3	10.5
Labour cost per employee	16.7	8.4	7.7	8.0	10.2
Wage per employee	16.9	8.8	7.9	7.6	10.2
Social security contributions per employee	16.2	7.4	7.2	9.0	10.1
% of social security contribution on L.U. ingre (4)	41.5	40.4	39.8	41.2	40.9
Labour cost per employee(5)	-1.2	-1.9	2.9	1.3	0.1
Labour cost per employee (6)	0.2	-0.2	2.3	1.3	0.8
Input prices (7)	16.1	8.1	5.7	6.9	9.2
Cost of labour per unit of output	19.2	8.1	5.4	6.4	9.7
Output prices	17.5	9.7	5.7	7.0	10.0
% of gross profits on value added (4)	37.0	38.1	40.1	40.1	39.2

(1) At factor cost.
(2) At constant prices.
(3) At current prices
(4) Average figure.
(5) Deflated by value added deflator.
(6) Deflated by final consumption of households deflator.
(7) At market prices.

5

Indirect Productivity of Business Services, Through Non-Material Investments.

Jacques De Bandt
University of Nice-Sophia Antipolis

1. Introduction

The major debate as concerns services has to do with the combination of the following three elements :

- a dominant (and increasing) share of GDP and employment;
- low (labour) productivity growth;
- higher than average price increases;

i.e. with the fact that a major proportion of activities have low (lower than average) productivity surpluses, for which they compensate with higher than average prices.

They are thus able to take away (part of) the surpluses generated in other (minority) activities, which are thus deprived of the benefit of these surpluses: the service activities are "grabbers"(J. De Bandt, 1989). The accumulation possibilities of the other activities are thus reduced or eliminated.

The usual explanation is as follows: because productivity (growth) is low - this is considered to be self-evident - relative prices have to increase in order to allow wages to increase like everywhere else.

As a matter of fact, things are even worse, as prices are generally increasing proportionately more than productivity is increasing proportionately less than average.

This would mean that they are "twice grabbers": not only are they compensating for low productivity surpluses, but they are doing more than that.
This would tend to show that overall growth of the economy is endangered, not only because the quantitatively dominating (2/3 or more) activities have low productivity growth, but also, and even more so, because these activities are taking away from others the surpluses which are so badly needed for accumulation purposes. There are not only "too few producers", but part of the products of these producers is "stolen" or diverted to non productive uses.
The general debate about services/productivity/growth is complemented by two other debates : one as concerns the (absence of) impact of new (information) technology on productivity, the other as concerns (external) competitiveness.
The first complementary line of debate has to do with what is usually called the Productivity Paradox (OECD). The problem is the following: notwithstanding huge and increasing - even more so in constant prices - investments and current expenditures in new technologies (particularly in informatics), these don't seem to result in productivity increases. Even while some localized productivity increases are visible (e.g. the number of accounts per employee in the banks), important overall productivity increases are seen to be lacking.
The second complementary line of debate is in terms of international competition and external trade balances. At first glance at least, there does seem to exist some kind of inverse relationship between external balances in manufacturing goods and in services : countries like the US or France have trade surpluses in services but deficits in manufacturing, while the opposite is true for countries like Germany or Japan. The interpretation is usually that the (excessive) development of or emphasis on services is at the cost of the manufacturing basis and thus of competitiveness, the danger being that in the longer run this will also threaten service exports because of the weakened manufacturing basis.
The major idea behind all this is, one way or another, that, in line with traditional thinking, services are not (or only poorly) productive.

The aim of this paper is to show, in exactly the opposite direction, that services, or at least (the largest proportion of) informational business services, are more and more conditioning the ways not only of producing products and values, but of extracting productivity surpluses within the productive system.

A preliminary remark is needed in order to take account of the heterogeneity of the tertiary sector. This paper is not concerned with services in general. It will concentrate on informational business services.

This means that one has to eliminate:

- within the tertiary sector overall (66.9/66.1%)[1] , the non-market tertiary activities (16.5/25.4 %);
- within the market tertiary sector (50.4/40.7 %), the trade activities (11.1/12.3 %);
- within the services activities proper (39.3/28.4 %), the consumption related service activities (10.4/11.3 %).

Within the "production related" service activities, one can distinguish:

- comfort (or accommodation) services: security, cleaning, office maintenance;
- accompanying services: (part of)[2] banking, transport, telecommunications;
- informational services: consultancy, R&D, marketing, training.

The last two categories of services activities - to which must be added the same service activities developed within the user or client firm - are, to a large extent, the ones which condition both productivity and dynamic performances of firms.

2. Measurement

I want to make briefly the following points:

[1] These figures are for France, 1991 (INSEE, 1992): the first % refers to GDP, the second to Employment.

[2] The "accompanying" services are also, for a significant share, consuption related services.

2.1 On the Basis of Current Measures, Productivity Increases in the Service Sector are Low(er), but Non Negligible

Account must be taken of the following.
Firstly, service activities are too heterogeneous to allow for any global or average measure of productivity in the service sector in general:

- some service activities are without production logic: nuns and priests, museum or mausoleum attendants, bandmasters, army personnel[3] . In those cases, productivity is of course without any meaning.
- the productivity of some service activities is zero by definition or calculus: as a matter of fact, in all those cases in which output is being measured by inputs, productivity is by definition constantly equal to one.
- productivity increases are or can be substantial in some particular service sectors, in which large investments are made in equipment. telecommunications, transport.

Secondly, the differences as concerns productivity growth in service activities compared with manufacturing are substantially lower in terms of total productivity, than in terms of labour productivity alone, because of the differentiated importance of the non-wage components [4] .
Thirdly, taking account of the sheer importance (share of GDP) of service activities, even so the volume of productivity surpluses tends to be larger for the service sector overall than for the other sectors taken together (the difference in shares is larger than the difference in growth rates).

---

[3] While the question of productivity can of course be raised for army personnel in specific tasks (food, transport), the army as such, while "producing" security and eventually some sub-products (training, roads), has no production logic.

[4] Of course, in some service sectors, investment in physical assets may be quite important: beside the importance of high cost urban office space, the major cases are telecommunications, transport and rentals. It is, of course, well known that a large share of productivity growth is due to "production detours", i.e. the substitution of equipment for labour, which means the substitution of labour in the capital goods producing sector for labour in the capital using sector.

2.2 Inputs can be Used to Indicate the Level of Activity, but Certainly not to Measure Output (the "Product")

It has of course no meaning to make - as many people do - observations as concerns the low rate of growth of productivity, or in those sectors where the product is measured by the inputs.
The national accounting convention which consists in measuring "output" of non market services by the salaries paid doesn't allow to use this "output" for measuring productivity. This should be quite clear.
The same is of course true for market services, whenever the product tend to be measured on an input basis. The fact that in many business services - consultancy of various types, or informatics - the bill is established on the basis of time spent (man-hours or man-months), doesn't allow to use this for measuring output.
That inputs cannot measure output and that, when this is done, productivity is by definition constantly equal to one should be quite clear. It must however be noted that what is often said about the absence of any systematic relation between development or income level and the share of tertiary activities in "real" GDP is partly based on such measurements[5] .

---

[5] See for example, R.Summers (1985). The documents explaining how Purchaising Power Parities have been calculated clearly show both that differences in "real" products are systematically underestimated and that differences in prices are systematically overstimated. On the one hand, for many services for which no direct evaluations of output are available, outputs are measured by inputs. In such cases, it is clear that, for a given volume of services provided (e.g. for a given number of medical operations) - independently of quality - the lower the productivity, the more man-hours are needed, and the higher the "real" product appears to be. On the other hand, the prices of services are seen to be systematically increasing with the level of development: quality being supposed to be equal (which is, of course, a daring hipothesis), and productivity differences in services being supposed to be only small, the differences in service output must necessarily be attributed to price differences. Of course, when output is being measured by inputs, prices are obviously quite different, if one refers to the level of wages which are obviously increasing with the level of development.

2.3 *But Current Measures of Productivity in Service Activities are Not Correct*

It should be known by now that it is not justified to measure productivity as is usually done. The measures which are proposed and used (OECD, 1987) - by analogy with what was done in the manufacturing sector - are arbitrary, because of the impossibility to define the unit product on the basis of technical specifications and thus to identify the unit price. This makes it impossible to separate quantity (or volume) and price elements on a rigorous basis.

It is even more difficult to isolate the quality elements. These measures fail to catch the qualitative dimension of the services. The major dimension of services consists in the qualitative adaptation of the service to the specific needs or requirements of the customer: customization is the essence of services.

Taking account of the impossibility to strictly define unit products and prices and to catch the qualitative aspects of the service as such, when the (evolution of the) product in current prices is divided between the product (in constant prices) component and the price component, this is done arbitrarily.

It must however be added that to say that measures showing low productivity growth are not correct doesn't mean ipso facto that correct measures would necessarily indicate strong productivity growth.

2.4 *Productivity Measures in Service Activities do Systematically Underestimate Productivity Growth and Overestimate Price Increases in Services*

There are as a matter of fact two more or less systematic biases.

Firstly, the quality component in the evolution of the product, being not taken into account as such, is for the main part wrongly considered as a price component: this is so because higher quality is translated (mainly) into higher salaries or honoraria, which are used for measuring the evolutions of prices (e.g. a man-month of a senior engineer). Paradoxically, when the quality of services is improved - because e.g., on the basis of learning processes, the service providers are better able to handle the required informations - productivity doesn't appear to be increasing.

Secondly, when output is, one way or another, measured in terms of inputs, the product cannot increase more than the inputs, by definition, while the "price" is seen to increase as the wages or honoraria do.

It is usually said that, because productivity is increasing more slowly in service activities, prices have to increase faster in order to allow for similar wage increases. Beside the fact that for many services, price increases are more than compensating for the productivity bias, this compensation mechanism should take account of other factors as well: differences in cost structures, in skill and wage levels and evolutions, and other price determining factors (supply-demand relations).

But what is said here is completely different. The so-called compensation mechanism is only a mathematical trick: the value of the product being given, the price (or quantity) component can only be increased (or reduced) at the expense of the other. This decision being arbitrary, there is no a priori reason why relative prices would compensate for the productivity bias.

But, this all means that special emphasis must be put on the elements which are autonomously influencing both prices and products, i.e. relatives prices and productivities.

2.5 Productivity in Value (Current Prices) or in Relative (both Output and Inputs in %) Terms is Higher in Service Activities, and Much More so in (Informational) Business Services

Let us first eliminate the distinction between prices and products (in constant terms).

While productivity cannot be measured over time in value terms (because of the evolution of prices), the only means for comparing productivity between different activities[6] (at each point of time) is

---

[6] The same is, of course, true for productivity comparisons between different countries. See for example McKinsey Global Institute, *Service Sector Productivity*, Whashington, October 1992.

in actual or current prices (in absolute or relative terms). The various products are evaluated with reference to relative prices.

In these terms, relative productivity is systematically higher than average in services (higher than in manufacturing) and much higher in the case of informational business services (J.De Bandt, 1989)[7] .

For example, in the case of France (1991), while relative productivity is only 0.56 in agriculture and 0.64 in non-market services, relative productivity is approximately equal to 1 in industry (1.06), but relative productivity is at the level of 1.69 for production related services and at the level of 2.17 in business services.

How can relative productivity be systematically higher than average, while productivity growth in the service sector is systematically lower than average? This is of course due to the fact that relative productivities include actual relative prices.

But one has to take account of the fact that relative prices are necessarily included, one way or another. At each time basis used for the calculation of products in constant prices, actual relative prices are incorporated as weights. Whatever the evolution of prices, relative prices are used as they are, as reflecting the relative values of products.

2.6 Relative Prices do Reflect Relative Values, while Monopoly Rents do Seem to be of Secondary Importance

Prices of services are often said to be high, too high, increasing fast. Beside those cases in which decreasing returns are increasing costs and prices, prices are likely to deviate from their true value only when competition is insufficient. On this basis, higher prices in services would thus tend to reflect a lack of competition.

But why would competition be systematically weaker in the service sector? And is competition weaker?

---

[7] If one eliminates the non-market tertiary sector, relative productivity is systematically higher in the tertiary sector. It must be added that while the superiority of relative productivity in the tertiary sector is very important in low income countries, the difference is decreasing, one could say asymptotically, with development, relative productivity remaining however higher than average.

On the whole (there are of course exceptions) competition appears to be strong. It is certainly so, if one refers to the absence (in most cases) of barriers to entry and more so to effective entries and exits.
For example, in the case of France (1991), only 52,5 % of enterprises in the business services sector exist for more than 4 years, the figure being only 34.4 and 34.8% respectively in the informatics and marketing subsectors.
Fundamentally, in the case of services - contrary to goods, whose value is referring, one way or another, to (minimum) inputs or costs - prices are referring to user values. Once again, this is due to the absence of technical specifications allowing for a clear definition of the unit product: comparisons being difficult or even impossible, the customer is evaluating how much he is ready to pay for the expected solution of his specific problems. This means that the client pays what he considers to be the "users value", with reference to the expected benefit.

2.7 Standardization of Services doesn't Seem to Lead to Higher Productivity Growth, but Leads to Lower Prices

One major explanation of the supposed low productivity growth in service refer to the labour intensiveness of customization, and the absence of "roundabout" methods of production. The idea is that only the "production detours" which industrialization implies would lead to stronger productivity growth.
There are indeed permanently two complementary (contradictory?) tendencies at work within most service activities (or service relations): on the one hand, the tendency towards customization: the service product consists essentially in solving the problems of the customer or client in their most specific aspects; on the other hand, the tendency towards standardization of the product and rationalization of the process: aiming at solving problems in their common aspects, standardization (or "industrialization") allows for a lower priced service.
Of course, products are different, meeting different needs, or at least different ways and levels of meeting needs. Taking account of the way productivity is measured, productivity growth doesn't seem to

be different in either of these cases. This is of course the case whenever the product is measured on the basis of inputs (including for the "production detour" which standardization implies). But this seems to be the case more generally.
Cost and prices are different. This raises for the customer the usual choice of price-quality relation, depending on the relative weight he attaches to the specificity of his needs. But this doesn't seem to affect productivity growth[8] .

2.8 But, while Referring to User Values, Relative Prices May Well Include Various Elements, which Are More or Less Artificial and Have Nothing to do with Real User Values

But, even while referring to expected user values, relative prices can include very diverse elements:

- reputation rents: the importance of entries and exits doesn't prevent, in most cases, imperfect competition on the basis of image (reputation) and high prices (which are supposed to demonstrate both professionalism and non material investments). What the customer is paying in order to increase the probability or guarantee of a (good) solution to his specific problems means reputation rents for the high tariff service providers.
- "bubbles" are likely to develop because of the difficulty for the customer to identify and evaluate somewhat rigorously the product and because of the possibility for the service providers to build users values, more or less artificially, but in a sense cumulatively, i.e. to develop strong expectations beyond what the service providers can effectively perform. Service providers appear to be able to "produce demand", in the sense of convincing the customers, at least for some time, that they need some kind of service, which will appear afterwards as being more or less useless. This can develop for quite some time before the customers find out the artificiality of some of their needs or of some of the services they actually buy at high (and usually increasing) prices.

[8] Of course, one can also find here another illustration of the fact that the usual productivity measures are not correct.

Several examples of these "bubbles" can be shown: in finance, advertising, training, consultancy.

2.9 But User Values can also Correspond, in the Case of Business Services, to the (Expected) Productive Contribution of the Service Provider

Contrary to the above (in which artificial elements are included), (high) prices are likely to correspond, in the case of informational business services, to the awareness of the customer of the contribution of the business services used to their functioning and efficiency. Typically, the client is using informational business services, because he knows that he needs, for the sake of producing "values" (products which sell well), a variety of complementary competencies and informations, which he doesn't have. He knows the service provider can make a real contribution to the way his product is defined, produced or sold, and is ready to pay on that basis.
The situation is not the same for a final consumer. But, by analogy, one can easily imagine the contribution the customer can be expecting from the service provider to his personal satisfaction or utility.

2.10 The Productive Contribution of Informational Business Services Must be Measured in Terms of Indirect Productivity

Informational business services are not only simultaneously produced and consumed, but are co-produced, i.e. produced together/in close cooperation both by the service provider and the customer or client. While the service provider is helping the customer in finding adequate solutions to his specific problems, the customer must actively contribute to this, by making clear his specific needs or problems, by producing the relevant information and by implementing the proposed solution. Without this active participation of the customer, the service provider is helpless.
As a matter of fact, these informational business services are supposed to bring the necessary competencies in collecting and handling the complex set of information - be they scientific or technological, industrial or commercial, or information generated within the pro-

duction processes - which are required in order to contribute effectively to the solutions which are looked for.
This means that the service provider is participating in the functioning of the client firm: he is not selling a product form outside the firm, he is one of the actors within the client firm, representing part of the information dimension of the production process or of the technology creation process. From that standpoint, there is no real difference between the external and the internal service providers: they both participate in the effective working of the production process. Whether they are external or internal is secondary from the standpoint of their contribution to production and value added.
This means that the productivity of (external) service providers is indirect: while the amount of inputs (number of man-months) which is put at the disposal of the client firm indicates the level of activity or the volume of their participation (not their output), their output is their contribution to the production of value added at the level of the client firm.
While, on the basis of national accounting conventions, the services which are bought outside the client firm are registered as intermediate consumption, they should, from the standpoint of production be registered as "production factors", the same way internal service providers are measured. It is then possible to measure the partial (average and marginal) productivity of the service provider like for other production factors.

2.11 The Informational Business Services are Contributing Mainly through Non-Material Investments

The intervention of informational business service providers can in principle take place in two different perspectives. The first perspective corresponds to a situation in which firms tend only to reproduce identically what they were doing before: the firm is supposed to know how to do it, and if the firm needs the help of some external service provider, it would be in order to compensate for some internal structural weaknesses, because of newly generated adjustment needs. We know however that this is of no help, unless the client firm has internally enough resources and competencies in order to implement the necessary solutions. The second perspective corresponds to the situation in which the firm is involved in developing its basic resources and/or going through a process of technology creation or innovation (process or product). This implies the contribution of complementary competencies and information, and gives way to the building of specific assets.

The major contribution of informational business service providers is within the "production detour" which takes the form of building specific non material assets : non material capital is thus substituted for labour and increasing productivity within the client firm.

2.12 Are Different "Models" Affecting (Indirect) Productivity of Informational Business Services?

Services being co-produced, the ways the relationships between service provider and client are organized are likely to affect productivity to a very large extent. But what do we know about those ways and modalities?

Different "models" are seen to work, in different countries, sectors, periods:

- customization vs. standardization: while, as has been said above, the two tendencies are at work simultaneously, there are obviously large differences (e.g. between the "big eight" and a majority of firms in non Anglo-Saxon countries): the product being not the same, the question is whether the "indirect" productivity impact is different or not.
- The observation would be here that both standardization and customization are in many cases excessive (in opposite directions of course). But what about the future?
- internalization vs externalization: different factors are deciding whether to internalize, to externalize or to do both (transactions costs, production costs, co-production requirements, appropriation of information or assets, J.De Bandt, 1993). There are obviously big differences as concerns the productivity impact.
- service vs information: while we are speaking essentially of informational services, there are obvious differences between approaches consisting mainly in providing selective information and

other approaches consisting mainly in applying expertise to specific information at the client level. In the first case the relation to the information systems is decisive, while in the second case expertise and relational dimensions are dominant.

2.13 The (Extensive) Service Economy Hypothesis Revisited

According to P.Malaska (1985), we are entering a new development phase, characterized by the extensive growth phase of the emergent service economy.

I would like to suggest that this hypothesis is able to reconcile different phenomena which are apparently contradictory:

- the decisive role of business services;
- the "productivity paradox";
- the extensive growth of services;
- the non-maturity of service markets.

The interpretation is as follows.

We are really entering a new phase of development, implying new ways or modes of production. Informational business services which are central in this, are indeed developing rapidly: business services are growing fast, because the need is there. Their relative prices, corresponding to their expected contribution (indirect productivity), are decisively increasing. But in this phase in which the information or service economy is only emerging, extensive growth is dominating, both because needs are growing fast, but also because competencies and know how are still lacking or are quite poor.

While the firms are more and more conscious of their needs for informational services, actors and systems experience huge difficulties in mastering the production, co-production, organization and use of those informational service activities.

There is thus no contradiction between what can be said about the central role on informational business services on the one hand, and several questions which are raised as concerns the deficiencies and the low degree of maturity which is characterizing the service markets.

It can probably be said that - in the actual state of things - because of the still rather poor level of development and maturity of many in-

formational services, the interventions of service providers are, in many cases, only poorly efficient: lack of experiences and competencies, low degree of organization and transparence of the market, information asymmetries.
This would tend to mean that the actual contributions of business services can still be and probably are quite far away from their potential and expected contribution. Firms are willing to allocate - both internally and externally - large amount of resources to these informational activities, of course on the basis of their expected contribution. But they are doing so - and increasingly so - because of their needs, before having learned what the right conditions and ways are for producing the relevant information which they require. There does seem to exist a big gap between needs and capabilities.
Phenomena like the observed lack of maturity (difficulties in defining products, norms, relations, obligations) and the "productivity paradox" (large allocation of resources together with inefficiencies) can thus be explained by the extensive growth hypothesis.
If this interpretation is correct, the policy implications would seem to be quite clear. The main problem would be not to deregulate in order to increase competition, but to regulate in order to promote and accelerate the development and consolidation of learning processes.

3. Some Major Questions

Major questions related to service productivity have to be raised:

- the lack of maturity of service providers, clients and relations between them in many of the informational business service activities: while it is well known that market mechanisms are only poorly efficient in the case of those services (lack of transparency, uncertainty about he product, reputation phenomena) and while the product as seen by both the service providers and by the client is often hardly the same, this is not compensated by a sufficient degree of organization of the market. Many of the services which are provided are rather far away from what would be required from the standpoint of indirect productivity.
- There exists what I would call a service "paradox": informational business services and non material investments are obviously

very and increasingly important from the standpoint of productivity, competitiveness and industrial performances. The capacity to develop and to master those activities is an essential - if not the essential - part of the new modes of production corresponding to the information economy or society. Yet many observations tend to show that these activities are not up to the requirements of this information economy: the productivity paradox, the lack of competitiveness in those countries where service activities are apparently the most developed, the bubbles, etc.

- Information as public, quasi-public or collective goods vs. the merchandization of information: to a large extent, the informational business services correspond to the merchandization of various categories of information (including part of scientific information). At the same time however, more and more information tend to become more or less collective, at different levels, because of the necessity to cooperate and share information. What is the focal point of services: merchandization or informational function within networks or systems ?
- In what time horizon is the substitution likely of "expert systems" to informational services, which would mean a new step in the "production detour" or some new form of capital deepening ? Isn't it so that any move towards more organization of the market and of the relations between service providers and clients, in the form of norms and rules, would tend to accelerate the tendency away from services towards expert systems, but also towards the production of information and software.

References

J., De Bandt, (1993), "Services aux Entreprises: Informations, Produits, Richesses", (forthcoming).

J., De Bandt, (1989), "Can We Measure Productivity in Service Activities?" in A.Bressand and K.Nicolaïdis, *Strategic Trends in Services: an Inquiry into the Global Service Economy*, Harper & Row, New York.

INSEE, *Les Comptes des Services en 1991*, Paris, December 1992.

P., Malaska, (1985), "The Outline of a Policy for the Future, The Science of Complexity", United Nations University, Tokyo.

OECD, (1987), "Measurement of Value Added at Constant Prices", in *Service Activities, National Accounts: Sources and Methods*, Paris.

R., Summers, (1985), "Services in the International Economy", in R.Inman, ed., *Managing the Service Economy, Prospects and Problems*, Cambridge University Press, Cambridge.

PART II

International and Intersectorial Differences in Productivity: Catching-up or Divergence?

6

Structure and Change in Distribution System: An Analysis of Seven OECD Member Countries

Henry Ergas
OECD

1. Introduction

The distribution sector accounts for some 13 per cent of value added in the OECD area and for 16 per cent of total employment. The efficiency of this sector is therefore a matter of concern in its own right. These concerns are made all the greater by the impact which this sector can have on efficiency economy-wide, notably by affecting the extent to which the potential benefits to consumers of domestic and international competition are fully and promptly realised.
This report examines the structure and operation of the distribution sector in seven OECD economies: the United States, Japan, the United Kingdom, France, Germany, Italy and Sweden. The discussion is limited to the distribution of goods largely reflecting the fact that services, as usually defined, are not distributed, since their production and consumption is simultaneous; and it is limited to distribution in the sense of commerce, hence excluding those transport activities (such as the operation of freight companies) which provide inputs to distribution as defined here.
The distribution sector is regulated in almost all OECD member countries. In a few, explicit controls on entry act to slow structural change; in many others, constraints on zoning and siting, shop hours, and trade practices alter the functioning of competition. The impacts of these regulations need to be seen against the pressures for

change in distribution; understanding these impacts is the primary goal of the report.
The report is structured in five parts with this introduction being section 1. Drawing on papers on each of the countries covered, section 2 analyses current patterns and recent trends in distribution. Section 3 assesses the consequences of these trends for efficiency both in the distribution sector and in the economy more broadly. Section 4 examines the implications for public policy. Finally, section 5 provides an overview of trends and issues in industrial markets.

2. Distribution in Consumer Markets: The Changing Pattern

Distribution systems for consumer goods have changed dramatically over the last three decades. In the countries covered by this study, the density of retail outlets broadly, the number of shops per capita decreased at an average annual rate of 1 per cent over the period from the mid-1960s to the mid-1980s: a decrease which means that there are today some 1.5 million fewer retail outlets than there would have been if densities had remained constant (Table 1 provides data on the density of outlets). Five major changes have paralleled this decline in the number of outlets: average *size* has increased; *concentration levels* have risen; outlets and firms have *diversified* both within distribution and outside it; *new agents*, specializing in securing economies of agglomeration in distribution, have emerged; all combining to diminish the independent role of the *wholesaler*. This chapter reviews these changes and assesses the forces at work.

2.1 Density of Retail Outlets

Long term trends. Comparable data on the share of large outlets in retail sales, presented in Table 2, give rise to three observations. First, there is a strong trend towards high average shop sizes. In fact, the data presented in the table understate this trend because they do not reflect the shift towards larger outlets within the category described as "large".

Second, the data available highlight a disparity in terms of average outlet size between the "food" (which in most countries refers to groceries, rather than simply to food-stuffs) and "non-food" categories.

Table 1 Number and density of distribution outlets

	F	D	I	J	S (8)	U K (10)	U S.(11)
RETAIL							
Outlets (1)							
1970	--	450(5)	931(6)	1496(7)	--	560(6)	1420(7)
1980	411	406(3)	981	1674(3)	44(9)	410	1535(12)
1988	394	404(4)	983	1620	47	372	1930(13)
Density (2)							
1970	--	7.4	17.2	14.1	--	9.1	6.8
1980	7.6	6.6	17.4	14.4	5.3	6.5	6.6
1988	7.1	6.6	17.1	13.2	5.6	5.9	7.9
WHOLESALE							
Outlets (1)							
1970	--	120(5)	--	259(7)	--	--	370(7)
1980	79	109(3)	91	369(3)	21(9)	91	435(12)
1988	85	112(4)	122	436	27	115	467(13)
Retail/Wholesale ratio							
1970	--	3.8	--	5.8	--	--	3.8
1980	5.2	3.7	10.8	4.5	2.1	4.5	3.5
1988	4.6	3.6	8.1	3.7	1.7	3.2	4.1

Not available

(1) Thousand. Includes non-store (mail order, Kiosks, itinerant) except for France, which also excludes motor trade. The United States excludes non-employer direct selling.

(2) Outlets per thousand of population.

(3) 1979

(4) 1985

(5) 1968

(6) 1871.

(7) 1972

(8) Retail outlets as estimated by the Trade Research Institute (HUI).

(9) Great Britain.

(11) Data for 1972 and 1982 refer to end-year. 1987 data refer to numbers in business at any during the year. Retail excludes eating and drinking places. Retail includes, but wholesale excludes, non payroll outlets. Retail data for 1972 and 1982 are estimated.

(12) 1982

(13) 1987

Source: Contry reports, EC, Statistical Abstract of the United States, OECD Secretariat estimates

Table 2 Large outlets' share of retail sales (1) %

	Food						Non-food
	1968	1979	1987	1990	1968	1979	1990
France	5	26	47	53	1	9	15
Germany(2)	--	45	60	65	--	23	24
Italy(3)	2(4)	7	17	23(5)	4(4)	2	3(5)
Japan(6)	--	27	28(8)	--	--	--	--
Sweden	58(9)	60	62(10)	66	--	--	--
United Kingdom(2)	--	50	60	65	--	2	2
United States	--	71(11)	71(12)	--	--	--	--

(1) Hypermarkets and supermarkets. Generally, this refers to outlets exceeding 400m^2 (500m^2 in Japan). Estimates for the United States refer to supermarkets which are outlets providing a full range of departments and having annual sales of at least $2.5 million (1985 prices).
(2) Estimated. Germany includes speciality stores.
(3) Data for non-food are estimated by CESCOM and exclude autos.
(4) 1971
(5) 1989
(6) Total retail sales.
(7) 1982
(8) 1985
(9) 1970
(10) 1986
(11) 1980
(12) 1988
Sources: Country and communications of country experts.

The greater strength in the latter of the trend towards large outlet sizes is consistent with results of earlier analyses which point towards diseconomies of outlet scale in service-intensive goods.
Third, there are significant differences between countries in the degree to which the trend to larger outlets has progressed. As three of the countries covered have regulations aimed at protecting small shopkeepers from competition by larger stores, these differences may be at least partly due to the policy environment:

- The opening of large stores has been restricted by law in Italy since the late 1930s, with regulations being tightened in 1971.
- In Japan a first measure aimed at protecting small shopkeepers was adopted in 1948, and was followed in 1956 by a law regulating department stores. This law was extended to other types of large store through the "Large Scale Retail Store Law" of 1974, which, as modified in 1979, severely restricted the opening of stores larger than 500 square meters. (The typical North European hyper-market has around 4.000 square meters, while some U.S. hyper-markets exceed 14.000 square meters.)
- In France, some measure of protection for small shop-keepers has existed since the late 1930s, and a law restricting the opening of large stores, and notably of hyper-markets, was enacted in 1973. Though this law remains in effect, it has been less vigorously implemented since the administrative decentralization of the early 1980s.

However, there are also marked differences between countries that do not have specifically restrictive legislation in place - the share of grocery sales through large outlets in the United Kingdom is some 10 percentage points less than that in the United States. Policies are therefore not the only factor at work.

To assess the factors generating these differences between countries, a regression equation modelling retail density was estimated, drawing on analyses of population geography and on the main results of theories of spatial competition. On the demand side, these analyses emphasize the key role of the *effective size of the market*; five variables which appear to be especially important in this regard are included in the model:

i. population density, as measured by inhabitants per square kilometre;
ii. an indicator of the concentration of the population in the ten largest urban areas, as measured by the sum of the squared shares of each of these areas in total population; this is intended to capture the effect of agglomeration economies;
iii. the number of cars per capita, as a proxy for consumer mobility;
iv. the square of per capita consumption, which will give greater weight to larger changes in income;

and

v. the female labour force participation rate, which will proxy the opportunity cost of time spent shopping.

Variables i), ii) and iv) should have *positive* signs. An increase in the value of the third variable, however, will have three effects: it will increase the market facing all outlets; it will expand the market for outlets specifically related to the sale of cars and for petrol stations; and it will increase the competitiveness of large outlets, notably in the distribution of convenience goods. Consequently it should have a slight *positive* impact on the density of non-food outlets, but a *negative* impact on density in food distribution. Equally, an increase in the fifth variable, the female labour force participation rate, can be expected to raise the size of the average purchase and hence favour larger outlets, especially in the distribution of food; this variable should consequently have a *negative* sign, again notably in food distribution.

On the supply side, the key variables are those relating to the *input prices* facing outlets in different size classes. Larger outlets make especially great use of land and of part time, largely female, labour. We would consequently expect the balance between large and small outlets to vary with the price of land relative to other factors and with the supply of female labour. The latter will already be captured by the variable for female labour force participation and the effect this has on relative input prices strengthens the expectation that it will appear with a negative sign. This leaves the relative price of land which can be proxied by a sixth variable, namely:

vi. the price index of rents relative to the CPI.

The sign of this variable should be positive, with an especially strong effect on density in food distribution.

Finally, a set of dummy variables is included to capture the effects of regulatory restrictions on entry. These restrictions applied throughout the period in Italy and Japan; they applied in France from 1974 on, with special force in the decade following their enactment. By preventing the opening of large stores, these measures can be expected to have increased store density, and hence to have a *positive sign*, most notably in food distribution.

Equations relating the density of retail outlets (total, non-food and food) to these variables have been estimated using pooled annual observations for seven countries. The results are presented in Tables 3a and 3b. All the data points are normalized to their means, so that the magnitudes of the coefficients can be directly compared.

- In general, the results are good, even in equations without the dummy variables for regulatory intervention. The coefficients tend to be significant and have the right sign; the overall fit is good; and the variables that are expected to have their greatest impact on food distribution do so. As the literature predicts, the variable on female labour force participation is especially significant.
- Adding dummy variables for regulatory intervention, however, enhances the model's performance. The results suggest that the regulations in place in Italy and Japan have had a major effect on retail density, most notably in food distribution. The French regulations have had little impact on distribution outside food, and a weakly positive impact in food.
- The extent of these regulatory effects can be highlighted by examining what would happen in the absence of the restrictions. This can bc measured by the reduction in the number of outlets predicted by the model for Italy, Japan and France when the dummies are rendered inoperative - that is, when the data points for each of these countries is applied to the estimated coefficients without adding to this the value of the dummy. Compared with the number of outlets predicted when the dummies are taken into account, this results in a halving in the number of outlets in Italy and Japan (by about 400 and 800 thousand, respectively), and a reduction of some 5 per cent in France (Table 4)

2.2 Concentration and Economies of Scale

Paralleling the increase in the average size of stores has been an accelerated shift away from the small, independent operator as the dominant element in the retail system towards larger, multi-outlet entities.

Table 3 (a) Equations modelling the density of total retail outlets

	Retail outlet density		
Independent variable	**1**	**2**	**3**
Constant	2.1926 (0.4374)**	0.9325 (0.1728)**	1.0529 (0.1726)**
Car density	-0.117 (0.0892)	-0.006 (0.0333)	-0.025 (0.0331)
Relative price of land	1. 1981 (0.2457)**	0.1617 (0.0819)*	0.1337 (0.0804)*
Female labour force participation rate	-2.666 (0.2927)**	-0.616 (0.1292)**	-0.638 (0.1260)**
Population density	0.1062 (00483)*	-0.027 (0.0168)	0.0370 (0.0167)*
Personal consumption squared	0.0986 (0.0285)**	-0.004 (0.0086)	0.001 (0.0085
Japan dummy	-- --	0.6250 (0.0333) **	0.6289 (0.0325)**
Italy dummy	-- --	0.9526 (0.0300)**	0.9475 (0.0293)**
France dummy	-- --	-- --	0.0971 (0.0338)**
Summary statistics R^2	0.5434	0.9633	0.9654
Standard error of the regression	0.2637	0.0753	0.0734
F-stastic	27.170	442.85	415.77

NOTE: Standard errors are in parenthesis
* Indicates significance at the .99 level.
** Indicates significance at the .95 level.

Table 3 (b) Equations modelling the density of total retail outlets

	Retail outlet density		
Independent variable	**1**	**2**	**3**
Constant	1.6293 (0.3906)**	0.8946 (0.2521)**	0.9848 (0.2590)**
Car density	0.0722 (0.0588)	0.1301 (0.0321)**	0.0929 (0.0413)*
Relative price of land	-0.026 (0.0796)	0.1212 (0.0489)**	0.1075 (0.0498)*
Female labour force participation rate	-1.868 (0.2614)**	-0.406 (0.1895)**	-0.422 (0.1892)*
Population density	0.0017 (0.0432)	-0.135 (0.0247)**	0.142 (0.0251)**
Personal consumption squared	0.635 (0.0255)**	-0.024 (0.0127)*	-0.022 (0.127)*
Japan dummy	-- --	0.5911 (0.0489)**	0.5940 (0.0488)**
Italy dummy	-- --	0.7355 (0.0440)**	0.7317 (0.0439)**
France dummy	-- --	-- --	0.0722 (0.0506)
Summary statistics R^2	0.3914	0.8679	0.8699
Standard error of the regression	0.2355	0.1105	0.1101
F-stastic	14.685	110.90	99.554

NOTE: Standard errors are in parenthesis
* Indicates significance at the .99 level.
** Indicates significance at the .95 level.

Table 4 Simulated effects of removing regulations restricting the opening of large stores in Japan, France and Italy (1)

	Variation in outlet density (percentage)		
	Japan	France	Italy
Total outlets	- 48	- 5	- 55
Non-food	- 50	- 4	- 47
Food	- 44	- 8	- 65

(1) These calculations were carried out using the estimates of Table 3 without the specific country dummies.

This has been most apparent in the rise in concentration in retail distribution that is, in the share of the largest enterprises in retail sales. Table 5 sets out admittedly rough estimates of the four and ten-firm concentration ratios both for all retailing and for food taken separately[1] .

There are major differences between products and between countries. Thus, concentration levels in groceries are significantly higher than those in retailing as a whole; while concentration levels, both in food and in retailing overall, are lower in Italy and Japan than in the other countries examined, reflecting the impact of regulations on store size.

Seen as a whole, the trends to greater concentration have had two consequences.

First, in the distribution of convenience products (mainly food), tightly co-ordinated, integrated operations based on the common ownership of a large number of large-scale stores have come to the fore. The firms responsible for these larger operations are characterized by managerial hierarchies similar to those classically found in

[1] The rise in concentration is even more dramatic when it is seen against a longer run of years than is reported in the table. Thus, in France, the ten-firm concentration ratio in food in 1963 was of around 10 per cent; this ratio has consequently more than quadrupled in less than three decades. Equally, in Germany, the top 0.1 per cent of food retail firms accounted for some 20 per cent of food sales in 1960; this ratio had trebled by the end of the 1980s. Finally, in the United States, the top 0.1 per cent of firms more than doubled their share of retail sales over the period from 1958 to 1982.

manufacturing, and derive economies from buying power, superior logistics, and the ability to provide customers with "one-stop shopping".

Table 5 Retail market concentration (per cent share of largest enterprises)

	F	D	I	J	S	UK	US.
FOUR LARGEST							
Food							
1979	17	19	--	--	65(4)	17	--
1984	--	33	--	--	7(1)	24	15(6)
1988	36	35(2)	5	--	71	35	17(7)
All retail							
1979	7	11	--	4	--	11	--
1984	10(1)	12	--	4(3)	--	36	5(6)
1988	20	13(2)	--	4	50(2)	16	6(7)
TEN LARGEST							
Food							
1979	25	23	--	--	--	--	--
1984	--	39	--	--	--	41	--
1988	54	41(2)	--	--	85(2)	53	--
All retail							
1979	11	15	--	7	--	22(6)	--
1984	18(1)	18	--	7(3)	--	24	--
1988	29	19(2)	--	7	60(2)	30	--

Not available.
(1) 1983
(2) Estimated.
(3) 1985
(4) 1978
(5) Great Britain. Estimates for the four largest are calculated on the basis of C5 concentration data.
(6) 1982
(7) 1987

Source: Country reports, communications from country experts, Association of Department Stores in Japan (Japan)

Second, the effective degree of integrated management has also increased in other parts of the retail system but not solely or even principally through common ownership. Rather, the spread of franchise systems has allowed economies to be reaped even in retail contexts where the decentralization of ownership is essential to the efficient supervision of fairly service-intensive forms of retailing.

In practice, therefore, the concentration, or at least co-ordination, of *control* has increased even more rapidly than the ownership-based data suggest. But the process has not gone as far in some countries as in others.

In effect, the regulations in place in Italy and Japan have slowed the growth of large retail outlets; and hence impeded the emergence of integrated operators owning large numbers of these stores and dominating the market segments to which these stores cater.

The magnitude of this impact can be gauged by examining patterns of enterprise size in the countries where the growth of large stores has not been seriously impeded by policy. To obtain a point of reference, it is noted that in each of France, the United Kingdom and Germany, the average firm in the top four in the food market has annual sales of around $10 billion; while the average for the United States top four is around $18 billion (the lower U.S. concentration rates being at least partly a mechanical result of the larger size of the U.S. market).

Table 6 takes the European figure as a reference point, indicative of the long-run least-cost scale of operation at the more standardized end of the market. Given the size of the Italian market, four firms operating at this scale would result in a four-firm concentration ratio some 30 percentage points above current levels. All other things being held equal, achieving this level of concentration would require the four largest operators to displace over 100 000 smaller retail outlets. Applying the same approach, if four such enterprises operated in Japan, concentration ratios would rise by some 5 percentage points - which again would involve these top four displacing some 100.000 smaller rivals.

Table 6 Impact of greater food retail concentration on number of retail outlets, 1988

	Italy	Japan
Market share of 4 largest enterprises (%)		
Actual	5 (1)	10 (2)
With greater concentration (3)	36	14
Outlet numbers ('000)		
Actual	351	648 (4)
Reduction with greater concentration (5)	120	104

(1) See Table 5
(2) Estimated by reference to the relationship between concentration data for food and total retail in other countries in Table 5.
(3) Assuming that the four largest enterprises have an average turnover in 1988 of $10 billion --that is, in line with the turnover of the four largest enterprises in the other major European countries. See note 5 below.
(4) Estimated on the basis of 1985 data.
(5) Estimated as follows:
Italy: Private consumption of food and beverages is estimated at L 145.4 billion in 1988, while $40 billion sales for the four largest firms would imply turnover of L 452.1 billion compared with an actual estimated L 7 billion. Food retailers with more than 20 employees accounted of an estimated L 17.4 billion, implying a turnover of L 128 billion for businesses with 20 or less employees. Total employment in food retailing is estimated at 31.5 per cent of total retail employment; that is, at 740.7 thousand in 1988, of which an estimated 682 thousand in enterprises of less than 19 persons and hence an average tunover per employed person of about L 188 million. The counterpart loss in turnover for smaller enterprises implied by greater concentration would imply a loss of (44,287/188=) 235 thousand jobs.
Since small outlets in Italy employ on average two persons, this would entail the disappearance of around 120 thousand outlets.
Japan: Food/bevange retail sales are estimated at Y 36 175 billion in 1988, while $40 billion sales for the top four firms would imply turnover of Y 5 128 billion (and a market share of just over 14 per cent) or an increase of some Y 1 510 billion. If the counterpart sales loss were evenly spread among all outlets of less than 50 persons this would imply the disappearance of 27.4 thousand outlets (1.7 per cent of outlets). However, recent history shows that the decline in outlet numbers has been borne entirely by the smallest (1 to 2 persons) units.
If the counterpart loss were restricted entirely to this category, the loss would amount to 11.8 per cent of their turnover and entail the disappearance of 104 thousand outlets.

2.3 *Diversification and Economies of Scope*

The growth in the size of outlets and the expansion of multi-outlet firms has transformed the manner in which the retail system secures *economies of scope* that is, the efficiencies gained by undertaking distinct activities under common management, rather than separately. In traditional retailing, these economies were realized mainly through the location decisions of firms, the agglomeration at a single place of shops providing broadly complementary services. But while this provided customer convenience, it was an at best haphazard process, which especially as urban areas became more crowded could create or aggravate the diseconomies associated with congestion while hardly exhausting the benefits obtainable through co-ordination.

The attempt by firms to more systematically secure these benefits has led to three broad responses: diversification within individual establishments; diversification by multi-outlet enterprises; and the emergence and rapid growth of the planned shopping centre.

Greater diversification at the establishment level has been closely bound up with the growing size of stores.

As large food stores have increased their surface area, they have sought to give greater prominence to non-food items[2] which, though they have slower turn-over, are typically sold with considerably higher gross margins[3].

---

[2] Thus, non-groceries account for some 40 per cent of sales in French hyper-markets; but their share of surface area rises from slightly less than half in the smaller hyper-markets (those with more than 2.500 but less than 5.000 square metres) to over 60 per cent in the largest size class (exceeding 9.000 square metres). As these stores have expanded, so too has their share in all sales of non-grocery items, going from less than one-third of 1 per cent in 1968 to 12 per cent in 1991. Equally, in Germany, non-groceries account for some 30 per cent of hyper-market sales; but the proportion passes from 23 per cent in the smaller outlets to 36 per cent in the large ware-house type stores. Diversified assortments of this type account for a smaller share of sales in the United States - possibly because the much larger size of the U.S. market has accelerated the growth of large-scale specialist outlets in the non-foods sectors, which can under-cut the non-food sales of grocery chains. But even here, non-grocery items account for some 15 per cent of sales in superstores and in combination stores, and for 35 per cent of hyper-market revenues.

[3] Thus, while the average (across all products) gross margin in the typical U.K. supermarket in 1990 was of 23 per cent, the gross margin in supermarkets on toiletries was of 27 per cent. Equally, gross margins on non-grocery items in U.S. hyper-markets are around 20 per cent, as against the 10-15 per cent standard on food. See Colla (1992), page 133.

Diversification at the establishment level has been reflected in diversification in the business enterprise. A primary factor here has been the professionalization of management which, in this industry as in others, creates the ability systematically to identify and exploit diversification opportunities. Retail firms have sought these opportunities primarily in four areas.

The first is *backward integration* into the design, branding, and in some cases, even production of goods that form an integral part of the larger retailers' sales assortment. Second, retailers have diversified into providing *complementary services* to the sale of goods at their retail outlets, with financial services being especially important in this regard. A third type of diversification involves expanding the range of *business formats* or store types the firm operates within its core product market. This strategy has been especially pronounced where distinct formats are needed to provide the ambience and assortment which can attract the differing segments of the public; and it has allowed chains operating in these parts of the system to secure both economies of scale and of scope. Finally, a fourth type of diversification entails *moving into entirely new product segments*: that is, into operating stores selling in quite distinct product areas. In each case, several factors can be identified in the diversification decision: transferability of management systems, trading style or operational know-how across retail markets; constraints on further expansion in the firm's core business; attempts to secure the best use of the firm's property portfolio; the desire to share costs between similar trading outlets in distinct product markets; and the attempt to reduce risk by diversification.

In short, retail firms have acted through a range of strategies to internalize the economies of scope in consumption and production. The net impact of all these changes on the retail system has been accentuated by the rise of the *planned shopping centre*. This involves a cluster of outlets in a site selected to be readily accessible, designed to house a strictly complementary set of activities, and equipped to a standard level of comfort and security[4] . From the consumers' point of view, the centre facilitates "one stop shopping", but

---

[4] See Dawson (1983).

with a range of stores and hence of assortments, ambiences and levels of service. From the point of view of the retailer, it offers an environment in which inter-shop competition is limited and carefully controlled, with locations within a mall allocated so as to maximize the rental value of the mall as a whole; the opportunity to benefit from the traffic-attracting effects of other mall tenants; and savings in cost through sharing of expenses associated with security, the maintenance of common areas, and with public utilities.

The transfer of retail sales from unplanned environments (such as downtown shopping areas) to planned sites has gone furthest in the United States where, by 1985, shopping centres accounted for over 40 per cent of all retail sales, with the top 1 per cent of centres by floor space accounting for over 7 per cent of the U.S. total retail sales.

A close link exists between the planned shopping centres and the large, multi-site, diversified retail chains. Developing a shopping centre entails high sunk costs and hence considerable exposure to risk. To control this risk, developers seek tenants whose product mix and operating type are known and successful, and with a predictable ability to attract customers and generate revenue. At the same time, the centres provide the chains with an opportunity to locate optimally sized stores in an environment designed to support them.

The result is an equilibrium in which the centres are characterised by larger than average outlets, primarily operated by the national chains with one estimate being that in U.S. shopping centres, chains provide from 75 to 90 per cent of the tenants and generate over 90 per cent of the sales[5]. This link reinforces the chains' competitive advantage, further strengthening the overall trend towards greater concentration.

2.4 The Implications for Wholesalers

Greater concentration and integration in retailing has altered the position of the wholesale trade, the traditional intermediaries between manufacturers and retail outlets. The dominant trend has been

[5] Jones and Simmonds (1990), page 92.

for the wholesale functions to be absorbed by the retail chain and this trend is likely to continue. In the grocery trade, for example, where logistics costs are high, retail enterprises have tended to expand in such a way as to allow sites to be economically serviced from centrally located warehouses. This imprints a distinct regional pattern on the growth of chains with their geographical scope expanding in a concentric model from their original site[6]. As the chain grows, it becomes efficient for it to deal directly with the manufacturer, either by a wholesale subsidiary, by direct deliveries by the manufacturer to the individual store, or by some combination of both.

Developments in information technology have accentuated the pressures in this direction. Access to point of sale information allows the larger retail chains to forecast demand with a high level of accuracy, and hence to fine-tune their assessments of inventory needs by product, store, and region. This, in turn, is translated into physical delivery schedules which minimize packing and unpacking costs and cut holding times both in the stores (where space devoted to inventory has a high rental cost) and at the retailer's warehouse.

The larger the number of intermediate links, the greater the difficulties which this type of on-going adjustment will generally involve[7]. The resulting demand for "just in time" delivery places great strain on multi-layered logistic structures[8], and has resulted in a shift in control over inventories from wholesalers to retailers[9].

Faced with backwards integration by the larger retail chains, wholesale firms have restructured their operations with three strategies

---

[6] See Vance (1970), Brown (1981) and Laulajainen (1987).

[7] See Arrow (1975) and Carlton (1979).

[8] See Bowersox (1990).

[9] Thus, in the United States, where chains now control over 40 per cent of sales in the wholesale sector, the ratios of inventories to sales for manufacturers, wholesalers and retailers in 1969 were, respectively, 1.84, 1.27 and 1.44; by 1989, these ratios had become 1.58, 1.27, and 1.59 - evidencing a transfer of inventory holding to the retail level. Equally, in the United Kingdom, nominal inventory holdings (end-of-year stock values) for retail businesses with more than 100 outlets increased during the 1980s by some 12 per cent annually, three percentage points greater than their nominal growth rate of sales. Nonetheless, improvements in logistics allowed the largest grocery retailers to hold the nominal growth of stocks to just over 6 per cent annually, implying a significant reduction in real inventory levels.

being especially widespread; first, some wholesalers have sought to *diversify* their operations, notably (but not solely) into retailing; second, others have sought to upgrade the services they offer; while third, yet others have tried to control costs by moving from delivered trade (where the wholesaler performs the transport function on behalf of the retailer) to "cash and carry" warehouse arrangements in which the retailer selects and assembles the assortment, as well as transporting it.

These responses have come at a time when increased competitive pressure has been reducing rates of return in wholesaling. This has weakened the position of marginal firms and induced a rise in concentration. In France, for example, the ratio of operating surplus to value added in wholesaling decreased at an annual average rate of 1.4 per cent over the period from 1970 to 1987, stimulating exit and allowing larger firms to expand through acquisition. In the United Kingdom, gross profits in wholesaling are now barely a third those in retailing, and net margins for even the largest wholesalers are below 4 per cent of sales again, accelerating the moves to industry rationalization, with the two largest organizations in the grocery cash and carry trade increasing their combined market share from 27 per cent in 1983 to 40 per cent in 1989. In the United States, wholesalers have had to substantially up-grade their assets so as to remain competitive with the result that capital intensity in the wholesale food trade increased by over 50 per cent in the five years from 1982 to 1987. This has been associated with an apparent rise in the minimum efficient scale of operation, the four largest firms in the activity increasing their share of total sales by 1.4 per cent over the period.

3. The Implications for Efficiency

The changes under way in distribution systems for consumer goods affect efficiency both in distribution itself and in the economy as a whole. Within the retail system, productivity levels have risen, competition has been durably strengthened, and innovation and consumer choice have been enhanced. At the same time, the changes in distribution have acted to lower entry barriers economy-wide, improving market access for both domestic and foreign producers.

3.1 Efficiency and Competition within the Retail System

3.1.1 Increased Productivity

Increased concentration in the retail sector has transferred resources from establishments and enterprises with lower productivity levels towards establishments and enterprises whose productivity levels are higher. The indicators in this respect are far from complete and are subject to many sources of error: the measurement of productivity in service industries is notoriously difficult, and the problems affecting these measurements are accentuated in a context where the extent of the service provided has varied greatly over time[10]. Three points are, nonetheless, worth making:

i. Data presented in the country background studies suggest that average sales per employee tend to be 50 to 80 per cent higher in the largest size class of store than in the smallest. At the same time, value added per employee can be as much as 100 per cent higher. This suggests that larger stores are achieving significant economies of scale - a presumption borne out by the academic literature[11].

ii. The transfer of resources can therefore be expected to increase productivity levels by at least the extent of the transfer multiplied by the extent of the productivity disparity. This too is borne out by the studies available. An analysis for France, for example, finds that over the period 1980-1986, this shift effect accounted for just over 1 per cent of labour productivity growth in retailing annually, equivalent to some 40 per cent of the observed system-wide gain[12].

iii. The transfer of output can be expected to intensify the competitive pressures on the smaller firms, and thereby encourage them to adopt more efficient ways of working. To the extent that they increase productivity *over their output as a whole* rather than merely at the margin, the system-wide productivity gain will be

[10] See especially Schwartzman (1971).

[11] See, in addition to the sources cited above, Betancourt and Gautchy (forthcoming), where the authors correct for the various dimensions of the quality of service.

[12] Noyelle (1990).

all the greater.The evidence for France again suggests that such a "catch up" response is occurring: since the early 1980', when the restrictions on the opening of large shops were *de facto* liberalized, the independents have increased value added per employee nearly three times more rapidly than the hyper-markets and decreased their inventory ratios at a time when these were rising in the largest stores.

Given these processes, one would expect two factors to differentiate those countries where rationalization has gone furthest from those with significant regulatory obstacles to change:

i. Levels of *gross margins* (the difference between the price of goods at delivery to the retail system and their price at sale) should *decline* in those countries where rationalization is most advanced, and should be *lower* than those observed elsewhere.
ii. Because the shift in resources within the distribution system should not only increase *average* productivity but also reduce its inter-sectoral *variance*, productivity measures should have a narrower spread in those countries where structural change has gone furthest. The persistence of a wide spread in productivity could therefore be taken as an indicator of technical inefficiency.

Data on gross margins are set out in Table 7. Interpretation of these figures is subject to many caveats, but the following observations can be made:

- Gross margins are highest in the United States, followed by Japan. But retailers in Japan bear a lower share of overall distribution costs than those in the United States, both with respect to inventories and to the costs of disposing of unsold goods. The ranking of both countries in terms of gross margins and rates of return is therefore not clear-cut.
- Margins have tended to rise slightly in the United Kingdom and to a lesser extent in France and Germany. This may reflect cyclical developments, changes in sectoral capital intensity, or trends in market power.

The persistence of inter-sectoral disparities in productivity provides a second indicator of technical efficiency. Two points emerge from estimates of the coefficient of variation in productivity levels for different size classes of firms for five countries (data for Italy and Sweden are not available):

- The coefficient of variation in productivity levels is considerably greater for Japan than for the other countries covered;
- It has been rising in Japan, while declining for France, the only other country for which time series data are available.

This provides some support for the view that the failure to adapt industry structure does create inefficiencies - with consequences, it is argued below, that may go well beyond the distribution system itself.

3.1.2 Strengthened Competition

The growth of larger firms has also changed the dynamics of competition within retailing. Concerns have been expressed that rivalry in distribution may be stifled as concentration levels rise - with three factors, each taken to increase the barriers to entry, being seen as contributing to this risk:

i. The first is the prospect that as concentration rises, the larger retail enterprises will switch into investments in vertical product differentiation - that is, into distinguishing the attributes of their products from those offered by their rivals. These investments - for example, in advertising - will create sunk costs which discourage entry[13], encouraging the dominant retail firms to increase margins by "trading up"[14].
ii. The spatial dimension of retailing may also create entry barriers. To the extent to which the dominant firms succeed in securing the best sites within each local market, they will create a cost asymmetry between themselves and rivals, further increasing the scope

[13] See Bresnahan and Reiss (1990), Sutton (1986, 1990).

[14] This is the "wheel of retailing" theory which has figured prominently in marketing theory since the 1950s. See, for example, Bucklin (1972), McClelland (1963), McNair and May (1978) and (1982), and Spranzi (1991).

for increases in margins[15].

iii. Lastly, it has been argued that the dominant firms may be at an advantage because of their ability to extract more favourable terms from suppliers[16].

These hypotheses cannot be tested against the evidence available on trends in margins - evidence which is too sparse in the period of its coverage, does not provide enough sectoral detail, and is of uneven quality. There are, however, good reasons to believe that they seriously over-state the risks to competition. Three factors underpin this assessment.

First, the market for retail services has become more efficient thanks to: i) increased consumer mobility that has reduced the degree of local monopoly; ii) increased information available to consumers (most strikingly as a result of the spread of comparative advertising, an innovation pioneered by the retail chains); and iii) reduced consumer vulnerability to purely perceptual product differentiation - a trend visible in the declining elasticity of demand with respect to advertising[17].

Second, product diversification by large chains has increased the threat of entry. This operates most quickly at the level of the outlet, where lines can be added fairly readily when margins become attractive. The French hyper-markets offered a particularly clear example of this in the mid-1980s when they moved into the then heavily regulated petrol market: they were willing to bear the costs of campaigning for the regulations to be dismantled; and as this campaign succeeded they entered the market and grabbed market share - virtually eliminating the disparity between the petrol price before tax and the Rotterdam corresponding price.

---

[15] There are two aspects to this: i) pure spatial competition - that is, competition for sites which differ in their attributes; see, for example, the empirical model of retail location in West (1983), pages 129-143 as well as Eaton and Lipsey (1979) and West (1981); and ii) the ability of a chain with several concentric locations to deter entry by the threat of predation; see Selten (1975), pages 127-159.

[16] Note, however, that these purely pecuniary economies of scale would, in effect, transfer supra-normal earnings from the producers of the goods being sold to the dominant distributors - which presumably reflects rather than causes differential entry barriers.

[17] Pushing advertisers to shift resources into sales promotions - but at high cost; see, for example, Jones (1990), pages 145-152; and McKenna (1991), pages 65-79.

Table 7 -Gross margins in distribution (per cent)

	Retail								Wholesale			
	Food				Total							
	1979	1982	1986	1988	1979	1982	1986	1988	1979	1982	1986	1988
France (1)	18.4	17.4	19.3	19.0	28.0	27.9	29.3	29.6	19.5	19.2	22.9	22.8
Germany (2)	18.9	19.1	19.2	19.8	30.6	31.1	30.9	31.1	23.0	24.7	23.8	25.3
Italy (3)	--	16.8(4)	17.5	17.5	--	--	--	--	--	20.2(4)	22.8	22.4
Japan	25.2	--	25.4	--	27.0	--	27.1	--	11.9	--	11.2	--
Sweden (5)	19.2	19.6	19.7	20.0	--	--	--	--	--	--	--	--
United Kingdom (6)	19.7(7)	19.4	21.2	22.8	26.5(7)	26.6	28.3	29.4	--	--	13.4(8)	--
United States	--	24.4	25.6(9)	--	--	30.8	32.3(9)	--	--	17.8	20.1(9)	

(1) Non-specialized food outlets

(2) According to the Institut für Handelsforschung

(3) Businesses with more than 20 employees. Food retail refers to non-specialized outlets (largely packaged groceries as opposed to fresh food). The numerator excludes the cost of goods used in production.

(4) 1983.

(5) Self-service outlets.

(6) Great Britain.

(7) 1980

(8) 1984

(9) 1987

Source: Country reports

The same entry processes can operate between store types, as already diversified firms seek to capitalize on their management skills by moving into areas with excess returns.
Third, the emergence of foreign direct investment in retailing has also further strengthened the pressure of potential competition. The largest German and French retailers have been at the forefront of this process - the French accelerating their presence on foreign markets once the regulations restricting their expansion in France came into effect. By 1990, the largest French hyper-market group, Carrefour, derived 30 per cent of its revenues from foreign operations; while by 1991 foreign revenues matched domestic revenues for the diversified retail/wholesale group Promodes. These firms have invested heavily in modernizing the distribution system in Spain (where foreign firms now account for over 50 per cent of large store sales) and in Italy[18].
Combined, these factors mean that size does not shelter large chains from competition - a result empirical analyses largely bear out. Thus, in France, rates of return for the larger retailers do not appear to have persistently exceeded the all-industries average[19]. Equally, in the United Kingdom, gross profits for the larger retailers increased significantly in the 1980s: but this seemed to reflect the coincidence of an economy-wide pick-up in rates of return with far-reaching rationalization and cost-cutting within retail firms, rather than the exercise of market power. In the United States, retailer profitability rises with market share; but this reflects higher margins on (what are at least perceived as) superior products, rather than an ability to extract higher mark-ups on standard lines[20].

3.1.3 Innovation and Consumer Choice

The pressures of rivalry in retailing are even stronger when competition through innovation is taken into account. In effect, the mana-

[18] Equally, the German firm Aldi demonstrated the power of rapid entry in 1989 when, in the face of a move to higher margins by the established British discounter Kwik-Save, it decided to enter the U.K. market establishing some 30 sites within a year and reversing the trend towards rising real prices. The episode and its long term consequences are discussed in Colla (1992) pages 104-106.
[19] See Chappert and Ecalle (1989).
[20] See Buzzell and Dew (1990); and Buzzell and Gale (1987).

gerial and financial assets of the large retail chains are sufficient to support the systematic search for improved ways of doing business; and these firms are capable of rapidly transferring innovations throughout their operations[21]. This has allowed them to play an especially important role in three broad types of innovation:

i. The larger retailers have encouraged an acceleration in product innovation - by spotting market trends and creating shelf space to accommodate them[22]; by themselves developing entirely new products, as does the AMS buying organization (which groups seven of the largest European retailers); and by reducing the loyalty of consumers to established product brands, thereby inducing the owner of these brands to accelerate new product introductions as a means of coping with greater competition[23].
ii. At least in Europe (the data for Japan and the United States are not fully comparable), they have taken the lead in the implementation of new technologies in retailing: most notably those based on telecommunications and data processing[24].
iii. Finally, they have made organizational innovation a normal part of their operations: as evidenced in the rapid spread of Direct Product Profitability (DPP) analysis[25] and the widespread diffusion of new store formats and of techniques of product promotion.

---

[21] Examples are given in Samiee (1990), pages 54-76.

[22] Thus, Sutton (1992) describes the role retailers played in the very rapid emergence of the market for mineral water.

[23] Thus, McKenna (1991) cites evidence that the number of new products introduced into U.S. supermarkets increased by 60 per cent between 1985 and 1989.

[24] Thus the penetration of optical scanner technology is highest in the countries where retailing is most concentrated - with Sweden having a ratio of scanners per outlet fifteen times that of Italy, while the United Kingdom and France exceed Italy by a factor of four (calculated from data reported in Pilotti (1991) page 37, using data on the number of outlets derived from the country reports), with a similar pattern prevailing in the diffusion of networks for Electronic Data Interchange. At the end of 1991, there were (according to a BIS market study) only 40 users of EDI in Italy, as against 4.100 in the United Kingdom, 610 in Germany, 450 in France and 150 in Sweden.

[25] DPP is a technique of financial analysis which uses detailed, computer-generated sales information to allow retailers to assess profitability by product and by display area. It provides a systematic basis of pricing and promotion decisions and for choice of assortment.

Ultimately, it is a feature of retailing that innovators have difficulty in securing effective property rights in their innovations: imitation is generally easy, and the pressure to adopt innovations is strong. The consumer benefits of structural change have therefore been secured especially rapidly - making the costs of impeding these changes all the greater.

3.2 Retail Distribution and Economy-Wide Competition

The changing structure of the distribution system has also altered the conditions of competition economy-wide. The effects centre on an increase in the degree to which markets are contestable and workably competitive. Overall, the changes observed have gone broadly in the right direction: reduced costs, greater choice and lower prices. Combined, these must yield consumer benefits; but there have been significant differences between products and countries in the extent to which these changes have progressed.

Greater contestability arises because the increased scale of the distribution activity helps diminish the market power of incumbent producers of goods. In consumer markets, producer power typically arises from product differentiation, branding and product advertising. Strong brands increase total rents and the share of these rents captured by producers rather than distributors. Individual distributors consequently have an interest in countering strong producer brands to secure margins which they would otherwise have to transfer to the supplier of the branded goods. By reducing the power of a brand, they increase the competition it faces in the market, and hence promote lower prices, so that the net effect is to enhance consumer welfare.

Increased scale has significantly enhanced distributors' ability to secure these gains, notably by launching their own brands. This entails high fixed costs and requires a fairly broad product line. Size provides at least two advantages in this respect: it increases the range of shops and customers to which the own-brand can have immediate and "free" access, largely eliminating the barrier to entry which distribution costs would otherwise create; and the larger a distributor is, the greater the likelihood that it will already have a brand reputation of its own among its customers, making them more willing to experiment with the new product range.

Where own-brands have developed, they have had four direct impacts. First, there have been some purely *re-distributive* effects between producers and distributors, as producers of branded goods have had to relinquish some part of their margins in various ways. Second, there have also been effects on *consumer prices*. Thus, own-brands under-price national brands by a margin which goes from around 30 per cent in Germany, to nearly 20 per cent in the U.K. and 10 per cent in France[26], with the effective rebate being substantially greater in some instances. Equally, in the United States, generics (unbranded goods), which are available at some 80 per cent of supermarket outlets, sell at a discount of 25 to 50 per cent relative to the leading national brands. Third, own-brands have come to play an increasingly important role in *extending consumer choice*, with retailers seeking to increase their margins both by taking the lead in introducing new products and by up-grading their existing own-brand items. Fourth, they have created a *low-cost entry route* for new manufacturers, as the distribution expenses are covered by the retailer whose label appears on the product.

Producers of established brands have responded to increased competition by improving the services they provide to distributors, by seeking to reinforce consumer loyalty through promotional campaigns, and by accelerating new product introductions. The late 1980s appear to have marked a peak in this respect, with the number of new products introduced annually at retail rising by some 60 per cent from 1985 to 1989. Since then, numbers have stabilized but at very high levels[27].

Estimates suggest that "distributor owned brands" now account for some 30 per cent of sales of packaged groceries in the United Kingdom, and for around 25 per cent of these sales in France, Germany and Sweden. They are less significant in the U.S. (where their share of the market is about half that in the U.K.) and play little role in

[26] Estimates given in Colla (1992), page 286.

[27] See McKenna (1991) page 66.

Italy and apparently, Japan (though very little data is available on this).

As far as Italy and Japan are concerned, the primary factor appears to be the absence of intermediaries of sufficient size to act as credible entrants into markets for heavily branded products. Fragmented as it is, the retail sector does little to offset market power elsewhere in the economy.

The U.S. case is more complex, and it can be thought to reflect three, partly offsetting, factors. First, especially in the grocery industry, U.S. retail chains tend to be regional rather than national, whereas entry into heavily branded goods may require access to the entire national market. Second, established brands may have a firmer hold on U.S. consumer preferences than their European counterparts. Third, the growth of discounters of branded products may have reduced the incentive for retailers to introduce own-brands, since margins even on heavily branded items have fallen as low as 5 per cent of sales

Conversely, the high share of own-brands in the U.K., Germany and France may partly attest to the weakness, in these markets, of the other sources of contestability. These are markets which, for many years, were shielded to a considerable degree from import competition, with disparate technical standards and labelling requirements preventing prices from being equalized across frontiers. There is a long tradition of collusion among domestic manufacturers, until recently tolerated by the authorities in some cases, and actively promoted in others. The last two decades have seen significant concentration occurring in manufacturing, further increasing the risks to competition. All of this has increased the importance of retailers as a source and promoter of entry, and hence as a check on the persistence of supra-normal earnings.

3.3 Retail Systems and International Competition

The evolution of retail distribution systems affects the degree of openness of OECD economies through three channels. First, the development of substantially larger outlets has contributed to the steady broadening in the assortments made available to customers.

To the extent to which greater variety is secured by drawing on differentiated products from overseas (as recent models of international trade suggest), changes which reduce the transactions costs of expanding assortment contribute to higher imports. Second, retailers can themselves act as significant importers. Third, a relatively concentrated retail structure may reduce the costs importers face in identifying and securing foreign distribution channels.

Though references to distribution systems as factors affecting imports are frequently found both in industry case studies[28] and in studies of international trade[29], there is little consensus as to distribution's practical significance. An attempt to determine such significance is made here by assuming - in the spirit of the "new" trade theories - that import penetration primarily responds to income and relative prices; but that it also responds to distribution costs. The higher these costs, the lower the observed import penetration rate at any given level of the other variables.

The equation to be tested takes as the dependent variable the ratio of imports of final consumption goods (excluding food but comprising, in addition to consumption goods as narrowly defined, household capital goods, including vehicles) to domestic private goods consumption. Four explanatory variables are then used, namely:

i. domestic GDP (like the other variables, this is measured at constant prices) - which can be taken to determine the share of domestic producers in the range of differentiated goods available to consumers;
ii. the difference between world GDP and domestic GDP - which can be taken to determine the share of foreign producers in the range of differentiated products available to domestic consumers;
iii. the relative price of imported to domestic goods: proxied by the ratio of import prices to the private goods consumption deflator net of imports (noting that this proxy has the disadvantage of including distribution costs as well as indirect taxes in the denominator);

and lastly,

[28] See, for example, Sutton (1991), pages 414 and 478.
[29] See, for example, Lawrence R. (1991).

iv. a measure of the structure of the distribution system: either the volume of consumption per outlet or outlet density.

The equation has been estimated using a pooled sample for the seven countries covered by this study - the results are out in Table 8.

Table 8 Equations modelling import penetration in consumption goods

	M/ (D.M) ratio for consumption goods		
Independent variable	**1**	**2**	**3**
Constant	-19.388 (1.9260)*	-10.133 (1.8100)*	-14.323 (1.7229)*
Relative price variable	-0.0323 (0.2481)	0.2319 (0.2126)	-0.0678 (0.2169)
Domestic GDP	-0.2987 (0.0452)*	-0.3431 (0.0351)*	-0.3518 (0.0358)*
Rest of world GDP	1.2950 (0.1139)*	0.7717 (0.1075)*	1.0658 (0.1024)*
Volume of private consumption per outlet	-- --	0.4715 (0.0457)*	-- --
Outlet density	-- --	-- --	-0.0645 (0.0065)*
Summary statistics R^2	0.4925	0.6837	0.6737
Standard error of the regression	0.4745	0.3527	0.3582
F-stastic	59.850	87.549	83.640

NOTE: Standard errors are in parenthesis
* Indicates significance at the .99 level.

The two GDP variables have the right sign, highlighting the distinction between the impact of product differentiation and the standard income effects. Adding the distribution variables increases the explanatory power of the equation without modifying greatly the effect of the other variables, excepting the price variable (which is never significant). The distribution variables have the right sign - greater density reducing import penetration, greater consumption per outlet increasing it - and are consistently highly significant.

While the relation between distribution costs and import penetration is significant, the absolute magnitude of the impact is not large. This is shown in Table 9 which summarizes the main outcomes of simulating the effects on import penetration in consumer goods of reducing the density of outlets in Italy and Japan.

Table 9 Simulated effects of 50% negative shock to outlet density on import penetration in Japan and Italy (1)

	Change in	
	Retail outlet density	Import penetration
Japan	- 0.006606	+ 0.1263
Italy	- 0.009087	+ 0.3789

(1) These calculations were carried out by using the estimates of Table 3.

The extent of the reduction is based on the results reported in Table 4 - that is, the estimates of the outlet density levels expected on the basis of underlying economic and demographic characteristics. Using these levels rather than the current ones would increase import penetration in consumer goods in Japan by just over one-tenth of 1 percentage point, and in Italy by around four-tenths of a percentage point.

4. Retailing and Public Policy

Overall, developments in the distribution of consumer goods have yielded considerable gains in consumer welfare. Looking to the future, there is every reason to expect that structural change in distribution will continue, with three factors being especially important.

First, the shopping preferences of consumers will continue to evolve. Thus, the trend towards significantly smaller families, and the very rapid growth of one person family units, may well shift demand away from "trolley shopping" (large purchases of standard items) towards the smaller unit purchases often referred to as "basket shopping", located at sites closer to the place of work and with an emphasis on variety and ambience. This could, in part, be offset by a widening in the income distribution, which would bolster that segment of demand which is especially price-sensitive; so that the retail system may need to adapt to further segmentation in the pattern of demand.

Second, rapid change will also continue in the technology of distribution. The greatest advances are likely to arise from the systematic application and use of information technology. In a first phase, this technology was deployed primarily to control inventories, reduce pilfering, and speed up payment; but it is now apparent that the data being collected provide the retailer with an extraordinarily rich base of information about customers. As retailers use this data to modify assortments and develop new product lines, the boundaries between distributors and manufacturers are likely to blur further.

Third, the structure of the retail industry will itself change. The last two decades have seen major modifications in the actors on the supply side; these include: the rise of vertical marketing systems; the emergence of large-scale retail franchising; the continued growth of the largest operators, and their expansion from the grocery sector to other, less concentrated, parts of the distribution system. These developments have been closely tied up not only with technical innovations but also with organizational change - the rise of direct product profitability analysis being a striking case in point. Experience with and mastery of these innovations is an important source of competitive advantage for the leading-edge firms in the industry; and it is clear that they are moving to make the best use of this asset through internationalization. In this industry as in others, internationalization should provide a powerful means for the transfer of skills; and as retailers go international, they tend to bring their suppliers with them, providing further impetus to the growth of trade[30]. Combined, these factors will create on-going pressures for change; what matters is that the distribution system be in a position to adapt to these pressures as they emerge. This requires that the participants in this sector be free to experiment among alternative approaches, and that consumers be able to select those which best match their needs. All of this is unlikely to happen in a tightly regulated environment; yet the distribution sector is subject to considerable regulation in the countries covered. These regulations centre on four aspects of the sector:

i. entry into retailing;
ii. zoning and the siting of shops;
iii. anti-social or anti-competitive conduct by retailers;
iv. vertical relations, both between levels in the distribution system and between distributors and producers.

4.1 Entry into Retailing

The greatest obstacles to change have been the regulations restricting entry into retailing. Notably in Italy, Japan and France, these were adopted so as to protect small shop-keepers from what was perceived as the "unfair" competition of the larger stores; as modified in the 1960s and 1970s, the relevant legislation in each of these countries made reference to promoting adjustment in distribution[31] - but its practical effects have been very largely at odds with the stated intentions. Rather, the restrictions have durably slowed the adjustment in the number of shops; where larger outlets have been allowed, they have acted to increase their operating costs; and they have hindered the development of competition among larger stores, creating rents for those operators able to clear the regulatory hurdles.

---

[30] On the internationalization of retailers see Burt S. (1991), pages 487-516; and Colla (1992), pages 65-136.

[31] The development of these policies is discussed for Japan in Yoshino (1971), pages 251-271; for Italy, in Spranzi (1991) pages 193-225 and Zamagni (1982); and for France in the country study on France.

The Italian case usefully demonstrates these impacts. Law 426/71 created formidable barriers to the opening of large stores, notably in the South, where the regulatory commissions empowered to grant approval for store opening have been most heavily dominated by small shop-keepers. The effect on the density of retail outlets has been discussed above; but the Law's impacts go beyond this. Three of these impacts are especially important.

First, the Law has led to a highly distorted pattern of large store location. The central and western parts of the North, which account for less than 35 per cent of population, account for over 60 per cent of large outlets; and even within this part of the country there are areas where large store penetration is very low. The fairly inconsistent way in which the Law has been applied has meant that large stores have not been able to site outlets so as to derive economies in the use of storage and transport facilities; so that inventory costs at Italian hyper-markets rise sharply with size of store[32], and the gains attainable from improved logistics are largely foregone.

Second, the Law has distorted the allocation of large store ownership. There appears, in effect, to have been a preference for spreading widely the right to operate large outlets; and within this spread to give special preference to cooperatives. Moreover, the Law has treated especially favourably larger units established through the merger of existing smaller outlets. The result is that the more efficient firms have not been able to expand - with the largest single operator controlling a sales surface less than 10 per cent of that of any one of the top 10 German retailers; while the cooperatives have managed to maintain a higher share of the market than many observers believe warranted by their relative efficiency.

Third, the Law has sheltered what large stores there are from the disciplines of competition. It has, in particular, been extremely difficult to site a new large store within the catchment area of another; with the consequence that larger outlets do not compete as vigorously, notably on price, as they do elsewhere. As a result, the rate of return on investment in Italian hyper-markets has been one-third higher than that in France.

---

[32] See the data presented in Colla (1992), page 218.

Recent years have seen some liberalization of restrictive regulations in each of the countries where they exist. Thus, in France, the transfer of powers of regulatory approval to regional levels of government has been associated with a more liberal attitude to the granting of approval. In Italy, a number of automatic exemptions have been introduced, mainly raising the size limit beyond which approval for the opening or extension of an outlet must be sought. Finally, in Japan, the Large Scale Retail Store Law has been amended, increasing the threshold at which approval must be sought, broadening the composition of the regulatory entities so as to dilute the representation of small shop-keepers, and increasing transparency in the receipt and processing of applications.

The practical impact of these changes differs:

- In France, the current application of the regulations seems broadly permissive; it is an open question whether, as now applied, they mainly protect small outlets from competition by larger stores, large outlets from competition by each other. In Italy, on the other hand, the regulations, though they now allow the opening of super-markets, still seriously impede the development of hyper-markets, notably in the Centre and South, with experts estimating that the Italian market could absorb some 300 to 400 more hyper-markets than currently operate.
- Equally, in Japan, even after the amendments, the thresholds at which special approval must be sought are still low by the standards of most OECD countries - with stores larger than 500 square meters needing approval at Governor level, and those exceeding 1.500 square meters (or 3.000 square meters in the case of large cities) needing approval by the Minister for International Trade and Industry; and the backlog of applications remains high.

This raises the question of whether there is, in fact, a need for special processes to govern the opening of retail outlets. In effect, where a special process exists, separate from the normal operations of the zoning system (discussed below), there will inevitably be pressures for it to be used to stifle the development of competition in retailing - with the proven ability of small shop-keepers to act as effective lobby groups making it all the more likely that these pressures will at least partly succeed.

4.2 Zoning and the Siting of Shops

It may consequently be desirable to rely solely on the zoning system to control the opening of retail outlets; but it is fair to note that in practice, the operations of this system have in many cases conflicted with goals of economic efficiency.

The issues involved partly relate to *land use* policy more generally. Thus, in Japan, the special tax treatment of agricultural land within areas zoned for development has reduced the willingness of farmers to convert land from farming to other purposes - with the result that agriculture continues to account for a significant share of land use even within densely populated areas (as much as 18 per cent in some parts of Tokyo), and that when sites do become available, they are typically extremely small[33]. Equally, in the U.K., the rigid approach adopted to the development of land zoned for the "green belt" has undoubtedly affected urban land values, and contributed to greater congestion in the main urban areas. In each case, the impacts go well beyond retailing; but the limited availability of large sites with adjacent transport must distort the competitiveness of different types of store.

These impacts may be magnified by zoning processes bearing specifically on retail development. In Sweden, for example, local authorities generally only make space available for two large-scale grocery stores, on the assumption that these will be sufficient to meet local requirements. As a result, the Swedish grocery market comes close to being a duopoly, with each urban area having one store affiliated to the ICA chain and another affiliated to the co-operative movement. with the scope for entry being severely limited, the duopolists are under little real pressure to compete. Similar constraints on competition arise from the manner in which the planning laws are administered in France, increasing the rents available to the hyper-markets which manage to obtain sites.

It is undoubtedly the case that the development of large outlets can create congestion externalities, primarily due to the additional traffic

---

[33] See especially Hebbert and Nakai (1988).

both of customers and for deliveries - these outlets entail[34]. Regulating these externalities is an important function of land use policy in all the countries covered. The pursuit of this goal would not, however, be compromised by greater transparency - for example, by seeking to more systematically evaluate, on a cost-benefit basis, the land use choices being made; and it should be possible to reconcile the objectives of land use policy with greater flexibility in the way in which the policies are applied. This is especially important if the development of spatial monopolies in retailing is to be avoided - which requires that entrants be able to secure the inputs (including land) needed to contest the established outlets' position.

4.3 Anti-Social or Anti-Competitive Conduct by Retailers

In addition to controlling entry into retailing, regulations have also acted to control major aspects of conduct. These regulations pursue a variety of objectives; but their practical effect has often been to reduce competition and consumer choice.

Restrictions on *shopping hours* illustrate the forces at work. The stated goal of these policies - which, among the countries covered here, are especially tightly enforced in the U.K., France, Italy, Germany and Sweden - is usually to prevent anti-social conduct. Historically, their function was to censure that the distraction of shopping was not available on designated days and to obtain the social benefits of a common pause day; virtually everywhere, this has evolved towards an emphasis on social protection of shop employees.

There are legitimate concerns in this respect; but it is also clear that there are employees willing to work at the times which are currently restricted; that many stores are willing to pay some measure of a penalty rate for employing the staff needed; and that many customers - indeed, thanks to the growth of two-income families, a rising number - wish to shop at those hours. The persistence of the restrictions is consequently not due to a lack of potential gains from their relaxation.

---

[34] Though note that proximity to a large outlet may also increase residential land values, thereby conferring a positive externality on current owners.

Rather, a major factor appears to be the impact which this would have on competition in retailing. Extending opening hours would allow fuller use to be made of floor space - since the same fixed space could be utilized for a longer period. It is unlikely that this would be matched by an increase in the overall volume of sales, so that total floor space needed would probably diminish. In assessing the competitive impact this would have, it is important to bear in mind that the cost savings from fuller utilization of space would be greatest for those types of outlets with the highest share of land costs in their total costs; and that these are generally the largest stores. The effect would therefore be to further increase these stores' attractiveness - explaining at least in part the strength of the opposition to proposals which (by allowing better use of land) would reduce costs and would receive widespread consumer support.

The link between the regulations on conduct and the control of competition is even more apparent in limits imposed on the *pricing and promotion policies* of stores.

Here too, regulations, while few in the United States, are widespread in the European countries; an indication of their coverage is given in Figure 1.

Many of these restrictions have the effect of limiting competition:

- Controls over mail-out advertising, and over comparative advertising more generally, cannot but reduce the incentives stores have to cut prices.
- Prohibitions against special rebates, be they offered directly or through vouchers, and the requirement to maintain advertised prices, will facilitate tacit collusion between stores by i) preventing chiselling - that is, the granting of discounts from the reference price - and ii) by forcing stores to grant reductions not only to the most price-sensitive customers, but to their customer base as a whole - thereby increasing the cost, to the store, of price competition.
- Restrictions intended to curtail the use of "loss-leaders" create the risk that retailers engaged in promotional discounts will be subject to legal action by their competitors - further increasing the disincentives to aggressive price cutting.

Figure 1 Restrictions to retail trade practices in European countries

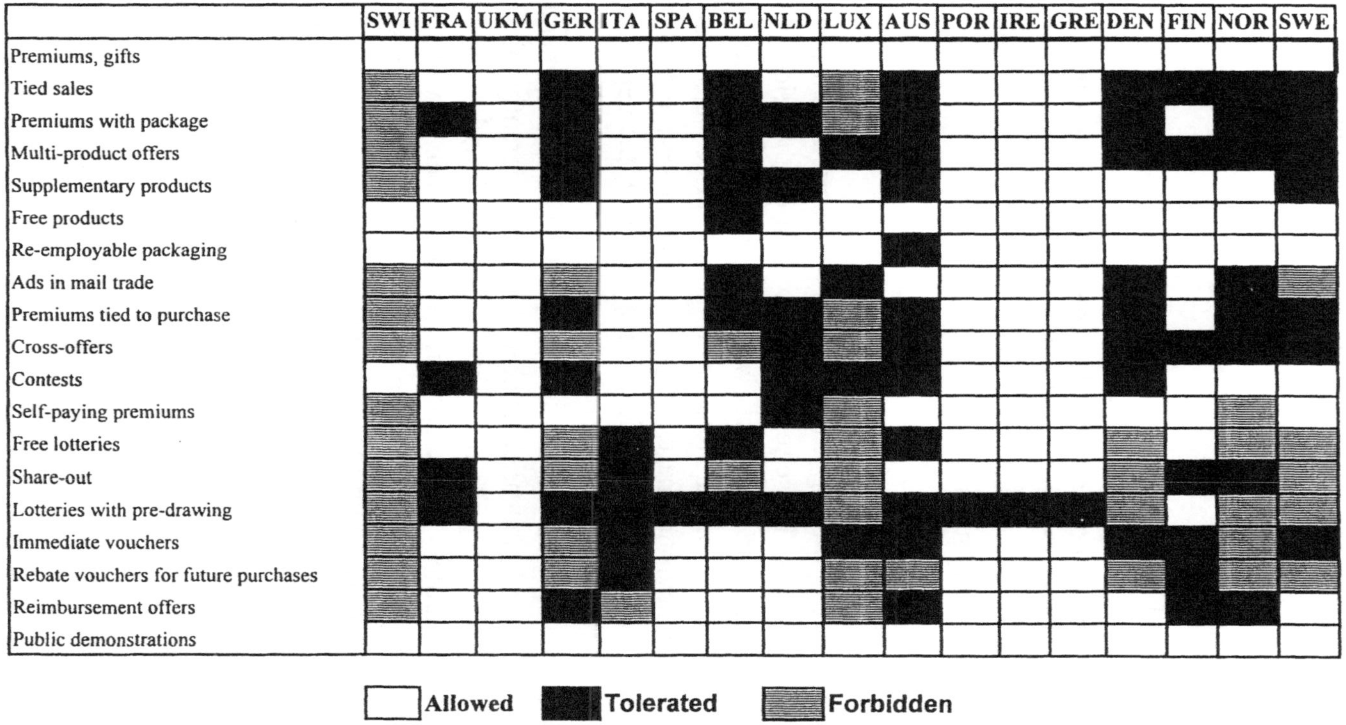

Source: Marketing Mix, No 43, June 1990

In short, these restrictions do little to promote efficiency in retailing; and their legitimate goals could be better met through the application to distribution of the general regulations preventing anti-competitive trade practices.

4.4 Restrictions on Vertical Relations

A final set of controls regulates the vertical relations between different layers in the distribution system and between producers and distributors. These controls, implemented through the trade practices authorities, have the broad objective of preventing vertical relations from being used to distort competition; they seek to achieve this objective by two means

4.4.1 Vertical Restraints

The first is by limiting the restraints which producers may impose upon distributors. These restraints may bear on the prices a distributor can charge for a product (where "price" covers every aspect of the terms of sale or transfer), or on the non-price aspects of the distributor's behaviour (the territory or customer segments to which it may sell, the ancillary services it may provide, the depth or breadth of the assortment it must carry).

Competition policy authorities in the OECD area generally treat these price and non-price restraints quite differently: they take a hostile attitude to price restraints, which are largely banned *per se* (that is, regardless of the specific circumstances in which they are adopted), while being willing to tolerate non-price restraints in some, though by no means all, cases.

Underpinning the hostility to price restraints is the view that restrictions such as resale price maintenance are likely to reduce competition both at the retail level and among suppliers - and hence should be banned *per se*; while non-price restraints are seen as more ambiguous in their effects, reducing competition in many instances, but promoting it in others (as when they serve to ensure that distributors offer a reasonable standard of service within a designated territorial area) - so that they need to be assessed on more of a case-by-case basis. Two points can be made in this respect.

The first is that the *per se* prohibition of vertical price restraints seems unjustified. In effect, such a prohibition:

- Takes no account of whether the firms engaged in the conduct have significant market power. It is difficult to see how vertical price restraints entered into between firms each of which had no market power could confer such power upon the firms acting together, and thereby distort competitive conditions.
- Moreover, it overlooks the fact that vertical price restraints may have goals supportive of competition and consumer welfare: they may, for example, serve to prevent retailers with market power from engaging in double marginalization, support a new distributor undertaking investments in building or expanding a distribution network, or prevent the "free riding" which occurs when some retailers (but not others) reduce services and prices, thus allowing consumers to benefit from the information and display services of higher priced distributors without having to pay for these services.

It is indeed the case that vertical price restraints may reduce competition in some circumstances - for example, when the contractually mandated resale price set in a market by a dominant firm, or by a number of firms with market power, facilitates collusion by largely eliminating the incentive each of the firms has to secretly cut its price to retailers. Yet here the offence should be collusion rather than resale price maintenance for the harmful effects flow from the former rather than the latter.

Second, specific problems arise from the differential treatment of different types of restraints. The distinction between price and non-price restraints is in effect somewhat arbitrary. In practice, the goals being sought through vertical price restraints can often be achieved through non-price means - for example, by specifying the grade of service a retailer is to provide. By prohibiting the one in all cases, while being at least willing to tolerate the other, the competition authorities will distort the choice of contractual arrangements.

At the same time, the manner in which non-price restraints are often treated by the competition policy authorities also seems unduly restrictive:

- Here too, it is questionable whether a firm which itself lacks market power could use a vertical restraint - say, over which firms it chooses to act as its distributors, or how it goes about choosing them - to create power for itself in the market.
- Moreover, even if the firm had market power, it is rarely the case that it would maximize its profits by engaging in a vertical restraint (such as forcing distributors to carry one item of its output if they wish to carry another) rather than by simply charging higher price in the market which it dominates.
- Finally, it is only under exceptional circumstances that even a dominant firm can strengthen its hold over a market by binding distributors in vertical relations - indeed, the lower the barriers to entry into distribution, the more difficult such market foreclosure will prove to be.

Overall, though few empirical studies are available, there is reason to believe that the constraints imposed by competition policy on vertical agreements have had two effects on the distribution system.

To begin with, they have, in several instances, slowed the emergence of competition in retailing. Thus, the harsh initial treatment of franchise contracts in the E.C. discouraged firms from entering into such arrangements, contributing to the large gap between the U.S. and the European countries in this respect[35].

At the same time, they have induced uneconomic choice of distribution channels. In particular, the prohibition on resale price maintenance encourages producers to rely on wholly-owned intermediaries, rather than on contracts with independent agents when either double marginalization (for example, market power at both the manufacturer and wholesale/importer level) or market power at only wholesaler/importer level is a factor. The U.K. automobile market provides an illustration. That market, isolated geographically and by technical standards from the Continental market and subject to a VER agreement limiting imports from Japan, is characterized by

---

[35] See Korah V. (1989), and Mendelsohn M. (1992).

high prices to consumers. Unable to force distributors to lower retail prices, manufacturers in recent years have given rebates directly to the final consumer. This tactic is now being supplanted by the buy-out of independent importers - foregoing economies of specialization in exchange for a greater measure of control.

There is, therefore, a case for reviewing the treatment of vertical restraints under the competition policy laws. Such a move has already begun in the United States, notably with respect to non-price restraints; and some significant changes have also occurred in the EC. However, several important aspects of the status of franchise contracts remain uncertain within the EC, despite a "Block Exemption" granted in 1988; and experts view the tendency within the EC to allow vertical restraints through case-by-case exemptions (which imply that the action involved is anti-competitive, but confers other advantages), rather than by simply finding that the conduct does not distort competition, as creating unnecessary uncertainty and (given the long delays required to secure such exemptions) limiting the use of efficiency-enhancing clauses in distribution contracts[36]. At the same time, resale price maintenance remains very largely prohibited - even when it involves a firm seeking to establish a maximum price for its product; and the greater enforcement of competition law in the countries now affiliating to the EC, and in Japan, seems set to broaden rather than narrow the scope of this regulatory prohibition.

Looking to the future, more far-reaching reform appears necessary. It would, in particular, be desirable to abandon the current distinction between price and non-price restraints; to shift from *per se* prohibitions to a rule of reason approach; and to apply this rule with a degree of toughness corresponding to the market power of the producer in question - with small firms in concentrated markets, and large firms entering new markets being given great latitude (effective *per se* legality) in establishing vertical restraints. A move in this direction would increase the ability of firms, including foreign firms, to establish new distribution networks.

[36] See, for example, Korah (1990), pages 120-123 and 222-237, and Whish (1989), pages 551-630.

4.4.2 Preferential Dealing

Competition laws also regulate the degree to which a producer or other supplier can differentiate the terms and conditions on which it is willing to deal with various suppliers. The goal of these laws is to prohibit "undue" price discrimination; but their practical impact is more often to protect the market position of smaller retailers.
In the United States, these regulations are mainly enforced (at least at a Federal level) through the Robinson-Patman Act of 1936, which was championed by opponents of the "chain store monopolists".
The manner in which the courts have interpreted the Act was largely set down in Federal Trade Commission versus Morton Salt Co. (1948), where it was stated that:

> *"The legislative history of the Robinson-Patman Act makes it abundantly clear that Congress considered it to be an evil that a large buyer could secure a competitive advantage over a small buyer solely because of the large buyer's quantity purchasing ability. The Robinson-Patman Act was passed to deprive a large buyer of such advantages except to the extent that a lower price could be justified by reason of a seller's diminished costs.."*[37].

In practice, the Act's exemption of price differentials based on differences in cost has had relatively little effect, since the courts have imposed such stringent tests as to make this escape clause largely unusable. As a result, the Act, as it has been interpreted, does not prohibit price discrimination in an economic sense: that is, the securing by a supplier of different rates of return on the same good provided to differing customers; rather, it *mandates* discrimination by creating a presumption in favour of uniform pricing: that is, the practice of charging the same price to customers causally responsible for different levels of cost. In addition to large direct welfare losses, this has had two, somewhat perverse, effects.
The first is that it has encouraged vertical integration by larger enterprises. The relations between a firm and its affiliate - for example,

[37] Areeda and Kaplow (1988), page 947.

the transfer prices set by different divisions of an enterprise - are exempt from the Act. As a result, the Act encourages larger U.S. firms to integrate vertically; which in the case of large retailers, takes the form of own-brands.

The second is that it has encouraged direct sourcing from overseas. These too, are largely outside the Act's application; so that a large U.S. retailer can be freer in negotiating special terms with a foreign supplier than with a U.S. firm.

Greater awareness of the Act's effects has led to a significant relaxation in its application in recent years. In particular, since the early 1980s, the Federal Trade Commission has not sought to prosecute actions under the Act; and the courts have substantially expanded the scope of the defences which may be used by a defendant and limited the applicability of treble damages. However, the fact that the Act remains in place encourages considerable private litigation under its provisions and constrains the degree to which larger retailers can secure volume discounts, even when these do reflect cost differentials.

Provisions similar to those of the Robinson-Patman Act now form an integral part of the competition policy laws of virtually all OECD countries. Thus, the EC competition policy authorities have sought to prevent undue price discrimination under the provisions of Article 86 of the Treaty of Rome. These provisions have been interpreted as limiting the discounts which may be offered by a dominant firm to reductions which i) are clearly related to differences in cost, and ii) are functionally available to all the participants in a market. In practice, the threshold of dominance has been set low; the burden of proof that a rebate is cost-justified has been placed on the defendants; and the evidentiary standard established for determining the cost base has less to do with economics that with accounting. Provisions along these lines have long figured in the Japanese Anti-Monopoly Law, though they have not been vigorously enforced; but the authorities now seem set to enforce them[38].

Empirically, it is far from clear whether such regulations serve a useful purpose. Thus, studies of volume rebates granted to even the

[38] See Matsushita (1990), pages 56-57.

largest retailers find that the discounts are usually quite small, and are in any case generally severely constrained by arbitrage. These studies confirm that in practice, suppliers have little interest in engaging in "undue" price discrimination; where they do discriminate, it usually reflects differences in cost and in the effective elasticity of demand, as well as the use of price variations as a way of chiselling from the relatively rigid prices which characterize many oligopolies. Discrimination of this type will usually be welfare-enhancing, expanding consumption in the most price-sensitive segments of the market; it is hardly clear why it should be subject to regulation except in situations where it is closely linked to a pressing threat of monopolization. This suggests placing the emphasis squarely on whether the conduct being alleged is likely to durably reduce competition; and treating the relations between producers and distributors within the general terms of prohibitions on monopolization, rather than as requiring special regulation.

4.5 Promoting Contestability in Distribution

Overall, the distribution sector in the OECD economies remains highly regulated, though the form and intensity of this regulation differs from country to country. What differs less is its anti-competitive effect.

This is not to suggest that, left entirely to its own devices, the distribution system would be perfectly contestable. It would not: there are elements of spatial monopoly; sunk costs of entry can be high; and it can take considerable time for an entrant to seriously challenge a well-entrenched incumbent. Yet the purely economic barriers to entry into retailing are by no means exceptionally large; and the international expansion of large retail firms adds an increasingly powerful force for competition.

The greatest barriers, however, come from public policy. In Italy, Japan and, to a lesser extent, France, restrictions on entry into the sector severely limit the growth of the most efficient firms. In the U.S., France, Italy, and Sweden, and to a lesser extent Germany, zoning laws make it more costly for entrants to acquire the sites needed to compete. In all of Europe, limits on shop opening hours artificially reduce the efficiency of larger stores and perpetuate profligate use of land. Equally, most strikingly in continental Europe, restrictions on promotions and discounts limit price competition - with consequences which must be greatest for entrants. Finally, in virtually all countries, the treatment by competition law of vertical relations between producers and distributors restricts efficient contracts and limits the ability of larger distributors to fully benefit from economies of scale.

There have been moves to liberalize some of these regulations. The laws restricting the opening of large stores in Italy, Japan and France have been eased - though they are far from having been entirely relaxed. In the EC, the changes forming part of the completion of the internal market have facilitated cross-border investment, and should promote further foreign direct investment.

Finally, some of the greatest changes have come in the U.S., as zoning laws have been implemented more liberally, partly as a result of the budgetary constraints on local government; and as anti-trust restrictions on vertical relations have been loosened and a generally more permissive attitude taken to the pricing and supply decisions of individual firms.

These changes should contribute to greater competition in distribution, and hence to lower prices for consumers. Especially in the U.S., as regulations have been relaxed, there are clear signs of strong rivalry in distribution, reflected in prices for many consumer goods which are low by international standards. There is no reason why a similar degree of rivalry should not prevail in other countries - but this will require further progress in reforming the policies which make the distribution system far less competitive than it need be.

5. Distribution in Industrial Markets

In contrast to the distribution of consumer goods - which occurs very largely through the "long channels" associated with the retail system - industrial goods are traded in a broad variety of ways, many of which do not immediately fit into the standard concept of distribution. In some cases, the transactions occur entirely within a firm, as when one unit in an enterprise transfers part of its output to another;

in others, the transactions are negotiated directly between firms - as when a firm markets its output to a user enterprise; in yet others, intermediaries, such as dealers or agents, play a role. Understanding why firms choose to operate through one of these means rather than another, and the consequences of these choices, is the primary focus of this section.

5.1 The Structure of Industrial Markets

Conceptually, the factors affecting the structure and functioning of transactions in industrial markets are clear. Firms, it can be assumed, will in the long run choose the mode of transaction which provides them with the greatest benefits: that is, they will seek to minimize the costs which the distribution of goods imposes. These costs include the costs of search, of contract, of procurement and of support; together, they are frequently referred to as the "transaction costs" involved in exchange[39].

The extent and nature of these costs, and their effect on the way transactions are structured, is very largely a function of the context in which the product is traded. Three elements, that are summarized here are especially important: the nature of the product; the size and strategy of the company; and the main features of the national industrial structure:

- As far as *product type* is concerned, vertical integration and quasi-integration are most likely where the transactions are frequent and supply involves product-specific assets.
- Vertical integration is also most likely when the *company* using the product concerned is large relative to the size of the market and is operating in a fairly mature industry.
- Finally, vertical integration is most likely in *national contexts* where the costs of organizing transactions through markets is high, for example because obligations are frequently disputed and are costly to enforce.

The combined effect of these patterns can be illustrated by examining the motor vehicle industry. The production of motor vehicles is

[39] See Williamson (1975) and (1986). An especially clear re-statement is in Rubin P.H. (1990).

an extremely complex activity, centred on the manufacture and assembly of some 10 to 30.000 parts. The assembly task is characterized by significant economies of scale, the conventional estimates being that the minimum efficient scale of an assembly plant is in the order of 1 million vehicles per annum, with a 5 to 10 per cent unit cost penalty for plants operating at about half that scale. The assemblers themselves are therefore typically large firms, operating high-throughput processes; but scale economies are less significant in many of the parts they assemble, and there is no reason in principle why the same firms should carry out both assembly and the tasks of parts production. In practice, the extent to which they do so reflects the interaction of the product, company and national context factors discussed above.

Thus, the U.S. assemblers are relatively highly integrated, with two patterns emerging from the data:

- The larger firms are more integrated than the smaller. According to one study, for example, in-house sources accounted, in the late 1980s, for 70 per cent of parts supply at General Motors, 50 per cent at Ford and 30 per cent at Chrysler[40].
- Looked at by product, the degree of vertical integration is higher for parts which are produced using "specific" or "idiosyncratic" assets and account for a large share of the total cost of a vehicle[41].

Four features of the U.S. industry's context seem important in explaining the high overall levels of integration:

- The U.S. industry achieved large scale relatively early, and already before World War II had attained a level of output where it could build component plants operating at efficient size. The cost penalties of integration therefore had less deterrent effect than in other countries.
- Industry structure also stabilized early, with a fixed pattern of price leadership, centred on the annual cycle of (largely cosmetic) model changes, persisting into the late 1970s. In a steadily growing market, stable price leadership ensured relatively high cash

[40] Womack et al. (1990).

[41] See Monteverde and Teece (1982).

flow, especially at GM, reducing the costs of internal expansion through integration - a strategy which was attractive to management teams primarily oriented to "empire building"[42].

- The broader regulatory context may also have encouraged integration into parts supply. Anti-trust constraints prevented the three leading firms from expanding by taking over other assemblers. At the same time, the Robinson-Patman Act imposed constraints on the volume rebates the larger assemblers could secure from suppliers. Internal supply was therefore seen as a way of securing scale-related cost advantages.
- Relations with suppliers had been poor in many instances, and notably in the case of GM - there had been circumstances where suppliers had seemed to engage in short-term profit maximization, regardless of the impact on good-will. Yet, other than vertical integration, there were few structural options for controlling opportunism: the most obvious solution, cross-equity holdings, was far less attractive than elsewhere because under U.S. corporate law, it exposed company directors to charges of conflict of interest and insider trading.

Combined, these factors have led to a situation in which inside sourcing has been the strategy of choice for U.S. assemblers. Where the assemblers do use outside suppliers, contracts are fairly short-term - generally one year; they are allocated giving great weight to competitive bidding, notably on price; and, in over 80 per cent of cases, the specifications are set down in fine detail by the assembler, the supplier acting essentially as a subcontractor. The net effect is to segment the supply chain into two parts: one governed largely by vertical integration; the other by what comes close to spot transactions.

This picture stands in marked contrast to the pattern in Japan. Assemblers there have low levels of vertical integration, with even the largest obtaining 70 per cent or more of input requirements from outside sources. Relations between assemblers and suppliers have four salient features:

---

[42] See White (1971), pages 109-116 and 126-33; and Boyle S.E. and Hogarty T.F., pages 81-95.

- They extend beyond the product market, with the purchaser generally providing some technical support and, in many instances, equity. The amounts of equity involved are almost always small: a recent survey of parts suppliers showed that at 80 per cent of the companies surveyed, assemblers accounted for no more than 20 per cent of outstanding equity.
- They are hierarchically structured. In the usual case, the assembler deals mainly or even solely with firms producing major components or sub-assembly units (such as engines, instrument panels and suspension systems); these suppliers - of whom there are somewhere between two and four hundred - then deal with some 5.000 smaller, more specialized enterprises, which in turn have the primary role in managing relations with some 32.000 "third tier" companies. Moreover, within each tier, there is some hierarchical ordering, as suppliers with more seniority in a product are recognised as having a stronger claim on orders.
- They are long term, though by no means immutable. Procurement contracts generally last four years, but a supplier would have a reasonable expectation that good performance would lead to renewal into a new contract cycle. The supplier would, however, be expected to maintain a target rate of productivity growth sufficient to ensure that its prices diminished as its cumulated production rose.
- External suppliers are more than subcontractors. They carry out the detailed design and engineering tasks for some 70 per cent of parts externally sourced. Engineering advice, including the loan of skilled personnel, provided by the purchaser plays an important part in co-ordinating the flow of information and technology through the supply chain.

The Japanese industry therefore relies primarily on relational transactions: that is, multi-period exchanges in which the parties develop assets specific to the relationship. Each of the features described above supports this type of transaction: by ensuring that the parties have some common financial interest, and access to "insider" status; by facilitating the flow of information; and by sustaining social norms of conduct which inevitably affect management's response to changing circumstances.

This in part reflects factors which have discouraged vertical integration in Japan. Thus:

- The Japanese automobile industry developed late and then grew very rapidly. Management attention has been focused very largely on expanding the scale of the assembly activity, rather than on moving into other markets. Full vertical integration has been seen as detracting scarce assets - of skills and cash - from expansion; and in a market which was and remains intensely competitive, there has been no slack to draw on.
- The segmentation of the labour market has also discouraged vertical integration. As major employers, the assemblers have a far greater commitment to job security than smaller suppliers. Integration would have added to this core labour force, increasing the firms' fixed costs. Moreover, labour costs are considered to be higher at the assemblers than at smaller firms, again limiting the incentive for production to be brought in-house.

Spot transactions have not, however, been a viable alternative to integration both because of the product factors discussed above and because they would not support the industry's growth. In effect:

- With rising capital intensity in the industry, the assemblers could not expect the component producers to rely solely on internal resources to expand their scale of production in line with market growth. Especially in the 1950s and 1960s, distortions in capital markets favoured access to capital by the larger firms; this increased the pressure on the assemblers to act as non-bank intermediaries, and channel funds, albeit on a small scale, to the best of their suppliers.
- Distortions in the capital markets have also made it easier and cheaper for the large firms to maintain access to liquidity in down-turns. Given the sunk costs of exit and entry, this has encouraged a form of risk-sharing in which the large firms absorbed some of their suppliers' risk by sustaining purchases and prices through the cycle[43].
- It would have been difficult for the parts suppliers to carry out fully independently the R&D needed to keep pace with the as-

[43] See especially the empirical results reported in Asanuma and Kikutani (1992).

semblers. Though smaller companies do undertake a larger share of the R&D effort in Japan than elsewhere[44], economies of scale in R&D[45], which must partly reflect distortions in capital markets and more limited access by small enterprises to highly trained personnel, have undoubtedly affected the distribution of the capacity to innovate. The assemblers have therefore had to bolster the technical ability of their suppliers through the loan of personnel and the exchange of information.

Finally, it may have been easier to make relational transactions work smoothly in the Japanese context than in, say, the United States. Broader socio-cultural factors may be at work; but the evolution of industry structure has also played an important part. Many of the key components producers started as offshoots of the assemblers; as they grew, the parent reduced its involvement, retaining an equity interest sufficient to have "insider" status but not necessarily to comprise a controlling interest. However, the links with the former parent and (often but not always) largest client usually remain strong, and senior staff retiring from the parent are frequently re-employed by the supplier. This translates into an ethos which emphasizes shared interests and, more broadly, into strong norms against opportunism.

The European picture, though varying greatly from country to country, tends to lie between these extremes. On average, the European assemblers source internally some 30 to 50 per cent of their components: less than the larger U.S. firms but more than those in Japan. The components suppliers tend to be larger relative to the assemblers than they are in the U.S. or Japan, and the largest and best established among these - firms such as Bosch, Lucas, Essex and Bendix - operate major R&D facilities and have very largely autonomous technical skills. These firms tend to supply most of the assemblers, often on a stable, long-term basis - with Germany and Sweden being closer to the relational contracting mode of operation found in Japan, while the relatively more protected assemblers in France, the U.K. and Italy have been somewhat more vertically integrated.

---

[44] See Clark R. (1984), page 15.

[45] See Link A.N. (1980), pages 771-782.

In short, common structural constraints can be met in differing ways, depending on the country context - a pattern which recurs throughout the industries for which studies are available. This raises two questions: the first is whether the differing outcomes in terms of industry structure lead to differences in industry performance: the second, what their specific implications are for the degree to which markets are genuinely contestable.

5.2 Effects on Industrial Performance

There is no systematic evidence linking the way in which firms organize their supply transactions to the efficiency with which they perform. It cannot, in other words, be taken as a fact that one mode of structuring relations in industrial markets universally or even generally performs better than others - rather, the outcomes in terms of performance will reflect features which vary significantly from product to product and market to market[46].

Broad changes in the overall context for economic activity may, nonetheless, create greater adjustment difficulties for some ways of organizing transactions than for others - inducing a shift in the balance between these. Two trends stand out in this respect.

- There has, to begin with, been a shortening in the life-cycles of many industrial products . The increase in the R&D capital stock, the development of technologies (such as computer aided design) which reduce the costs of product development, and the entry of new players on to the world market, have led to a rise in the rate at which new products are introduced.
- At the same time, there has been an increase in product variety, as rising income have lead to a growing demand for product differentiation and as new technologies, notably for computer aided manufacturing, increase the product-range economies of scope relative to the single-product economies of scale.

Combined, these developments have increased the importance to firms of being able to support rapid innovation across a broad product range - all while keeping costs under control. There is evidence

---

[46] See Buzzell and Gale (1987) for a review of a rich base of empirical evidence on the importance of fitting strategy to circumstance.

to suggest that long-term contracting may yield significant efficiency benefits in terms of the ability to meet these goals. Three factors seem to be at work.

First, successful innovation generally requires change not only in the single product or process which is being redesigned but also in a number of other elements in the structure of production and consumption. Thus, equipment and intermediate inputs may need to be changed; goods and services which are complementary to the new or modified product developed; and sales and distribution channels retrained. Mobilizing these "complementary assets" requires a degree of co-ordination above and beyond that feasible in short-term transactions.

Second, in many cases full vertical integration is not a cost-effective way of securing these complementarities. In effect, integration is accompanied by a blunting of market forces (as administrative hierarchies impose allocation rules different from those which might emerge under competitive conditions) and leads to a loss of focus in governance structures; it may cause cost penalties if in-house needs fall short of the efficient scale of production; and it cuts the integrated firm off from the information which it would normally obtain from its suppliers.

Third, long-term contracting may offer many of the advantages of integration without its costs. It allows for on-going co-ordination between the enterprises involved; but the relations between these enterprises remain transparent, and market mechanisms are not entirely suppressed; governance can be specialized, as can personnel management; and the innovating firm, by participating in transactions with a range of external agents, can introduce a measure of "yardstick competition" in the evaluation of its suppliers and insure itself against unsuccessful adaptation within its supply chain.

These factors are clearly at work in the case study material available. Thus:

- In the Italian textiles industry, the larger enterprises, many of them State-owned, which in the 1960s moved towards higher levels of vertical integration, proved largely incapable of surviving the transition to a more competitive environment in 1970s and 1980s. By contrast, highly specialized firms, generally clustered in the same town or region, were able to co-ordinate their efforts so as to invest in product differentiation while adapting extremely quickly to shifts in fashion.

- A similar pattern emerges in the machine tool industry, where the successful adaptation of the Japanese producers to numerical control has rested less on vertical and horizontal integration than on standardization of key components by an industry which remains relatively fragmented - in sharp contrast to the (unsuccessful) attempts by several European governments to bolster their domestic machine tool industry by promoting vertical and horizontal integration.
- Finally, a recent study of innovation in the car industry finds that the design of new models takes only 1.7 million work hours in Japan, as against 3 million in the U.S. - and that closer relations between assemblers and parts suppliers play an important part in reducing the time needed. Thanks to lower costs of product development, on average the Japanese producers introduced significantly new models every four years, as against six to seven years for the U.S. industry and closer to ten in Europe. At the same time, quality levels - as measured by the probability of obtaining a car with no defective parts per vehicle - where significantly higher in Japan than in the U.S.

Faced with rising competitive pressures, firms have therefore come to place greater emphasis on the strategic management of procurement. Both vertical integration and the more short-term focus of spot transactions have come under increasing scrutiny, as firms have sought ways of using long-term links with external suppliers to cut costs, extend access to market information, and improve the product development process.

There is, in short, a widespread trend towards the kind of long-term relationships which have characterized industry structure in Japan. Does this imply a reduction in the effective degree of competition, and notably, of exposure to the disciplines of international trade?

It is undoubtedly the case that long-term relationships reflect, and rely upon, some measure of sunk costs incurred by firms in learning to work with each other. Newcomers, not having incurred these costs, will need to qualify to join the club; and until they have demonstrated their staying power and credibility, they will not be granted the same trust as binds the firms which are already well-established. A hierarchical division of the gains from co-operation - in which the firms with more seniority as suppliers gain a larger share - may lengthen the time to break-even: though (much like an efficiency wage structure) it also increases the reward from success, and hence may actually serve to attract entry. The pattern of relationships may therefore display a measure of inertia; but this does not mean that it lessens competition.

It is, in particular, difficult to see why a structure based on long-term supply relationships between independent entities would be less contestable than one dominated by vertical integration. For such market foreclosure to occur, the firms involved in the relationship would need to be able to collude more successfully, and bringing along a broader range of industry participants, than could happen within a single integrated enterprise.There is no evidence to suggest that this has occurred or is likely to occur.

In effect, were such "foreclosure by collusion" occurring, one could reasonably expect to find three phenomena reflected in the data about Japan: the rate of entry by new firms should be lower than elsewhere; this is not the case - indeed, entry rates in Japan are relatively high by the standards of other OECD economies; profits should be more persistent than elsewhere: this too, is not borne out by the data, which shows that profits in Japan are contested away no more slowly than in the United States. The standard deviation of profits should be higher than elsewhere: as persistent rents are earned in industries where collusion is easy, while being bid away in industries where they are not. The data again show that this is not the case - rather, the inter-industry spread of rates of return is exceptionally low.

The evidence therefore does not support the view that the Japanese market, characterized as it is by long-term relationships in the supply of industrial products, is any less contestable than markets in other OECD countries. This does not mean, however, that it is necessarily an easy market to export to - indeed, the very strength of domestic competition may reduce the entry niches available to foreign providers, as well as lowering the expected return from entry. So long as domestic competition remains strong, the reluctance of foreign firms to enter the market need not be associated with losses in domestic welfare or efficiency; what counts is that foreign firms be free to enter should the disciplines of domestic competition wane.

5.3 Implications for Policy

The sourcing and distribution of industrial inputs has - at least to date - been subject to less regulation than has the distribution of consumer goods. The main result of this discussion is that markets, left to their own devices, can be relied upon to structure these transactions efficiently; so that there is no case for policy intervention.

Recent developments raise a number of concerns in this respect. There is, on the one hand, a trend towards the further rapid internationalization of the production and consumption of industrial inputs, both through the growth of trade and of foreign direct investment. As the more efficient manufacturers expand their production base overseas, they bring their suppliers with them; this increases the degree of competition in the markets in which foreign investment is occurring and makes for higher productivity, both directly and through the demonstration effect the new suppliers exercise on incumbent firms.

The trend to internationalization has, however, been paralleled by greater use of protectionist measures aimed at altering the decisions firms take about the sourcing of their industrial inputs. Thus, as was emphasized in the 1992 report to the Economic Policy Committee on *Progress in Structural Reform*, local content requirements are being used more frequently to incite foreign-owned firms to increase their demand for host-country components. The measures adopted often lack transparency; little is known, or at least is released to the public, about their extent or incidence. Equally, anti-dumping measures have been applied in a number of cases to goods which, it is claimed, have too little value added in the country or region where they are being consumed; again, the basis for the measures, and the processes by which they are taken, are rarely open to public scrutiny. Finally, pressures are being applied for individual countries to meet "trade targets" in particular markets; such approaches, best described as managed trade, can have little to do with the underlying principles of a liberal trading order. A continuation in these trends would jeopardize the gains which, in this area as in others, international trade and production can bring; reversing the rise in these often covert forms of protectionism should be a priority for economic policy-makers.

References

Alter M., (1989), "The UK Retail Technology Market: Applications, Benefits and Future Developments in EPoS/EFTPoS Systems and Software", *Business International*, London.

Anderson E. and Coughlan A.T., (1987), "International Market Entry and Expansion via Independent or Integrated Channels of Distributions", *Journal of Marketing*, 51(1), 71-82.

Areeda P. and Kaplow L., (1988), *Antitrust Analysis: Problems, Text, Cases*, Little, Brown and Company, Boston.

Arrow K.J., (1975), "Vertical Integration and Communication", *Bell Journal of Economics*, 6, 173-183.

Asanuba B. and Kikutani T., (1992), "Risk Absorption in Japanese Subcontracting: A Microeconometric Study of the Automobile Industry", *Journal of the Japanese and International Economies* 6, 1-29.

Berry B.J.L. and Garrison W.L., (1958), "Central Place Theory and the Range of a Good" in *Economic Geography*, vol.34.

Berry B.J.L., Parr J.B., Epstein B.J., Ghosh A. and Smith R.H.T., (1988), *Market Centres and Retail Location: Theory and Application*, Prentice Hall, Englewood, New Jersey.

Betancourt R. and Gautshi D., (forthcoming), "The Outputs of Retail Activities: Concepts, Measurement and Evidence from U.S. Census Data", in *The Review of Economics and Statistics*.

Bluestone B., Hanna P., Kuhn S. and Moore L., (1981), *The Retail Revolution*, Auburn House, Boston.

Bork R.H., (1978), *The Antitrust Paradox: a Policy at War with Itself*, Basic Books, New York.

Bourne L.S., Sinclair R. and Dziewonsky, (1984), *Urbanization and Settlement Systems: International Perspectives*, Oxford University Press, Oxford.

Boyle S.E. and Hogarty T.F., "Pricing Behaviour in the U.S. Automobile Industry" in *Journal of Industrial Economics*, vol. 24.

Bradley K. and Taylor S., (1992), *Business Performance in the Retail Sector: The Experience of the John Lewis Partnership*, Clarendon Press, Oxford.

Bresnahan T.F., (1992), "Sutton's Sunk Costs and Market Structure: Price Competition, Advertising, and the Evolution of Concentration", *RAND Journal of Economics*, 23 (1), 137-152.

Bresnahan T.F. and Reiss P.C., (1990), "Entry into Monopoly Markets", *Review of Economic Studies*, 57, 531-553.

Brown L.A., (1981), *Innovation Diffusion: A New Perspective*, New York, Methuen.

Brusco S., (1989), *Piccole Imprese e Distretti Industriali*, Rosemberg and Sellier, Torino.

Bucklin L.P., (1972), *Competition and Evolution in the Distributive Trades*, Prentice Hall, Englewood Cliffs.

Bucklin L.P., (1990), *The Gray Market Threat to International Marketing Strategies*, Marketing Science Institute, Cambridge, Mass.

Bucklin R.E. and Schmalensee D.H., (1987), *Viewpoints on the Changing Consumer Goods Distribution Scene: Summary of a Marketing Science Institute Conference*, Marketing Science Institute, Cambridge.

Burt S., (1991), "Trends in the Internationalization of Grocery Retailing" in *International Review of Retail, Distribution and Consumer Research*, vol. 1, no. 4.

Butaney G. and Wortzel L.H., (1988), "Distributor Power Versus Manufacturing Power: The Customer Role", *Journal of Marketing*, 52(1), 52-63.

Buzzell and Gale, (1987) and Harrigan K.R., (1984), *Strategies For Vertical Integration*, Lexington Books, Lexington Mass.

Buzzell R.D. and Gale B.T., (1987), *The PIMS Principle: Linking Strategy to Performance*, The Free Press, New York.

Buzzell R. and Dew M., (1980), "Strategic Management Helps Retailers Plan for the Future", in *Marketing News*, March.

Carlton D.W., (1979), "Vertical Integration in Competitive Markets Under Uncertainty", Journal of Industrial Economics, 27(3), 189-209.

Caves R.E., (1989), "International Differences in Industrial Organization", in Schmalensee R. and Willing R. (eds.), *Handbook of Industrial Organization*, North Holland, Amsterdam.

Caves R.E. and Bradburd R.M., (1988), "The Empirical Determinants of Vertical Integration", *Journal of Behaviour and Organization*, 9, 265-279.

Chandler A.D., (1977), *The Visible Hand: The Managerial Revolution in American Business*, The Belknap Press of Harvard University, Cambridge.

Chandler A.D., (1990), *Scale and Scope: The Dynamics of Industrial Capitalism*, Belknap Press of Harvard University, Cambridge.

Chappert A. and Ecalle F., (1989), "Les Relations entre Producteurs et Distributeurs: Une Approche Empirique", Economie et Prévision, 2/3(88/89), 73-98.

Clark K.B. and Fujimoto T., (1991), *Product Development Performance: Strategy, Organization and Management in the World Auto Industry*, Harvard Business School Press, Cambridge, Mass.

Clark R., (1984), *Aspects of Japanese Commercial Innovation*, The Technical Change Centre, London, 15.

Cohen R., (1992), "GM Reformer Takes on U.S.", *International Herald Tribune*, 10 June 1992.

Colla E., (1992), *Gli Ipermercati: Sviluppo e Maturità delle Grandi Superfici di Vendita in Italia e in Europa*, Etaslibri, Milano.

Collis D., (1988), "The Machine Tool Industry and Industrial Policy" in Hazard H. and Spence M. (eds.), *International Competitiveness*, Ballinger Books, Lexington, Mass.

Connor J., Rogers R.T., Marion B.W. and Mueller W.F., (1985), *The Food Manufacturing Industries: Structure, Strategies, Performance and Policies*, Lexington Books, Lexington, Mass.

Corey E.R., Cespedes F.V. and Rangan V.K., (1989), *Going to Market: Distribution Systems for Industrial Products*, Harvard Business School Press, Boston.

Cuoumano M., (1985), *The Japanese Auto Industry: Technology and Management at Nissan and Toyota*, Harvard University Press, Boston.

Danso A., (1992), "International Advertising Strategies: Global Commitment to Local Vision", *Journal of Advertising Research*, January 1992, 10-14.

Davies S.W. and Lyons B.R., (1991), "Characterizing Relative Performance: The Productivity Advantage of Foreign Owned Firms in the U.K." in *Oxford Economic Papers*, vol. 43.

Demsetz H., (1974), "Two Systems of Belief About Monopoly", in Goldschmid H.J., Mann H.M. and Weston J.F. (eds.), *Industrial Concentration: The New Learning*, Little Brown and Company, Boston.

Di Bernardo B. and Rullani E., (1990), *Il Management e le Macchine*, Il Mulino, Bologna.

Dixit A., (1992), "Investment and Histeresis", *Journal of Economic Perspectives*, 6(1), 107-132.

Dwyer F.R. and OH S., (1988), "A Transaction Cost Perspective on Vertical Contractual Structure and Interchannel Competitive Strategies", *Journal of Marketing*, 52(2), 21-34.

Eaton B.C. and Lipsey R.G., (1979), "The Theroy of Market Preemption: The Persistence of Excess Capacity and Monopoly in Growing Spatial Markets", *Economica*, vol.46, May, 149-158.

EIU Europe's Automotive Business, "Face to Face: With Prof. Dr. Ing. Walter Kunerth, President of Siemens Automotive Group", March 1991; "Production Purchasing at Ford of Europe", March 1991; "Production Purchaising and Supply of Automobiles Citroen", June 1991; "Production Purchaising at Volvo Car Corporation", December 1991.

Eliot S.J., (1984), "La Crisi nel Movimento Cooperativo Inglese", in Spranzi A. (ed.), *Problemi dell'Imprenditorialità Commerciale: Esperienze a Confronto*, Franco Angeli, Milano.

Fullerton R.A., (1988), "How Modern is Modern Marketing? Marketing's Evolution and the Myth of the 'Production Era'", *Journal of Marketing*, 52(1), 108-125.

Geroski P., (1991), *Market Dynamics and Entry*, Basil Blackwell, Oxford.

Geroski P.A., (1992), "Vertical Regulations Between Firms and Industrial Policy", *The Economic Journal*, 1(102), 138-147.

Hawley E.W., (1966), *The New Deal and the Problem of Monopoly*, Princeton University Press, Princeton.

Hebbert M. and Nakai N., (1988), *How Tokyo Grows: Land Development and Planning on the Metropolitan Fringe*, STICERD, London.

Helper S., (1991), "How Much Has Really Changed Between U.S. Automakers And Their Suppliers?", *Sloan Management Review*, 15, Summer.

Hover D.H. ,(1991), Jordan A/S, IMD, Lausanne.

Ito T., (1992), *The Japanese Economy*, The MIT Press, Boston.

Jefferys J.B., (1950), *The Distribution of Consumer Goods: A Factual Study of Methods and Costs in the UK in 1938*, Cambridge University Press, Cambridge.

Jones K. and Simmons J., (1990), *The Retail Environment*, Routledge, London.

Lones P.J., (1990) "The Double Jeopardy of Sales Promotions", in *Harvard Business Review*, September-October, 145-152.

Kida K. and Kiji M., (1991), *Japan's Distribution Stricture and Distribution Costs*, the MITI Research Institute.

Klein B., Crawford R.G. and Alchain A.A., (1978), "Vertical Integration, Appropriable Rents, and the Competitive Contracting Process", *Journal of Law and Economics*, 21, 297-326.

Klein M., King R. and Jones R., (1992), "The Chinese Economic Area: Economic Integration without a Free-Trade Agreement", *OECD Department of Economic and Statistics Working Paper* no.124.

Korah V., (1989), *Franchising and the EEC Competition Policy Rules*, European Competition Law Monographs, Oxford.

Korah V., (1990), *An Introductory Guide to EEC Competition Law and Practice*, ESC Publishing Limited, Oxford.

Laulajainen R., (1987), *Spatial Strategies in Retailing*, Dordrecht, D.Reidel Publishing.

Lawrence R., (1991), "Efficient or Exclusionist? The Import Behaviour of Japanese Corporate Groups" in *Brookings Papers on Economic Activity*, no. 1.

Lerner F.H., (1990), "Nonbank Banks: The Credit Card War" in *Bankers' Monthly*, vol.107, no.3

Levitt T., (1983), "The Globalization of Markets", *Harvard Business Review*, 61, May-June, 92-102.

Liberman M.B., (1991), "Determinants of Vertical Integration: An Empirical Test", *The Journal of Industrial Economics*, 39(5), 451-466.

Libowitz S.J., (1983), "Tie-in Sales and Price Discrimination", *Economic Inquiry*, 21(2), 387-399.

Link A.N., (1980), "Firm Size and Efficient Enterpreneurial Activity", in *Journal of Political Economy*, vol. 88, 771-782.

Matsushita M., (1990), *Introduction to Japanese Antimonopoly Law*, Yuhikaku, Tokyo.

McClelland W.G., (1963), *Studies in Retailing*, Basil Blackwell, Oxford.

McKenna R., (1991), "Marketing is Everything" *in Harvard Business Review*, January-February, 65-79.

McNair M.P. and May E.G., (1963), "The American Department Store 1920-1960", *Bureau of Business Research Bulletin*, no.166.

McNair M.P. and May E.G., (1978), "The Next Revolution of the Retailing Wheel", *Harvard Business Review*, 56, September-October.

McNair M.P. and May E.G., (1982*), The Evolution of Retail Institutions in the United States*, Marketing Science Institute, Cambridge.

McNeil I.R., (1980), *The New Social Contract: An Inquiry Into Modern Contractual Relations*, Yale University Press, New Haven.

Mendelsohn M., (1992), *Franchising in Europe*, Cassell, London.

Messerlin P., (1982), *La Revolution Commerciale*, Bonnel, Paris.

Miwa Y., (1991), *Keiretsu Trades and Products Imports*, Research Institute for the Japanese Economy, Tokyo.

Monteverde K.A. and Teece D.J., (1982), "Supplier Switching Costs and Vertical Integration in the Automobile Industry", *The Bell Journal of Economics*, Spring, Vol.13, no.1, 206-213.

Monteverde K.A. and Teece D.J., (1982), "Appropriable Rents and Quasi-Vertical Integration", *Journal of Law and Economics.*

Mueller B., (1992), "Standardization vs. Specialization: An Examination of Westernization in Japanese Advertising", *Journal of Advertising Research*, January, 15-24.

Nardin G., (1987), *La Benetton*, Edizione Lavoro, Roma.

Noyelle G., (1990), *Productivity in the Services: Preliminary Findings from a Comparative Study of France and the United States*, Bard College, Annandale-on-Hudson.

Odagiri H., (1992), *Growth through Competition, Competition through Growth*, Oxford University Press, Oxford, 207-232.

OECD, (forthcoming), *Competition Policy and Vertical Restraints: Franchising Agreements*.

Oliveira-Martins J., (1992), "Export Behaviour with Differentiated Products", in Dagenais M.G. and Muet P.A., (eds.), *International Trade Modelling*, Chapman and Hall, London.

Oxenfeldt A.R., (1964), *Marketing Practices in the TV Set Industry*, Columbia University Press, New York.

Palamountain J.C., (1955), *The Politics of Distribution*, Harvard University Press, Cambridge.

Perry M.K., (1989), "Vertical Integration: Determinants and Effects" in Schmalensee R. and Willig R. (eds.), *Handbook of Industrial Organization*, North Holland, Amsterdam.

Petersen C.E., "Trade Conflict and Resolution Methodologies", AER Papers and Proceedings, May 1992, 62-66.

Philips R. and Way A., (year?), *The West European Automotive Industry: Where Now in the 1980s*, The Economist Intelligence Unit Ltd., Special Press Report no.77.

Pilotti L., (1991), *La Distribuzione Commerciale*, UTET, Torino.

Pilotti L., (1988), "Technological and Informative Efficiency for Flexible Retail Services: Contracts, Firm-Specific Resources and Network Organizations", *Note di Ricerca no.15*, CESCOM, Milano.

Pilotti L. and Pozzana R., (1991), "Franchising Contracts in the European Community", *Series Studies, Commerce and Distribution*, no.18, EC Commission, D.G. XXIII.

Pilotti L. and Pozzana R., (1990), *I Contratti di Franchising*, EGEA, Milano.

Pilotti L., Rosolin M. and Rullani E., (1986), *La Rivoluzione Tecnologica nel Commercio*, CEDAM, Padova.

Pilotti L. and Rullani E., (1991), "Evoluzione e Innovazione nelle Forme Distributive: Doppia Elica o Servuction?", *Commercio*, no.43.

Porter M.E., (1974), "Consumer Behaviour, Retailer Power and Market Performance in Consumer Goods Industries", *The Review of Economics and Statistics*, 56(4), 419-436.

Porter M.E., (1976), *Interbrand Choice, Strategy, and Bilateral Market Power*, Harvard University Press, Cambridge.

Porter M.E., (1980), *Competitive Strategy: Techniques for Analyzing Industries and Competitors*, The Free Press, New York.

Porter M.E., (1983), *Cases in Competitive Strategy*, The Free Press, New York.

Posner R., (1976), *The Robinson-Patman Act: Federal Regulation of Price Differences*, American Enterprise Institute, Washington D.C.

Rubin P.H., (1990), *Managing Business Transactions*, The Free Press, Glencoe, Ill.

Samiee S., (1990), "Productivity Planning and Strategy in Retailing", in *California Management Review*, Winter issue, 54-76.

Saxonhouse G.R. and Yamamura K., (1986), *Law and Trade Issues of the Japanese Economy: American and Japanese Perspectives*, University of Washington Press, Seattle.

Saxonhouse G., (1989), "Differentiated Products, Economies of Scale and Access to the Japanese Market", in Feenstra R. (ed.), *Trade Policies for International Competitiveness*, The University of Chicago Press.

Schmalensee R., (1978) "Entry Deterrence in the Ready-To-Eat Cereal Industry" in *Bell Journal of Economics*, vol. 9.

Schwartzman D., (1971), *The Decline of Service in Retail Trade*, NBER, Washington.

Selten R., (1975), "The Chain Store Paradox", in *Theory and Decision, No.9*, 127-159.

Sheard P., (1991), "The Economics of Japanese Corporate Organization and the 'Structural Impediments' Debate: A Critical Review", *Japanese Economic Studies*, Summer, vol.19, no.4.

Skinner W., (1978), *Manufacturing in the Corporate Strategy*, Wiley, New York.

Spranzi A,. (1991), *La Distribuzione Commerciale: Economia del Commercio e Politica Commerciale*, Franco Angeli, Milano.

Stern L.W., El-Ansary A.I. and Brown J.R., (1989), *Management in Marketing Channels*, Prentice Hall, Englewood Cliffs.

Sutton J., (1986), "Vertical Products Differentiation: Some Basic Themes", *American Economic Review* (Papers and Proceedings), 76, 393-398.

Sutton J., (1991), *Sunk Costs and Market Structure: Price Competition, Advertising and the Evolution of Concentration*, The MIT Press, Cambridge.

Teece D., (1986) "Profiting from Technological Innovation" in *Research Policy*, vol. 15.

Vance J.E. Jr., (1979), *The Merchant's World: The Geography of Wholesaling*, Prentice-Hall, Englewood Cliffs, New Jersey.

Von Braun C.F., (1991), "The Acceleration Trap in the Real World" in *Sloan Management Review*, vol. 12, no. 4.

West D.S., (1979), "Tests of Two Locational Implications of a Theory of Market Preemption", *Canadian Journal of Economics*, vol.14, May.

Whish R. (1989), *Competition Law*, Butterworths, London.

White L.J., (1971), *The Automobile Industry Since 1945*, Harvard University Press, Cambridge.

Williamson O.E., (1975), *Markets and Hierarchies: Analysis and Antitrust Implications*, Free Press, New York.

Williamson O.E., (1986), "Vertical Integration and Related Variations on a Transaction-Cost Theme", in Stiglitz J.E. and G.F. Nathewson (eds.), *New Developments in the Analysis of Market Structure*, The MIT Press, Cambridge.

Wills L.R. and Mueller W.F., (1989), "Brand Pricing and Advertising" in *Southern Economic Journal*, vol. 56, no. 2.

Wiseman C., (1988), *Strategic Information Systems*, Irwin Publishers, Homewood, Illinois.

Womack J.P. et al. (1990), *The Machine that Changed the World*, MIT.

Yamawaki H., (1989), "A Comparative Analysis of Inter-Temporal Behaviour of Profits: Japan and the United States" in *Journal of Industrial Economics*, vol. 37, no. 4.

Yamawaki H., (1992), *Japanese Multinationals in US and European Manufacturing Industries: Entry, Strategy and Patterns*, IRES/Catholic University of Louvain.

Yip G.S., (1991), *Do American Business Use Global Strategy?*, Marketing Science Institute, Cambridge.

Yoshimo M.Y., (1971), *The Japanese Marketing System: Adaptations and Innovations*, The MIT Press, Cambridge.

Zamagni V., (1982), *La Distribuzione Commerciale in Italia fra le Due Guerre*, Franco Angeli, Milano.

Zandpour F., Chang C. and Catalano J., (1992), "Stories, Symbols, and Straight Talk: A Comparative Analysis of French, Taiwanese, and U.S. TV Commercials", *Journal of Advertising Research*, January, 25-38.

Comment

Carlo Pace
University of Rome "La Sapienza"

An evaluation of Dr. Ergas' report regarding the efficiency of retail distribution in some OCSE countries, including Italy, could be approached from two points of view: one in terms of method, the other in terms of its realism.

I will not address those issues upon which I am largely in agreement with Dr. Ergas; instead, turning my attention to a number of points which I found perplexing or questionable, may save time and avoid repetition. At the same time, I wish to clarify that by focusing attention on some matters is not to take anything away from the unchallenged merits of the author, to whom I extend my congratulations for the work presented here.

It is the first section of the report that is endowed with the most originality. Here, the retail points-of-sale are taken into consideration, noting the tendency towards an increase in average dimensions which is especially marked in the non-food sector.

This tendency, nonetheless, manifests itself differently from country to country. Dimensional growth, for instance, is less marked in Italy and Japan, where the density of retail outlets is greater. This situation is explained by the existence there of regulations which govern this sector of business. The original aspect of the research presented here is the attempt to single-out, using an estimate of a multivariate function, the explanatory factors (along with the relative significance) represented by the density of the points-of-sale, measured with reference to the population.

It is evident, first of all, that for the estimates the data employed seems to have been taken both from time series as well as from various nations. Here a question first arises. Resorting to the analysis of a time series would tend to highlight the effects of an existing dimensional evolution which is assumed by the explanatory variables, and based upon coefficients that reflect the *temporal* analogy within the structure of the relationships themselves. By contrast, a cross-sectional analysis would reveal the effects of the differences of the values taken on by the variables in different countries, assuming a *spatial* analogy in the relations. In effect, the method utilized here mixes the two kinds of effects, assuming, therefore, the existence of a double analogy: one temporal, the other spatial. I realize that if one had, instead, proceeded by estimating the equations for each nation separately (utilizing the relative time series data on the one hand, and the same year's relative data derived from different nations on the other), that one would incurred in a loss observations.

The price to be paid, however, for gaining a greater number of observations lies in masking the differences - differences of structure and evolution - occurring within the various actual situations.

A second observation has to do with the employment of a "dummy" variable to represent an existing regulatory system.

Before the starting date for the series of data employed here, regulatory systems already existed in Italy, Japan and France.

Nonetheless, a dummy variable appears for the entire data period for each of these nations. The report itself, however, explicitly acknowledges that the effect of the regulatory system has, in fact, diminished over time. This, among other things, confirms the perplexities involved regarding the use in the case study of data both from various years, as well as various nations. That the recourse to a dummy variable, which does not take into account the differing grade of effective strictness in the enforcement of a regulatory system, may lead to biases in the results obtained seems to be confirmed. This confirmation can come, for example, from an examination of how the role of the other explanatory factors changes following the introduction of the dummy variable. It seems, in particular, rather peculiar that the introduction of the dummy reduces the importance of the role which is attributed to the evolution over time of the relation between rents and consumer prices; a reduction that is stressed more in an analysis of the food sector.

A bit of explanation would seem to be called for regarding the choice made in the research of taking into consideration the quadratic per capita consumption rather than just the total amount. Even with the method adopted it seems to me that the consumption per person had but little influence upon the density of points-of-sale. Probably, before considering them in this way, Dr. Ergas had tried to utilize the per capita values in the regressions. It would be interesting to know what results he would have obtained.

The part of the report dedicated to the effects of concentration upon the economies of scale and scope, and contractual position of wholesalers is conducted by gathering some elements from observation, but without a true and proper inductive investigation, and by supplying a set of judgements based upon arguments that are essentially deductive. The use of a brief concentration index, like that of the share of sales that belongs to the four or ten largest units, does not seem to have been a particularly felicitous choice. If the objective set before us is that of revealing the effects of dimension, the index seems hardly appropriate. It is true that the choice of method for concentration measurement is made with reference to the objective proposed, and that, therefore, justifies the recourse to the most varied methods. In a case of this sort, however, the choice seems less appropriate since, among other reasons, the reference to the ordinates of the curve of concentration corresponding to numbers four and ten would make sense if one could consider (something that seems to us rather dubious) the hypothesis of a reduction of the operating units to four and ten, respectively. One wonders why was not employed, instead, the same index used to express the degree of urban concentration i.e. the Herfindel index (that at least has the advantage of synthesizing the whole distribution by dimension), or why reference was not made to another rather synthetic measure of the entire distribution: the average size. It seems to me necessary, moreover, to point out the somewhat easy passage made from firms to operative units when researching the effects of the concentration. In reality, one aspect of the "merits" that would be recognized regarding the concentration, according to the reasoning conducted in the report, is that they are valid when they refer to the concentration regarding companies, but not valid for those regarding local units.

Breaking the rule that I set for myself to highlight only those points of Dr. Ergas' report that raised problems for me, it seems to me proper to express my complete agreement with the negative assessment expressed regarding comparisons of those restrictions imposed by urban planning legislation that work (as an operative result) by raising property values and, consequently, the cost of business, thus limiting the expansion of the sales space. At the same time, I must point out that this restriction affects firms and points-of-sale differently.

One point that seems especially worthy of discussion is that of the effect that one would expect to come from an increase in competition. I can agree that a greater level of retail concentration can level-out, to its credit, the distribution of market power among producers, wholesalers and retailers. It remains to be seen, however, what consequences the consumers can produce regarding the contractual position of this head-to-head confrontation. In substance, the contingent gain of market power in respect to the industry does not translate automatically, nor (in my view) necessarily, into a reduction of the total market power of the enterprise system relative to the consumer. Instead, one is dealing with a simple matter of redistribution, as would seem to be indicated by the data given regarding gross margins which are higher where the degree of concentration is greater.

It is also evident how the report, while demonstrating an understanding of the possible differences regarding the content of services associated within the concentration, does not make any attempt to gather up such differences or to furnish any such evaluations regarding these. With this observation I would like to again underline the need to pay attention to, and to stress, research into the methods for calculating the value added by distribution services, or (if one prefers) into the definition of what, indeed, constitutes a service unit. This is a problem that, as is clearly apparent, is also reflected in all those considerations that are based upon the levels, as well as the evolution, of increased productivity.

Regarding the consequences that could be expected from a concentration process at the general level of the sector and of the economy, it seems to me useful to call attention to an aspect that is suggested by Italian experience. The presence of high unemployment rates indicates how imperfectly the labor market works. The most likely principal reasons for this are institutional and contractual constraints, but that is not the point of interest here. What becomes noticeable, instead, is how the distributive sector verifies the contemporaneous and consistent presence of independent, self-employment and regular, subordinate employment. The Italian experience has shown an irregular tendency towards self-employment, permitted (evidently) by the flexibility of the relative compensation. One can verify, therefore, a situation which might be called "second best". The missing concentration - as well as its reduction in later phases - in essence was actuated thanks to *both* the constrained and expensive capacity of self-employment. The excess of contractual wage with respect to the level of equilibrium in the employees sector is compensated by the acceptance of more restrained levels of profit - especially in recession periods - in the self-employed sector. The result is a level of production and employment that is higher than the distorted conditions of the market would have otherwise yielded.

In closing let me add some remarks regarding policy, for I believe that it is in this area that the report of Dr. Ergas needs some further integration. The freedom of works establishment in Europe and the easing or removal of regulatory systems poses the problem of the creation, in some states such as Italy, of large scale networks of distribution, of huge investments and of correspondingly huge financial needs. These needs could be met in a number of ways. One of these, consisting of the capital participation of industry in these distribution networks, bears the risk of a concentration of economic power and a consequent reduction in competition. It might be necessary, then, that concerted attention be dedicated to the system's evolution by those authorities responsible for the protection of open competition. Secondly, the character of the credit and financial markets is different throughout various nations. In the case of Italy, the recourse to credit is comparatively diffuse, and, in addition, the conditions (through the effect of strong pressure exerted from the issuance of public debt bonds) are also comparatively more burdensome. The result of this is an elevated average cost of financial resources for domestic networks, in comparison to those for foreign enterprises that can avail themselves of financial resources issued under better economic conditions. It is necessary, therefore (in my view), that the distribution sector carefully plan financing projects for its own networks which, in comparison to the system currently in place, would permit an innovative climate within the framework of a less-penalizing overall financial market policy. In my opinion, the challenge to efficiency passes precisely through this crucial point.

7

Does Productivity Converge Across Countries and Across Sectors? Empirical Evidences from Eight OECD Countries

Vincenzo Atella
University of Rome "Tor Vergata"

Furio Camillo Rosati
University of Rome "Tor Vergata"

1. Introduction

The increasing economic international integration that we have witnessed over the past fifteen years, lead many economists to study, from both the theoretical and empirical point of view, the existence and the determinants of convergence among the economies of different countries. In fact, at the basis of the hypothesis of convergence lies the role of international trade as a vehicle for the diffusion of technological progress among countries. Trade in goods and services should favour the transmission of technical innovation from one country to another, helping to explain an increasingly homogeneous set of knowledge. If countries are endowed with identical or very similar production technologies, then in the long run international trade should also guarantee that convergence in the productivity is reached.

In the recent past, a lot of attention has been devoted to economic literature to test if labor and or capital productivity tends to converge among countries at the same steady state value. This literature stems from the analysis of the classical Solow growth model and its stochastic generalization due to Brock and Mirman (1972). As we will discuss at some length later on, the tests of convergence have mainly been performed as tests of the catching-up hypothesis, using mostly cross section data. Recent work by Bernard and Durlauf (1992) has, however, proposed a test procedure based on the long run properties of time series, that appears appropriate to analyze economies that have a similar economic structure.

While large part of the literature is interested in analyzing if and to what extent less developed countries "converge" to more advanced economies, here we are interested in assessing convergence among developed countries. In particular we focus our attention on the group of the G-7 (with the exception of Canada) and on two small open economies like Denmark and Finland.

In this paper we extend previous work into two directions. On the one hand we do not consider aggregate output, per capita or per unit of capital, but we analyze separately manufacturing and selected service industries. On the other hand, we test for convergence not only in the level, but also in the rate of growth of productivity. By dis-aggregating among industries we pursue two aims: to test whether rejection of convergence could be due to the fact that the output of some industries, namely that of the service industries, is not or is less tradable than the output of the manufacturing sector and then, to assess the possible difference in productivity behaviour of the service sector with respect to the manufacturing sector. In fact the rejection of the hypothesis of convergence can be due, besides other reason, to the fact that all the studies we know, with the exception of Dollar and Wolff (1993), have tested it by employing aggregated output data. To the extent that services are not tradable or less tradable than manufactured products, and given the growing share of GNP that the service sector has in developed countries, failure to accept convergence can be due to the fact that production technologies in the service sector differ among countries. We have therefore tested convergence by considering separately manufacturing and some industries of the service sector. By proceeding in this way we are also able to verify if a different behaviour emerges in the service sector with respect to the manufacturing one. Moreover, as our test is based on the comparison of the productivity of the same sector for couples of countries and on the comparison of couples of sectors within the same countries, we are able to identify possible differences in the behaviour of productivity for the same sector among different countries and for the various sectors within the same country.

As far as the second aim of the analysis is concerned, it stems from the large attention that has been given recently to the macro-economic effects of a slower growth of productivity in the service sector, with respect to the manufacturing sector. In Italy the debate has been particularly intense and it has been based on the hypothesis, hardly tested, that the productivity in the service industries in Italy lagged behind not only that of the manufacturing industry, but also that of the service industries of other developed countries. The main reason advanced to support such difference in productivity growth can be expressed in the following way. If the production function of an industry is defined in a broad sense to include not only technological knowledge (assumed transferable among countries), but also the incentives to actually use such technical knowledge, then lack of such incentives may induce a country to lag behind the others. In particular it has been claimed that in Italy lack of competition, induced by restrictive practices and by regulation, has generated a lack of incentive to adopt more "productive" techniques. Therefore reduced to its barebones, the existence of a production function that is different from that of other developed countries is the hypothesis that has been advanced to claim a lower rate of growth of productivity in the italian service sector.

A natural way to assess whether, in the long run, countries share the same production function is to test whether there is convergence in productivity across countries. Therefore, we selected eight countries and five industries[1] over a period that ranges from 1960 to 1990, with some exceptions, with the goal to verify a) if there is convergence for labor and capital productivity across countries and across industries and b) if the service sector shows in aggregate and in its

[1] See the paragraph on data set for the country and industry specification.

sub-sectors a behaviour that is different in different countries and/or with respect to the manufacturing sector.

We finally turn to the problem of testing whether convergence is achieved in the levels or in the rate of growth of productivity. Rejection of convergence in level can be, obviously, due to the fact that the underlying theoretical model is not supported by the data. In particular, the neoclassical growth model has been strongly criticized for not being able to account for sustained growth and for the permanence of differences in income per capita among countries. Endogenous growth models have been developed to tackle such issues, by identifying a mechanism (economies of scale, accumulation of human capital, etc.) suitable to explain sustained growth in the presence of diminishing return to capital. One implication of this class of models, that is of interest to us, is that it allows to predict a convergence in the rate of growth, without implying necessarily convergence in the levels of productivity. In fact, as pointed out by Lucas (1988), an economy beginning with low levels of human and physical capital will remain permanently below an initially better endowed economy, while growing at the same rate, if preferences and technologies are the same. Therefore, testing for convergence in the levels and in the rate of growth of productivity can be considered as a (weak) test between competing models of growth. In other words, if two economies converge in levels and in rate of growth it means that microeconomic characteristics are equal and classical and endogenous growth models are both suitable to produce the data under scrutiny. On the other hand, if two economies do not converge in levels but converge in rates of growth it means that, even though microeconomic characteristics might be the same, initial endowments for some variables are different and only endogenous growth models should be compatible with the data. Finally, if two economies do not converge in both levels and rates of growth, then microeconomic characteristics and initial endowments are different and again both classical and endogenous growth models are coherent with the data.

Let us now briefly summarize the main results obtained in this paper, before discussing the analysis in detail. Convergence in the level of productivity can be rejected for all the countries and industries

considered. This is a strong result, as it relates to countries that have reached fairly similar stages of economic development and are heavily engaged in international trade. Moreover by dis-aggregating by industry we were also able to separate the generally more tradable goods from the generally less tradable services. Nonetheless, convergence was rejected not only for the latter, but also for the former.
A different picture emerges when we consider convergence in the rate of growth. In such a case we cannot reject convergence among most of the countries both for the manufacturing and for the services industries. There are, however, two exceptions, especially as far as the productivity of labour is concerned: Japan and Italy. In particular for Japan we can the reject the hypothesis of convergence in the rate of growth for the manufacturing sector with respect to all the other countries considered, while Italy shows a rate of productivity growth that does not converge with that of France, U.K. and USA.
The rest of the paper is organized as follows. Section two reviews the concept of convergence that, given the present evolution of the economic literature, needs to be clarified to avoid misunderstanding on the economic assumptions that are tested and on the interpretation of the econometric results. Section three gives some information about the data. Section four presents the econometric results.

2. Convergence

Over the past few years, a lot of attention has been devoted in literature, to the problem of convergence of per-capita output levels. Unfortunately, despite the growing attention on the subject, there is still not an established definition of convergence nor a general agreement on the test procedures to follow. To better understand the points of view that are currently supported by economists in the debate, it is fruitful to briefly illustrate how the problem of per capita GNP convergence across countries was born. According to Morawetz (1977, p.110):

> ... up to 1950 there had been little serious thought about the growth and development prospects of what were then called the "backward areas". The few peo-

> ple who had given the matter some thought did not have high hopes. After all, the industrialized countries, in their long period of economic growth unparalleled in human history, had managed to increase per capita income by only about 2 per cent per annum. There was no reason to expect that the so called "underdeveloped countries", many of which had experienced no growth for millennia, would do any better.

Despite this common belief, the GNP per-capita of these countries rose at an average of 3.4% per annum during the period 1950-75. This result was really unexpected from both official and private agents. It is also true that for a long period of time economists have been more interested in understanding what could have triggered development rather than be involved in measuring how close less developing economies were to industrialized economies (catch-up phenomenon). Moreover, a large emphasis was placed on equity and distribution effects of growth. The catching-up phenomenon as an indicator of economic progress was only marginally considered by development economists, for which any increase in the rate of growth of LDC per-capita output above the average rate of growth of per-capita output of industrialized countries could be considered as economic progress. In other terms, the attention of economists was more focused on the starting of the development process rather than on its ending (i.e. to achieve convergence with the developed countries). Catching-up was nothing more than a statistical result, with many drawbacks, in representing country economic development. It is for this reason that development economists have confined the concept of catching-up and have placed their attention on other aspects of development[2].

For more than twenty years catching-up and convergence have not been a leading topic among academicians or professionals. A new

[2] "The question to ask about a country's development are: What has been happening to poverty? What has been happening to unemployment? What has been happening to inequality? If all three of these central problems have been growing worse, it would be strange to call the result "development", even if per capita income had soared". (Seers, 1979, p.12)

wave of interest on catching-up and convergence emerged only at the end of the eighties[3], following the work by Baumol (1986), Delong (1988), Baumol, Blackman and Wolff (1989), Barro (1991) and Barro and Sala-i-Martin (1991a, 1991b, 1992), Durlauf (1989, 1991a, 1991b, 1992), Bernard and Durlauf (1991, 1992), and by Quah (1990, 1992a, 1992b). Despite the common use of the word "convergence" by these authors, a striking difference exists in the works above mentioned, in the meaning attributed to such a term. In fact, in the works by Barro, Sala-i-Martin, De Long, Baumol, Blackman, Wolff and Quah the concept of convergence should most properly refer to what is known as catching-up, while in the works by Durlauf and Bernard and Durlauf convergence is used to mean equality in the long run "characteristics" of the output measure considered.

This situation leads the authors to talk about different concepts that can produce, from the empirical point of view, different results. Due to these differences, the interpretation of the empirical results is not always in contrast. For example, as will be clearer later, non convergence in per-capita output according to Durlauf could not be in contrast with convergence of per-capita output according to Barro. Therefore, even though the aim for the authors is unique, testing if convergence of per capita income across countries and regions takes place, convergence definitions, economic assumptions and econometric strategies are quite different.

In classical models of growth various turnpike theorems suggest that steady state per capita output is independent from initial conditions. This conclusion was first extended to a stochastic environment in the pioneering work by Brock and Mirman (1972). The two authors developed a stochastic growth model in which convergence of economies with identical microeconomic parameters to a unique limiting

[3] This renewed interest on convergence and catching-up is probably due to two separate causes. The former is availability of more reliable data set for a wide range of countries (see for example the Heston-Summers data set) that can allow to produce more sophisticated empirical analysis. The latter is more related to an increased interest on economic integration across economies and to the attempt to check if 40 years of economic development policies have contributed to narrow the gap existing in the 50's between developed countries and LDC countries.

distribution is assured for a wide set of initial conditions. With Brock and Mirman the classical long-run equilibrium or "steady state" is replaced, in a stochastic environment, by the concept of "invariant distribution" (ID). An ID is a distribution where unconditional moments are independent of time. Given a neoclassical stochastic growth model, fulfilling regularity conditions, and given an arbitrary initial stock of capital, then the sequence of probability measures m_t, which characterize the aggregate output Y_t converge to a unique measure m. In other words, the stochastic process governing output is ergodic, or initial conditions do not matter asymptotically. As a consequence, if an economy has already converged to a steady state (as in the Solow classical case) or to an invariant distribution (as in Brock and Mirman), then the data generating process for the output possesses an invariant probability measure m.

It follows that, if two economies share the same microeconomic characteristics and probability distribution of shocks, then, according to the neoclassical growth model, the two economies converge. Of course, if microeconomic parameters are different across economies, divergences can occur. As a consequence, if the latter is observed, it is possible to deduce that either the economies have different structures or that these differences are transitory.

As just mentioned, tests of this hypothesis have been conducted along two different lines. On the one hand it has been tested under the form of "catching-up".

In other words it has been tested if one country, starting from an arbitrary initial condition, is reducing its gap, in terms of some objective variable, with respect to some specified level that is usually considered the long run equilibrium value. On the other hand, convergence can be tested by verifying if, with respect to some variables, the stochastic processes governing the two variables share a common trend (necessary condition) and the difference between the two series is a white noise stochastic process, with zero mean and constant finite variance.

Let us now discuss this issue in a more formal way, following the work by Bernard and Durlauf (1992)[4], the first authors to our knowledge to highlight the potential confusion that could arise between testing strategies of catching-up and convergence hypotheses and that gave a formal definition of the two concepts in a way that can allow us to nest the hypotheses.
In a stochastic environment, according to Bernard and Durlauf, a definition of convergence that most likely means "catching-up", can be stated in the following way:

> *Country i and j converge between time t and t+T if the income disparity at t is expected to decrease in value. If $Y_{i,t} > Y_{j,t}$, then*

$$E(Y_{i,t} + T - Y_{j,y} + T / I_t) < Y_{i,t} - Y_{j,t}$$

As already mentioned before, the approach that uses the definition of catching-up refers to a situation in which, starting from an arbitrary initial condition, one country is reducing its gap, in terms of some objective variable, with respect to some specified level, that is usually considered the long run equilibrium value. On the other hand, it does not add any information on how distant the two variables are or how different the rates of growth are of the two countries. For this reason we define catching-up as a "weak" convergence test.
In other words, given an initial condition, it should be quite easy to reject the hypothesis of no-convergence. On the other side, a stronger test of convergence can be based on convergence of a long term forecasts at all time (equality of microeconomic characteristics) can be stated in the following way:

[4] Quah (1993) also has contributed to clarify the meaning of the term convergence and perhaps he has given in that paper the broadest categorization of the term "convergence" in the literature. Moreover, in the same paper he proves the fallacy of Barro results or, more generally, of all those results obtained using cross-section regressions based on time averaged growth rate and initial level of income. However, Quah empirical interests differ from those of Bernard and Durlauf.

Country i and j converge if the long term forecast of per capita output for both countries are equal when computed at all time greater than or equal to t,

$$\lim_{k \to \infty} E(Y_{i,\tau+k} - Y_{j,\tau+k} / I_t) = 0 \quad \text{for all} \quad \tau \geq t$$

It can be easily seen that this second definition of convergence is stronger than the first. Two countries converge with respect to some variable, if the stochastic processes governing the two variables share a common trend (necessary condition) and the difference between the two series is a white noise stochastic process, with zero mean and constant finite variance.

The idea that lies behind this convergence definition is that two economies that converge with respect to some variables must have the same distribution parameters for the stochastic process determining the evolution of these variables.

A natural way to test the "catching-up" hypothesis is through cross-section regression of average rate of growth (dependent variable) on an initial level of income plus some ad hoc explanatory variables.

This strategy has been by now widely used in literature and it is usually referred to as "Barro regression".

According to Quah (1993), this definition of convergence[5] is equivalent to saying that "each country eventually becomes as rich as all the others - the cross-section dispersion diminishes".

The second kind of convergence test is carried out employing modern time series analysis to study the property of the stochastic processes that govern the variables under examination, as explained in

[5] Barro (1991), Barro & Sala-i-Martin (1991) and others have found that convergence takes place only after conditioning their regression upon some ad hoc exogenous variables. Therefore, it is more appropriate to refer to a concept of "conditional convergence".

Bernard and Durlauf (1991)[6].

Given these premises, a logical question arises: what convergence concept and what econometric methodology must be employed for the empirical analysis? As it will be clear later, the answer is not obvious nor arbitrary.

According to Bernard and Durlauf (1992), tests of convergence performed using cross-section and time series procedures tend to give different results when applied to aggregate data.

In particular, time series tests should reject, at least for the rates of growth, the null hypothesis of no convergence for industrialized countries (or more generally for groups of countries with very similar economic conditions), while cross-section tests should not reject this null hypothesis for the same data set, and contemporaneously they should reject it, for example, for the Heston-Summers data set[7].

The reason of this systematic behaviour in the acceptance or rejection of the null is strictly related to the concept of convergence and to the data set investigated. In fact, if the parameters of the distribution function that generated the data can be considered time-invariant, then time series tests can perform very well from the perspective of both power and size of the test. On the contrary, under

---

[6] There exists a third approach to convergence analysis. It originates from the following definitions of convergence given by Quah (1993): "a) countries originally richer than average are more likely to turn below average eventually, and vice versa - the cycle repeats; b) wheter a country income is eventually above or below average is independent of that economy's original position." These two definitions bring attention to study transitional characteristics, such as those used in income distribution and earning mobility literature. Quah (1990, 1992a, and 1992b) uses Markov matrices and random field theory to analyze the probability that one country has to remain /persist) in the same class of per capita income. It must be noted that the aproach used by Quah, even though it uses time series tests, is closer to the first one (cathing-up), rather than the second. However, due to the particular focus of our work, this approach will not be pursued in this paper.

[7] "If the data are generated by a process which is far from the model's steady state, then the sample moments of the data might inaccurately approximate the asymptotic population moments. For example, per capita output for an economy at a unique steady state will strictly exceed output of an economy converging to the same steady state from below. Hence the mean of the first economy will be strictly greater than the second, which violates Definition 2 and 3 when sample means are used to proxy for asymptotic mean. In such a situation, convergence may be erroneously rejected. In other words, time series tests may have poor size properties when applied to data from economies in transition...Cross-section tests naturally apply to transition data whereas time series tests more naturally apply to data with interpretable sample moments". (Bernard and Durlauf, 1992, p.16).

this assumptions, cross section tests perform poorly, while their performance is reversed when the group of countries examined is composed of evolving economies that are far from steady states and the convergence definition is closer to that of catching-up[8].

Therefore, the conclusions drawn by Bernard and Durlauf are that, given an initial definition of convergence and some prior beliefs on the parameters of the distribution generating the data, cross-section and time series tests can both provide reliable results on convergence or divergence. As we are considering convergence in productivity among developed countries, we can think of the data as stemming from very similar distribution functions and we therefore find it appropriate to use a time series test.

3. The Database

The data we used refer to eight countries from the OECD group, namely Germany, Denmark, Finland, France, Japan, Italy, United Kingdom and USA. For each country we analyzed two measures of productivity: output per worker and output per unit of capital. Moreover, we looked at five industries: Manufacturing, Wholesale and Retail, Hotel and Other Services, plus a fifth industry obtained as the aggregation of Wholesale and Retail and Hotel, because some countries lacked information at a disaggregated level. It is worth noting that we excluded from Other Services the following industries: Communication, Transport, and Finance.

All the data span over a period from 1960 to 1990, with some countries and some industry ranging over subsamples starting from 1966 or from 1970. The data is from two sources: OECD Sectoral Databank and EUROSTAT Cronos-Sec II.

- Due to the multi-country and multi-sector comparison that we want to obtain with this work, the visual investigation of the data can provide useful insights also for a better understanding of the empirical results. We report some graphs for both measures of

[8] A second reason to not employ cross-section regressions is due to the so called "Galton fallacy" of regression toward the mean, that from a theoretical point of view should yeld meaningless results as pointed out by Friedman (1992) and Quah (1993).

productivity in terms of index (levels). They should provide some intuitions of the phenomenon we are going to analyze.

In Figure 1 we present eight graphs reproducing, one for each country, labor productivity levels for each sector. All the data have been based on 1975, thus yielding for that year a value of one. As a general comment we can say that each country presents a fairly common pattern such as:

a) labor productivity increasing in all industries over the whole period with very few exceptions (Hotel industry in Germany and United States)
b) labor productivity in the manufacturing growing faster than in the other industries, with the only exception presented by Finland;
c) service sector and its sub-aggregates exhibiting a very similar pattern across country and sub-sectors (again Finland represents the exception).

On the contrary, capital productivity presents more differentiated patterns across countries (see Figure 2). In general, the positive trend of labour productivity is now replaced by a decreasing one and the similarity across countries and industries is now replaced by country and industry specific movements. Germany, France, Japan, United Kingdom and United States all present a marked decreasing and smoothed pattern for all industries with a more accentuated decrease over the period 1960-75 for Germany and United Kingdom. Italy presents two major differences with respect to those countries. The negative trend is less accentuated, and it is present only in the service sector and its sub-aggregates, while the capital productivity of the manufacturing sector increased from 1974 to 1990. Denmark and Finland show a time path that is less smooth and have a more pronounced cyclical behaviour. For the sake of clarity, it must be said that we are aware of the fact that data on stock capital is very eterogeneous despite the fact that it is collected from one data-base. This can probably be a cause of the apparent etereogeneity of the results about capital productivity.

Figure 1 Sectoral labour productivity indices by country

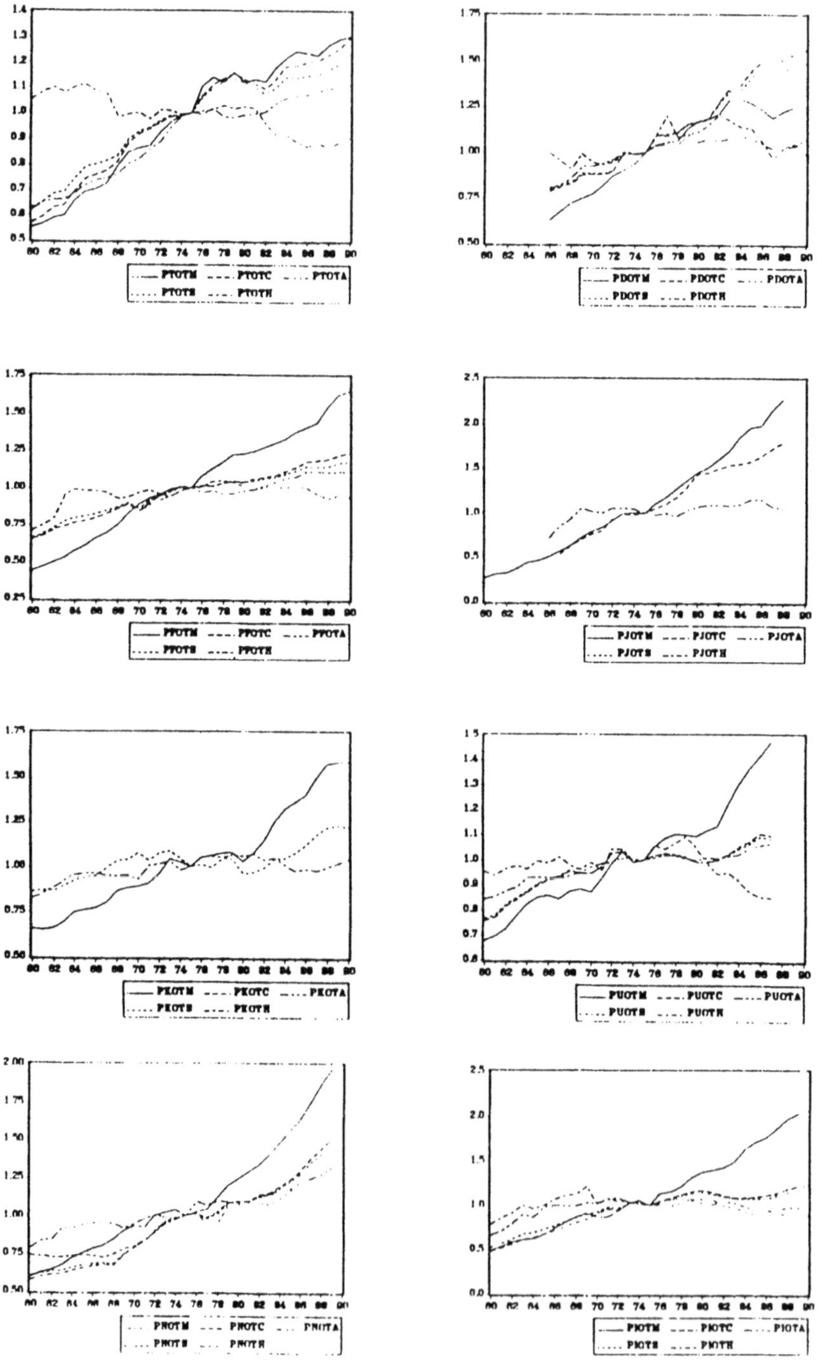

Figure 2 Sectoral capital productivities by country

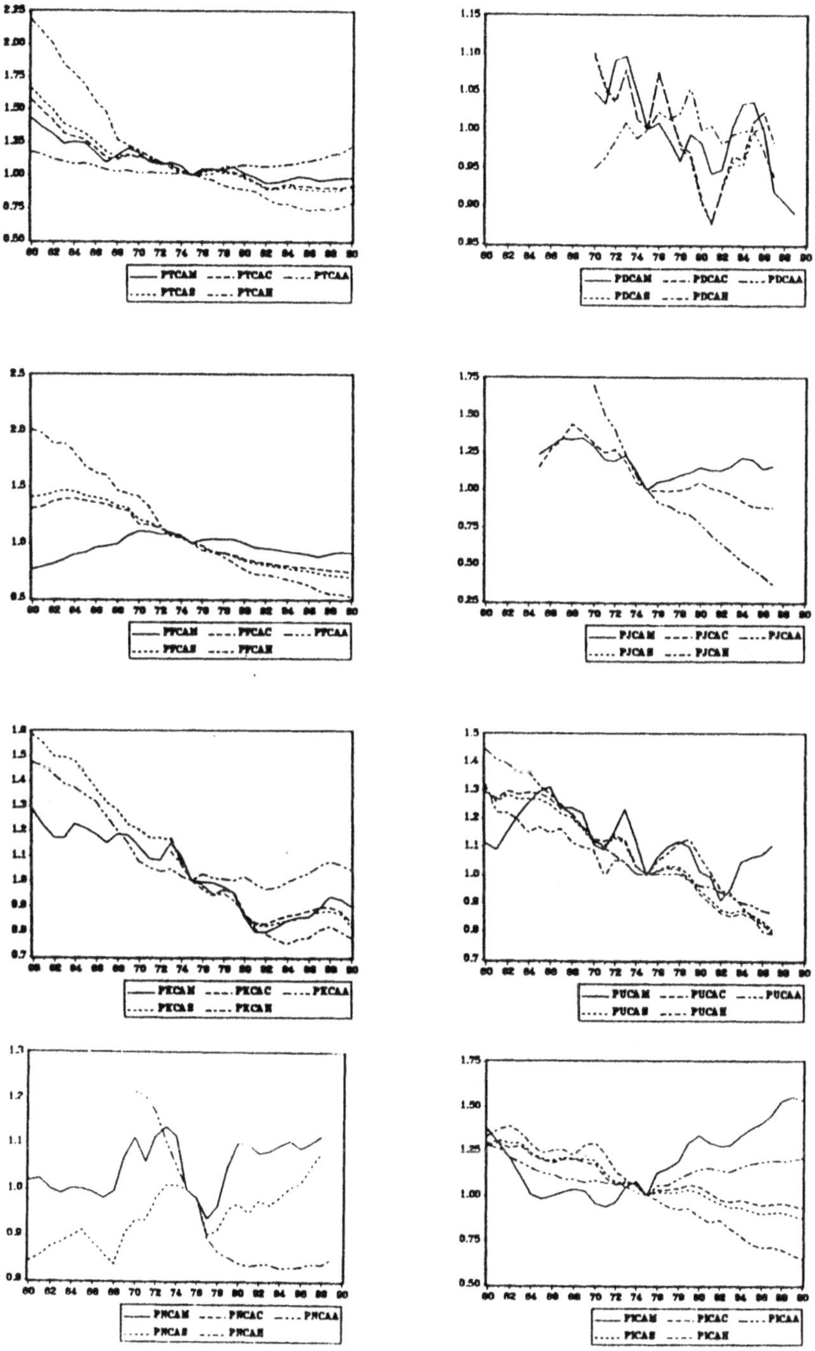

Figures 3 and 4 present similar data reorganized by industry rather than by countries. By looking at these charts it is possible to make industry comparisons across countries, therefore yielding an idea of the degree of convergence that can exist. From these graphs it is quite simple to conclude that convergence in productivity levels between countries is far from being achieved.

We have then analyzed productivity rates of growth. Some descriptive statistics, such as mean and standard deviation for rate of growth of the labour and capital productivity are reported in Table 1. It is clear that productivity rates of growth of the service sector have been lower than those of manufacturing. Hotel and Other Services industries, in particular, show the lower labour and capital productivity rates of growth across countries. The main conclusion that we can infer from this table is that rates of growth seem to be more similar across countries and industries than the levels, but still there are significative differences. Moreover, Japan represents an outlier with respect to our sample. In particular, we have a first group formed by Germany, Denmark and United States that shows an average rate of growth in manufacturing equal to 2.9% per annum, and a second group formed by Finland, France and Italy that shows a rate of growth ranging from 4.2% to 4.9%. United Kingdom and Japan are out of these two groups. As far as the service sector is concerned, the two groups are formed by Germany, Denmark, Finland and Italy with a rate of growth between 2.3% and 3.1%, and France, UK and USA with a rate of growth ranging from 1.2% and 1.9%.

The retail industry presents a more homogeneous pattern, with rate of growth ranging from 2.1% to 3.2% with the exception of Japan (6%) and USA (1.4%).

Other Service industries again present two groups. The first one is formed by Germany, Finland, France and Japan with rate of growth ranging from 1.9% to 1.4%; the second group is formed by Denmark, Italy, UK and USA with rate of growth ranging from 0.8% to 1.2%.

With respect to rates of growth of capital productivity, we observe the following. For the manufacturing sector all countries, with the exception of Germany and UK (-1%), present a rate of growth very close to zero.

Figure 3 Labour productivity indices by sector

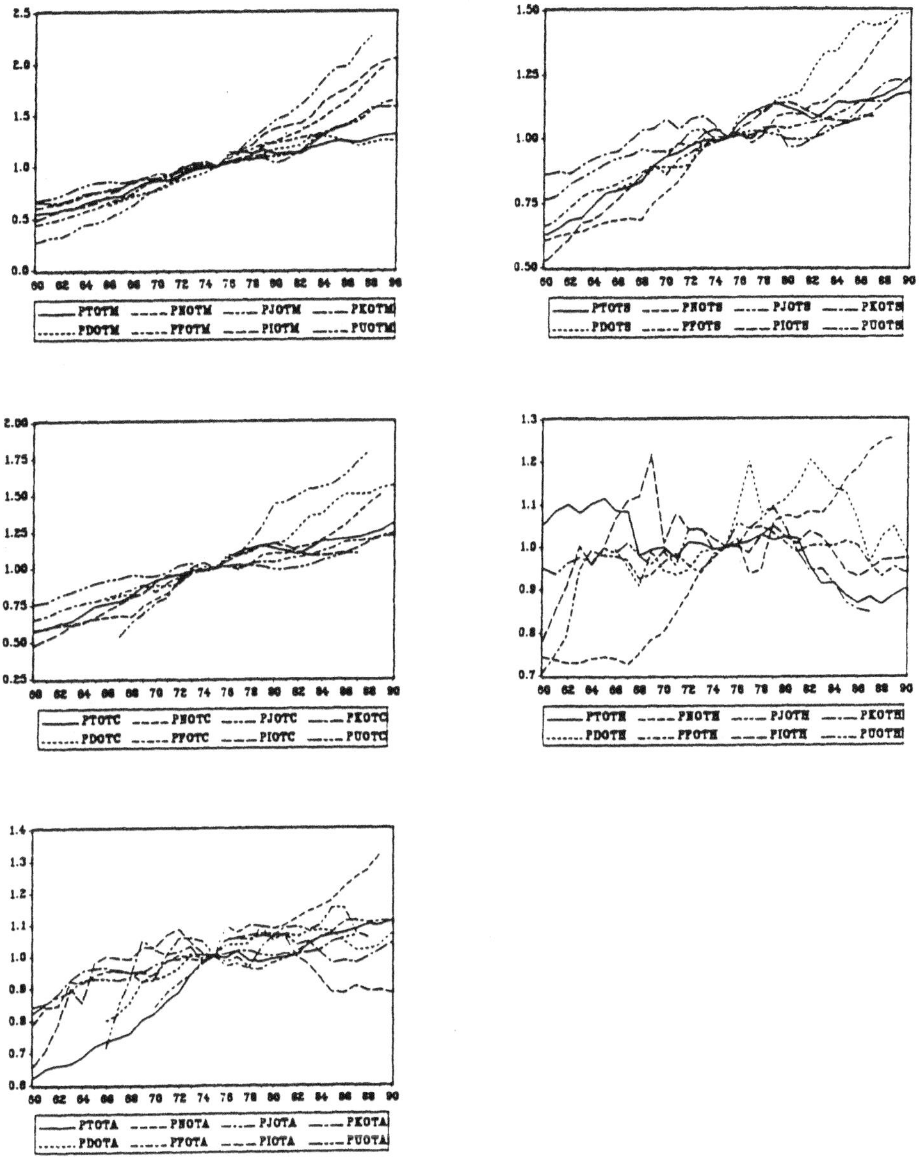

Figure 4 Capital productivity indices by sector

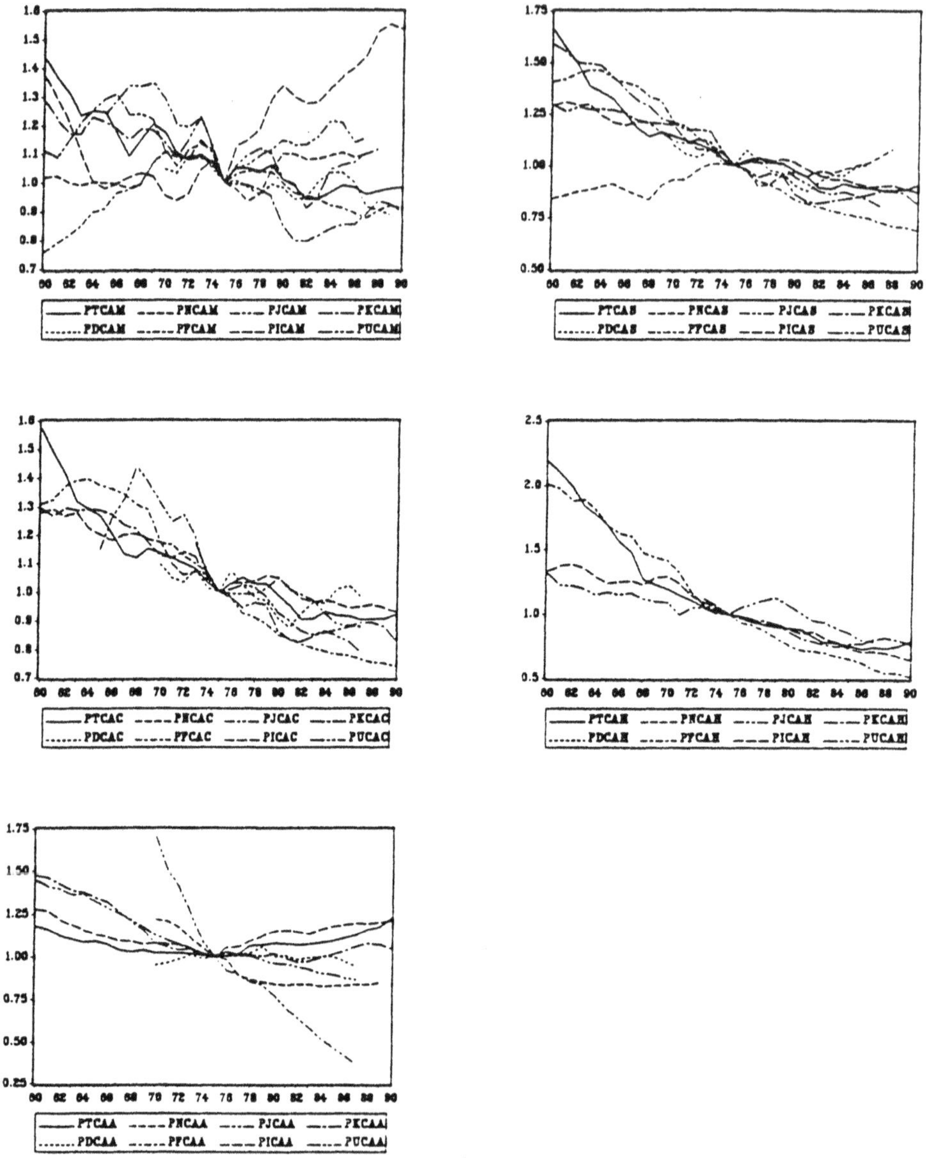

Table 1 Mean and standard deviation of productivity rate of growth

Labour	*productivity*			*Capital productivity*		
Sector	Mean	STDV	Country	Sector	Mean	STDV
			GERMANY			
MAN	0.029	0.032		MAN	-0.011	0.035
SER	0.023	0.024		SER	-0.019	0.026
RET	0.028	0.027		RET	-0.017	0.027
HOT	-0.004	0.028		HOT	-0.032	0.033
OTH	0.019	0.020		OTH	0.001	0.019
			DENMARK			
MAN	0.029	0.032		MAN	-0.007	0.035
SER	0.026	0.032		SER	-0.004	0.043
RET	0.029	0.033		RET	-0.005	0.044
HOT	0.001	0.055		HOT	---	---
OTH	0.012	0.027		OTH	0.000	0.024
			FINLAND			
MAN	0.042	0.025		MAN	0.003	0.038
SER	0.031	0.028		SER	0.009	0.031
RET	0.033	0.028		RET	---	---
HOT	0.018	0.034		HOT	---	---
OTH	0.018	0.028		OTH	-0.018	0.026
			FRANCE			
MAN	0.045	0.027		MAN	0.006	0.031
SER	0.019	0.022		SER	-0.023	0.020
RET	0.021	0.024		RET	-0.018	0.023
HOT	0.010	0.044		HOT	-0.044	0.027
OTH	0.014	0.020		OTH	---	---

(Table 1)

Labour	*Productivity*			*Capital*	*Productivity*	
			ITALY			
MAN	0.049	0.042		MAN	0.005	0.052
SER	0.028	0.033		SER	-0.012	0.020
RET	0.032	0.036		RET	-0.010	0.022
HOT	0.008	0.054		HOT	-0.023	0.029
OTH	0.011	0.051		OTH	-0.001	0.021
			JAPAN			
MAN	0.079	0.046		MAN	-0.002	0.045
SER	---	---		SER	---	---
RET	0.060	0.049		RET	-0.019	0.049
HOT	---	---		HOT	---	---
OTH	0.019	0.059		OTH	-0.086	0.033
			UNITED KINGDOM			
MAN	0.030	0.034		MAN	-0.010	0.039
SER	0.012	0.031		SER	-0.021	0.029
RET	---	---		RET	-0.019	0.037
HOT	---	---		HOT	-0.021	0.031
OTH	0.008	0.028		OTH	-0.011	0.023
			U.S.A.			
MAN	0.029	0.029		MAN	0.001	0.056
SER	0.013	0.021		SER	-0.017	0.023
RET	0.014	0.022		RET	-0.017	0.024
HOT	-0.003	0.036		HOT	-0.018	0.037
OTH	0.008	0.012		OTH	-0.018	0.012

The service sector is characterized by two groups of countries; the first one is represented by Germany, France, Italy, UK and USA with a rate of growth ranging from -1.2% (Italy) to -2.3% (France); the second group is represented by Denmark (-0.4%) and Finland (0.9%) with a rate of growth close to zero. The retail industry is perhaps the most homogeneous across countries, with a rate of growth ranging from -1.7% to -1.9%, with two exceptions: Italy -1.2% and Denmark -0.5%.

As general comment to these figures we can say that there are some clear patterns among different groups of countries according to different industries that are difficult to interpret in an unambiguous way. What clearly emerges is the Italian position in the service sector, that according to our data shows rates of growth that are the highest among the country panel.

4. Econometric Methodology and Empirical Results

In terms of the definition given by Bernard and Durlauf (1991), there exists a common stochastic element in per capita output of country i and *j* if $Y_{i,t}$ and $Y_{j,t}$ contain a stochastic trend and are cointegrated, i.e. there exists a constant γ such that

$$Y_{i,t} = \mu + \gamma Y_{j,t} + \nu_{ij,t} \tag{1}$$

where $\nu_{ij,t}$ is distributed $(0, s^2_{\nu_{ij,t}})$ and is stationary in levels. To achieve convergence the previous formula should be reduced to the following:

$$Y_{i,t} = Y_{j,t} + \theta_{ij,t} \tag{2}$$

where $\theta_{ij,t}$ is distributed $(0, s^2 q_{ij,t})$ and is stationary in levels.

From what we have just said, cointegration by itself is unable to produce convergence, unless the parameters μ and γ present particular values.

According to the framework presented above, the testing strategy is the following:

a) test for the presence of stochastic trends in the variables and that the order of integration of the series is the same;
b) if a) is not rejected test if the series are cointegrated (see results in Tables. 2 and 3);
c) if b) is not rejected test that $\theta_{ij,t}$ is distributed $(0, s^2 q_{ij,t})$ and is stationary in levels.

This strategy has been thought of for cases where the theory predicts convergence in the levels of productivity, such as neoclassical models. If convergence can be expected to hold for the rate of growth of productivity, but not for the levels, such as in the endogenous growth models, then the testing strategy should be modified to allow for the fact that, usually, rates of growth do not present stochastic trends.
If the series are stationary, we can use ordinary statistical techniques to see if there is any relationship between the variables. In particular, we looked at convergence by checking if the differences between the rates of growth across countries and industries,

$$\theta_{ij,t}, \text{ is white noise distributed } (0, s^2 q_{ij,t})$$

For this task we tested the hypothesis of $E(\theta_{ij,t})=0$ by means of t test (see Tables 4 and 5) and to assess whether such differences are while noise we used the Ljung-Box Q statistic (see Tables 6 and 7).
The main results can be summarized in the following way. If we consider the levels of the two productivity measures employed, namely output per head and output per unit of capital, we cannot reject, for all industries and countries considered, the hypothesis that they are I(1). We therefore proceed to estimate the cointegrating regressions and to test for co-integration. As shown in Tables 2 and 3, where ADF tests on the residuals of the cointegrating regressions are reported, it is possible to reject the hypothesis of cointegration. This implies that we can reject convergence for all industries and all countries. Note that these results substantially confirm those obtained by Bernard and Durlauf (1991) employing aggregated data.

Table 2 Cointegration test (ADF)

	Labour productivity									Capital productivity							
Manufacturing industry																	
	DEU	DNK	FIN	FRA	ITA	JAP	UK	USA		DEU	DNK	FIN	FRA	ITA	JAP	UK	USA
DEU	-								DEU	-							
DNK	-1.30	-							DNK	-0.71	-						
FIN	0.89	-1.34	-						FIN	-1.06	0.10	-					
FRA	0.33	-0.91	-1.63	-					FRA	0.50	-0.15	-0.35	-				
ITA	1.15	-1.17	-0.79	-1.09	-				ITA	1.37	-0.88	-0.85	-2.20	-			
JAP	0.97	-1.15	-1.18	-2.22	-1.80	-			JAP	-1.14	0.00	-0.57	-0.34	-0.1	-		
UK	2.18	-2.19	-0.99	-1.45	-1.64	-1.89	-		UK	-1.58	0.11	0.71	-1.94	-0.19	-1.89	-	
USA	1.13	-0.80	-1.48	-1.27	-1.58	-1.44	-1.37	-	USA	0.16	0.27	-0.59	-1.67	-0.08	-2.06	0.06	-
Service industry																	
	DEU	DNK	FIN	FRA	ITA	JAP	UK	USA		DEU	DNK	FIN	FRA	ITA	JAP	UK	USA
DEU	-								DEU	-							
DNK	-0.80	-							DNK	0.14	-						
FIN	0.25	-0.70	-						FIN	-1.68	-0.24	-					
FRA	1.22	-1.12	-0.63	-					FRA	-2.06	0.38	-0.88	-				
ITA	-0.33	-0.20	-0.90	-0.66	-				ITA	-1.22	0.18	-1.19	-1.33	-			
JAP	na	na	na	na	na	-			JAP	na	na	na	na	na	-		
UK	1.96	-2.08	-1.95	-1.73	-1.92	na	-		UK	-2.20	0.23	-0.48	-1.43	-0.46	na	-	
USA	1.60	-1.07	-1.12	-1.67	-1.12	na	-2.10	-	USA	-1.63	0.37	-0.91	-1.12	-0.88	na	0.34	-
Wholesale & Retail																	
	DEU	DNK	FIN	FRA	ITA	JAP	UK	USA		DEU	DNK	FIN	FRA	ITA	JAP	UK	USA
DEU	-								DEU	-							
DNK	-0.90	-							DNK	-0.23	-						
FIN	-0.25	-0.86	-						FIN	na	na	-					
FRA	-1.00	-0.92	-1.01	-					FRA	-1.96	0.08	na	-				
ITA	-0.12	-0.18	-0.92	-1.01	-				ITA	-1.40	-0.11	na	-1.29	-			
JAP	0.83	-1.05	-2.30	-1.63	-1.53	-			JAP	1.27	-0.32	na	-1.77	-1.79	-		
UK	na	na	na	na	na	na	-		UK	na	na	na	na	na	na	-	
USA	1.59	-1.17	-1.26	-1.57	-0.93	-1.34	na	-	USA	-1.81	-0.51	na	-1.41	-0.98	-1.62	na	-
Hotels																	
	DEU	DNK	FIN	FRA	ITA	JAP	UK	USA		DEU	DNK	FIN	FRA	ITA	JAP	UK	USA
DEU	-								DEU	-							
DNK	-1.00	-							DNK	na	-						
FIN	-1.80	-1.12	-						FIN	na	na	-					
FRA	-1.33	-1.24	0.24	-					FRA	1.38	na	na	-				
ITA	-1.53	-1.51	-0.31	-1.29	-				ITA	-	na	na	-1.46	-			
JAP	na	na	na	na	na	-			JAP	na	na	na	na	na	-		
UK	na	na	na	na	na	na	-		UK	-1.67	na	na	-1.38	-0.79	na	-	
USA	2.06	-1.50	0.49	-0.33	-3.52	na	na	-	USA	-1.44	na	na	-1.60	-1.71	na	-0.98	-
Other services																	
	DEU	DNK	FIN	FRA	ITA	JAP	UK	USA		DEU	DNK	FIN	FRA	ITA	JAP	UK	USA
DEU	-								DEU	-							
DNK	-1.44	-							DNK	-0.53	-						
FIN	-1.67	-1.51	-						FIN	-0.06	-0.83	-					
FRA	-1.69	-1.80	-3.02	-					FRA	na	na	na	-				
ITA	-1.51	-1.18	0.15	-1.15	-				ITA	-0.98	-2.11	-1.35	na	-			
JAP	-0.96	-2.15	-0.41	0.36	-0.19	-			JAP	0.66	-0.88	-1.59	na	-2.38	-		
UK	-1.66	-1.41	-1.20	0.24	-1.09	-1.26	-		UK	-0.50	-1.00	-0.46	na	-0.40	-0.67	-	
USA	-1.06	-1.63	-1.66	-1.32	-0.48	-1.76	-1.79	-	USA	-0.56	-1.01	-1.14	na	-0.66	-0.45	0.00	-

Reported values are t-stat of leggend error coefficient on ADF regression

Table 3 Cointegration test (ADF)

	Labour productivity						Capital productivity				
GERMANY											
	MAN	SER	RET	HOT	OTH		MAN	SER	RET	HOT	OTH
MAN	-					MAN	-				
SER	-1.14	-				SER	-0.85	-			
RET	-1.48	0.51	-			RET	-0.88	-1.45	-		
HOT	0.87	0.78	0.12	-		HOT	-1.73	-2.23	-2.11	-	
OTH	-1.98	-1.52	-1.78	-0.89	-	OTH	-0.72	-0.32	-0.41	-1.48	-
DENMARK											
	MAN	SER	RET	HOT	OTH		MAN	SER	RET	HOT	OTH
MAN	-					MAN	-				
SER	-1.57	-				SER	0.19	-			
RET	1.67	-1.49	-			RET	-0.01	0.12	-		
HOT	-0.36	-0.43	-0.43	-		HOT	na	na	na	-	
OTH	-1.84	1.65	-1.73	-1.33	-	OTH	0.18	-	-0.89	na	-
FINLAND											
	MAN	SER	RET	HOT	OTH		MAN	SER	RET	HOT	OTH
MAN	-					MAN	-				
SER	-1.71	-				SER	-0.98	-			
RET	-2.06	-0.91	-			RET	na	na	-		
HOT	-0.79	-1.03	-0.88	-		HOT	na	na	na	-	
OTH	-1.33	-2.00	-2.14	-1.25	-	OTH	-0.32	0.02	na	na	-
FRANCE											
	MAN	SER	RET	HOT	OTH		MAN	SER	RET	HOT	OTH
MAN	-					MAN	-				
SER	-1.44	-				SER	-1.89	-			
RET	-1.86	0.50	-			RET	-1.93	-2.00			-
HOT	0.42	0.15	0.22	-		HOT	-1.65	-1.84	-1.92	-	
OTH	-1.56	-2.52	-2.96	-0.53	-	OTH	na	na	na	na	-

Reported values are t-stat of lagged error coefficient on ADF regressions.

(Table 3)

Labour productivity / **Capital productivity**

ITALY

	MAN	SER	RET	HOT	OTH		MAN	SER	RET	HOT	OTH
MAN	-					MAN	-				
SER	-0.68	-				SER	-1.44	-			
RET	-0.81	-0.41	-			RET	-1.15	-2.11	-		
HOT	0.05	0.22	0.20	-		HOT	-1.67	-3.06	-3.09	-	
OTH	-0.76	-0.48	-0.41	-1.28	-	OTH	-1.71	-1.93	-2.22	-1.48	-

JAPAN

	MAN	SER	RET	HOT	OTH		MAN	SER	RET	HOT	OTH
MAN	-					MAN	-				
SER	na	-				SER	na	-			
RET	-0.18	na	-			RET	-1.01	na	-		
HOT	na	na	na	-		HOT	na	na	na	-	
OTH	-0.17	na	-1.17	na	-	OTH	-1.73	na	-0.16	na	-

UNITED KINGDOM

	MAN	SER	RET	HOT	OTH		MAN	SER	RET	HOT	OTH
MAN	-					MAN	-				
SER	-1.59	-				SER	-2.19	-			
RET	na	na	-			RET	-2.21	-1.34	-		
HOT	na	na	na	-		HOT	-2.15	-1.67	-1.32	-	
OTH	-1.24	-2.51	na	na	-	OTH	-2.57	-0.72	-0.87	-0.43	-

U.S.A.

	MAN	SER	RET	HOT	OTH		MAN	SER	RET	HOT	OTH
MAN	-					MAN	-				
SER	-1.31	-				SER	-0.83	-			
RET	-1.64	-0.72	-			RET	-0.80	-1.19	-		
HOT	0.23	0.18	0.19	-		HOT	-1.37	-2.15	-2.07	-	
OTH	-0.27	-1.50	-1.36	-1.20	-	OTH	-0.76	-0.17	-0.39	-1.47	-

Reported values are t-stat of lagged error coefficient on ADF regressions.

Table 4 Mean test

MANUFACTURING INDUSTRY

	Labour productivity								*Capital productivity*							
	DEU	DNK	FIN	FRA	ITA	JAP	UK	USA	DEU	DNK	FIN	FRA	ITA	JAP	UK	USA
DEU																
DNK	-0.2								-0.9							
FIN	-1.1	1.0							-1.7*	-0.8						
FRA	-1.5	-0.9	0.4						-1.8*	0.1	-0.2					
ITA	-2.0*	-1.5	-0.8	-0.4					-1.7*	3.4*	-0.1	0.1				
JAP	-4.8*	-3.9*	-3.7*	-3.3*	-2.7*				-0.9	-0.1	0.7	0.0	2.0*			
UK	0.0	0.1	1.0	1.5*	1.9*	4.7*			0.0	-0.1	1.4	1.7*	1.6	1.0		
USA	0.0	0.4	1.0	1.5*	2.1*	5.0*	0.1		-1.5	0.8	0.2	0.4	0.2	0.3	-1.4	

SERVICE INDUSTRY

	Labour productivity								*Capital productivity*							
	DEU	DNK	FIN	FRA	ITA	JAP	UK	USA	DEU	DNK	FIN	FRA	ITA	JAP	UK	USA
DEU																
DNK	-0.8								-1.0							
FIN	-0.8	-0.6							-3.1*	-1.0						
FRA	-0.3	1.1	1.1						0.3	2.4*	3.3					
ITA	-0.4	0.7	0.2	-1.0					-0.6	1.2	2.1*	-1.0				
JAP	na	na	na	na	na				na	na	na	na	na			
UK	1.1	1.5	1.8*	0.7	1.5*	na			0.2	1.5	2.9*	-0.1	0.8	na		
USA	0.9*	2.0*	1.7*	0.7	1.5*	na	-0.1		-0.5	1.2	2.5*	-0.6		na	-0.4	

WHOLESALE & RETAIL

	Labour productivity								*Capital productivity*							
	DEU	DNK	FIN	FRA	ITA	JAP	UK	USA	DEU	DNK	FIN	FRA	ITA	JAP	UK	USA
DEU																
DNK	-0.6								-0.7							
FIN	-0.6	-0.5							na	na						
FRA	0.6	1.0	1.1*						0.2	1.8*	na					
ITA	-0.4	0.6	0.0	-1.0					-0.6	0.6	na	-0.8				
JAP	-3.8*	3.0*	-2.3*	-4.2*	-3.8*				-0.3	1.6	na	-1.5	0.0			
UK	na	na	na	na	na	na			1.0	1.2	na	-0.3	1.0	-0.2		
USA	1.4*	2.3	1.8*	0.8	1.8*	1.8*	na		-0.2	1.4	na	-0.1	-0.3	1.0	0.5	

HOTELS

	Labour productivity								*Capital productivity*							
	DEU	DNK	FIN	FRA	ITA	JAP	UK	USA	DEU	DNK	FIN	FRA	ITA	JAP	UK	USA
DEU																
DNK	-0.8								na							
FIN	-2.0*	-2.0							na	na						
FRA	1.4	-0.2	0.7						1.1	na	na					
ITA	-1.3	0.3	0.9	0.1					-0.9	na	na	-2.0*				
JAP	na	na	na	na	na				na	na	na	na	na			
UK	na	na	na	na	na	na			0.5	na	na	-2.0*	0.8	na		
USA	-0.2	0.6	2.2	1.5	1.2	na	na		-2.0*	na	na	-2.6*	-2.3	na	-0.3	

OTHER SERVICES

	Labour productivity								*Capital productivity*							
	DEU	DNK	FIN	FRA	ITA	JAP	UK	USA	DEU	DNK	FIN	FRA	ITA	JAP	UK	USA
DEU																
DNK	-0.4								0.6							
FIN	0.1	-0.2							2.5*	2.0						
FRA	0.1	0.6	0.2						na	na	na					
ITA	0.8	1.7*	0.6	2.1*					0.3	-0.6		na				
JAP	0.0	0.7	-0.6	1.2	-2.4				9.2*	8.6*	6.5*	na	9.2*			
UK	1.1*	0.9	1.0*	0.7*	0.2	1.7			1.2	0.0	-1.8*	na	0.9*	8.5*		
USA	1.2*	0.5	0.8	1.1*	0.4	1.4	-0.2		1.7*	1.4	-0.6	na	1.6*	-7.1*	0.6	

(*) Indicate that the mean is significantly different from zero.

Table 5 Mean test

	Labour productivity						*Capital productivity*				
					GERMANY						
	MAN	SER	RET	HOT	OTH		MAN	SER	RET	HOT	OTH
MAN						MAN					
SER	0.6					SER	0.7*				
RET	0.1	-0.5*				RET	0.5	-0.2*			
HOT	3.4*	2.7*	3.3*			HOT	2.1*	1.3*	1.5*		
OTH	0.9*	0.3	0.8*	-2.4*		OTH	-1.3*	-2.1*	-1.8*	-3.4*	
					DENMARK						
	MAN	SER	RET	HOT	OTH		MAN	SER	RET	HOT	OTH
MAN						MAN					
SER	0.2					SER	0.2				
RET	0.0	-0.3*				RET	-0.1	-0.1			
HOT	2.8*	2.5*	2.8*			HOT	na	na	na		
OTH	1.6*	1.3*	1.6*	-1.1		OTH	-0.6	0.6	-0.3	na	
					FINLAND						
	MAN	SER	RET	HOT	OTH		MAN	SER	RET	HOT	OTH
MAN						MAN					
SER	1.0*					SER	-0.5				
RET	0.8	-0.2*				RET	na	na			
HOT	2.3*	1.2*	1.5*			HOT	na	na	na		
OTH	2.3*	1.2*	1.5*	0.0		OTH	2.1	2.8*	na	na	
					FRANCE						
	MAN	SER	RET	HOT	OTH		MAN	SER	RET	HOT	OTH
MAN						MAN					
SER	2.5*					SER	2.9*				
RET	2.3*	-0.2				RET	2.5*	-0.4*			
HOT	3.4*	0.9	1.1			HOT	5.0*	2.0*	2.5*		
OTH	1.7*	0.2	0.5	-1.5*		OTH	na	na	na	na	

(*) Indicate that the mean is significantly different from zero.

(Table 5)

Labour productivity							*Capital productivity*				
						ITALY					
	MAN	SER	RET	HOT	OTH		MAN	SER	RET	HOT	OTH
MAN						MAN					
SER	1.7*					SER	1.2*				
RET	1.5*	-0.2*				RET	1.7*	-0.2			
HOT	2.8*	1.0*	1.3*			HOT	1.8*	1.2*	1.1*		
OTH	0.6	-1.1*	-0.8*	-0.7*		OTH	0.6*	-1.7*	-0.4*	-0.5	
						JAPAN					
	MAN	SER	RET	HOT	OTH		MAN	SER	RET	HOT	OTH
MAN						MAN					
SER	na					SER	na				
RET	0.7	na				RET	0.8	na			
HOT	na	na	na			HOT	na	na	na		
OTH	5.1*	na	4.9*	na		OTH	8.1*	na	6.4*	na	
						UNITED KINGDOM					
	MAN	SER	RET	HOT	OTH		MAN	SER	RET	HOT	OTH
MAN						MAN					
SER	1.8*					SER	1.1				
RET	na	na				RET	0.7	0.0			
HOT	na	na	na			HOT	0.7	0.1	0.2		
OTH	2.1*	0.3	na	na		OTH	0.0	-1.0*	-1.9*	-2.1*	
						U.S.A					
	MAN	SER	RET	HOT	OTH		MAN	SER	RET	HOT	OTH
MAN						MAN					
SER	1.6*					SER	1.8				
RET	1.5*	0.0*				RET	1.9	0.0			
HOT	3.3*	1.6*	1.7*			HOT	1.9	0.0	0.0		
OTH	2.0*	0.4	0.5	-1.2*		OTH	2.0	0.1	0.1	0.0	

(*) Indicate that the mean is significantly different from zero.

Table 6 White noise test - Ljung-Box Q Statistics (**) Not significant at 5% level

Manufacturing industry

Labour productivity	DEU	DNK	FIN	FRA	ITA	JAP	UK	USA	*Capital productivity*	DEU	DNK	FIN	FRA	ITA	JAP	UK	USA
DEU									DEU								
DNK	**								DNK	**							
FIN	8.26	**							FIN	**	9.81						
FRA	**	**	10.84						FRA	12.10	**	9.39					
ITA	8.08	**	9.85	**					ITA	**	**	8.25	**				
JAP	**	**	**	**	**				JAP	**	na	**	**	**			
UK	**	**	**	**	**	**			UK	**	**	7.84	9.62	10.09	**		
USA	**	**	8.42	9.69	**	**	**		USA	**	**	**	**	10.54	**	**	

Service industry

	DEU	DNK	FIN	FRA	ITA	JAP	UK	USA		DEU	DNK	FIN	FRA	ITA	JAP	UK	USA
DEU									DEU								
DNK	**								DNK	**							
FIN	**	**							FIN	**	**						
FRA	**	18.37	**						FRA	11.01	**	**					
ITA	**	**	9.00	**					ITA	**	**	**	23.12				
JAP	na	na	na	na	na				JAP	na	na	na	na	na			
UK	**	**	**	**	**	na			UK	**	**	**	**	**	na		
USA	**	**	**	**	**	na	**		USA	**	**	7.84	**	**	na	**	

Wholesale & Retail

	DEU	DNK	FIN	FRA	ITA	JAP	UK	USA		DEU	DNK	FIN	FRA	ITA	JAP	UK	USA
DEU									DEU								
DNK	**								DNK	**							
FIN	**	**							FIN	na	na						
FRA	**	16.15	**						FRA	10.55	**	na					
ITA	**	**	**	8.24					ITA	**	**	na	**				
JAP	**	**	**	**	**				JAP	**	**	na	**	**			
UK	na	na	na	na	na	na			UK	**	**	na	**	**	**		
USA	**	**	**	**	**	**	na		USA	8.15	**	na	**	**	**	**	

Hotels

	DEU	DNK	FIN	FRA	ITA	JAP	UK	USA		DEU	DNK	FIN	FRA	ITA	JAP	UK	USA
DEU									DEU								
DNK	**								DNK	na							
FIN	**	**							FIN	na	na						
FRA	**	**	**						FRA	**	na	na					
ITA	**	**	**	**					ITA	9.74	na	na	**				
JAP	na	na	na	na	na				JAP	na	na	na	na	na			
UK	na	na	na	na	na	na			UK	**	na	na	**	**	na		
USA	**	**	**	**	**	na	na		USA	**	na	na	**	**	na	12.59	

Other services

	DEU	DNK	FIN	FRA	ITA	JAP	UK	USA		DEU	DNK	FIN	FRA	ITA	JAP	UK	USA
DEU									DEU								
DNK	**								DNK	**							
FIN	**	**							FIN	**	7.92						
FRA	**	**	**						FRA	na	na	na					
ITA	**	**	8.25	**					ITA	**	**	12.14	na				
JAP	**	**	**	**	**				JAP	**	8.95	7.84	na	**			
UK	**	**	15.00	**	**	**			UK	**	**	**	na	8.05	**		
USA	**	**	**	**	**	**	**		USA	**	**	**	na	**	**	**	

Table 7 White noise test - Ljung-Box Q Statistics (**) Not significant at 5% level

	Labour productivity						*Capital productivity*				
						GERMANY					
	MAN	SER	RET	HOT	OTH		MAN	SER	RET	HOT	OTH
MAN						MAN					
SER	**					SER	**				
RET	**	**				RET	**	**			
HOT	**	**	**			HOT	**	**	**		
OTH	**	**	**	**		OTH	**	**	**	**	
						DENMARK					
	MAN	SER	RET	HOT	OTH		MAN	SER	RET	HOT	OTH
MAN						MAN					
SER	**					SER	**				
RET	**	**				RET	**	**			
HOT	**	**	**			HOT	na	na	na		
OTH	**	**	**	**		OTH	**	**	**	na	
						FINLAND					
	MAN	SER	RET	HOT	OTH		MAN	SER	RET	HOT	OTH
MAN						MAN					
SER	**					SER	**				
RET	**	**				RET	na	na			
HOT	**	**	**			HOT	na	na	na		
OTH	**	**	**	**		OTH	8.21	**	na	na	
						FRANCE					
	MAN	SER	RET	HOT	OTH		MAN	SER	RET	HOT	OTH
MAN						MAN					
SER	**					SER	8.46				
RET	**	**				RET	**	**			
HOT	**	**	**			HOT	**	**	**		
OTH	**	**	**	**		OTH	na	na	na	na	

(Table 7)

Labour Productivity						*Capital Productivity*					

ITALY

	MAN	SER	RET	HOT	OTH		MAN	SER	RET	HOT	OTH
MAN						MAN					
SER	**					SER	11.04				
RET	**	**				RET	10.75	**			
HOT	**	**	**			HOT	8.43	**	**		
OTH	**	**	**	**		OTH	**	**	**	**	

JAPAN

	MAN	SER	RET	HOT	OTH		MAN	SER	RET	HOT	OTH
MAN						MAN					
SER	na					SER	na				
RET	**	na				RET	**	na			
HOT	na	na	na			HOT	na	na	na		
OTH	**	na	**	na		OTH	**	na	**	na	

UNITED KINGDOM

	MAN	SER	RET	HOT	OTH		MAN	SER	RET	HOT	OTH
MAN						MAN					
SER	**					SER	**				
RET	na	na				RET	**	**			
HOT	na	na	na			HOT	**	**	**		
OTH	**	**	na	na		OTH	**	**	**	**	

U.S.A.

	MAN	SER	RET	HOT	OTH		MAN	SER	RET	HOT	OTH
MAN						MAN					
SER	**					SER	**				
RET	**	**				RET	**	**			
HOT	**	**	**			HOT	**	**	**		
OTH	**	**	**	**		OTH	**	16.94	**	**	

We then turned to test for convergence in the rate of growth. Not surprisingly, these series turned out to be stationary, and we were therefore able to use the simpler testing procedure outlined above.
According to our econometric strategy, we tested that the pairwise differences between the rate of growth of productivity for each industry in different countries and for different industries in the same country have a zero mean and are governed by white noise stochastic process. All the series, with a few exceptions (see Tables 6 and 7), are white noise, thus showing that the differentials in the rate of growth do not have any systematic component that help to predict them. However, not all have a zero mean, and this leads us to reject convergence in some cases.
Let us now consider these results in more detail. Table 6 shows the mean for the differential in the growth rate of productivity across countries, where an asterisk indicates that the mean is significatively different from zero. Observe that the differential is computed as the difference between the rate of growth of the countries shown in the column and the rate of growth of the country shown in the row. We consider first output per head. For the manufacturing sector we can reject convergence in the rate of growth for a) Japan with respect to all other countries, and b) among Italy, France, UK and USA. For the service sector in aggregate we can reject convergence for USA, that shows a significant negative differential with respect to the rest of the countries. In all the other cases we can accept convergence. For the retail industry we can accept convergence for all the countries with the exception of USA and Japan. While for the Hotel and for the Other Services industries we are able to not reject convergence, with only a few exceptions for this last industry.
If we consider capital productivity, we can accept convergence, in the rate of growth, even more often than in the case of labour productivity. Moreover the systematic patterns, that appear to emerge for the latter, are not present in the case of capital productivity. Only for the Other Services industry can we observe a significant differential for Japan, that shows a productivity growth substantially smaller than that of the other countries.
Two tentative conclusions emerge from the results presented above. First, with some exceptions (that being systematic deserve further

scrutiny) we can accept convergence in the rate of growth, but reject it in levels. Such a finding seems to indicate that the data are more coherent with the endogenous growth model than with the neoclassical growth model.

The second conclusion is related to the "Service" sector. As far as convergence is concerned we observe that, notwithstanding the fact that services are less tradable than manufacturing products, the rate of growth of their productivity converges across countries. Moreover it converges among countries that have very different productive structure and systems of regulations. Consider for example the retail industry: its productivity growth is, in the long run, the same in Italy, in Germany and in France. This seems to indicate that the Italian retail industry does not show, in terms of dynamics of productivity, a behaviour that is significantly different form that of the rest of the European countries. A similar comment applies to the other industries of the service sector considered.

A different picture emerges if we consider convergence in the rate of growth of the different industries within a country. In this case we are able to reject convergence basically for all the countries considered. This seems to indicate that possible differentials in the rate of growth between the manufacturing and the "service" sector are to be attributed more to technological factors than to the "institutional" characteristic of the single countries. For the latter hypothesis to be true we should also have rejected convergence across countries, at least for those countries, like Italy, that are known to or thought of having a service sector which has a structure and/or is subject to regulations very different from those of the rest of OECD countries considered in this study.

References

Barro, Robert J., (1991), "Economic Growth in a Cross-section of Countries", *Quarterly Journal of Economics*, 106, 280-305.

Barro, Robert J. and Xavier Sala-i-Martin, (1991a), "Convergence across States and Regions", *Brookings Papers on Economic Activity*, no.1, 107-182.

Barro, Robert J. and Xavier Sala-i-Martin, (1991b), "Economic Growth", *Manuscript*, Harward University, Cambridge Ma.

Barro, Robert J. and Xavier Sala-i-Martin, (1992), "Convergence", *Journal of Political Economy*, 100, 223-254.

Baumol, William J., (1986), "Productivity Growth, Convergence and Welfare: What the Long Run Data Show", *American Economic Review*, 75, 1072-1085.

Baumol, William J., Blackman, S. and Wolff, E., (1989), *Productivity Growth: The Long View*, MIT Press, Cambridge, MA.

Bernard, Andrew B. and Durlauf, Steven N., (1991), "Convergence in International Output", *NBER Working Paper*, no. 3717.

Bernard, Andrew B. and Durlauf, Steven N., (1992), "Interpreting Tests of Convergence Hypothesis", *Working Paper in Progress*, Stanford University.

Brock, William A. and Leonard J. Mirman, (1972), "Optimal Growth Under Uncertainty: the Discounted Case", *Journal of Economic Theory*, 18, 479-513.

De Long, Bradford J, (1988), "Productivity Growth, Convergence and Welfare: Comment", *American Economic Review*, 78, 1138-1154.

Dollar D., Wolff E.N., (1993), "Competitiveness, Convergence and International Specialization", *Cambridge and London: MIT Press*, 228.

Durlauf, Steven N., (1989), "Output Persistence, Economic Structure, and the Choice of Stabilization Policy", *Brooking Papers on Economic Activity*, no.2, 69-136.

Durlauf, Steven N., (1991a), "Path Dependence in Aggregate Output", *NBER Working Paper*, no. 3718.

Durlauf, Steven N., (1991b), "Non Ergodic Economic Growth", *NBER Working Paper*, no. 3719.

Durlauf, Steven N., (1992), "A Theory of Persistent Income Inequality", *NBER Working Paper*, no. 4056.

Lucas, Robert J., (1988), "On the Mechanics of Economic Development", *Journal of Monetary Economics*, 22, 3-42.

Morawetz, David, (1977), "Twenty-Five Years of Economic Development", *Finance & Development*, 25, 10-13, 1977.

Quah, Danny, (1990), "International Patterns of Growth: I. Persistence in Cross-Countries Disparities I", *Working Paper*, MIT.

Quah, Danny, (1992a), "International Patterns of Growth: II. Persistence, Path Dependence and Sustained Take-Off in Growth Transition", *Working Paper*, Economic Department, LSE.

Quah, Danny, (1992b), "Empirical Cross-Section Dynamics in Economic Growth", *Discussion Paper*, no. 75, Institute for Empirical Macroeconomics, Fed. Res. Bank of Minneapolis, University of Minnesota, (Forthcoming in *European Economic Review*).

Quah, Danny, (1993), "Galton's Fallacy and Tests of the Convergence Hypothesis", *CEPR Discussion Papers*, no.820.

Romer, Paul M., (1986), "Increasing Return and Long-Run Growth", *Journal of Political Economy*, 94, 1002-1037.

Seers Dudley, (1972), "The Meaning of Development", in Lehmann David (ed.), *Development Theory*.

Appendix

The graphs reported in this paper refer to labour and capital productivity expressed in term of Index (level). The names of the variables shown in these graphs can be obtained using, sequentially, the following code:

p	=	is productivity and is common to all variables;
t, d, n, f, j, i, k, u	=	refer respectively to countries: Germany, Denmark, Finland, France, Japan, Italy, United Kingdom and USA.
ot	=	refer to labour productivity
ca	=	refer to capital productivity
m, s, c, h, a	=	refer respectively to sectors: Manufacturing, Service, Retail and Wholesale, Hotels, Other Services.

Therefore, the variable PTOTM refers to labour productivity (OT) in the manufacturing sector (M) in Germany (T).

The graphs reported in this paper refer to labour and capital productivity expressed in terms of indexes (in level). In Fig.1 and 2 the legend refers to the industries according to the following scheme:

OTHSER	=	Other Services
RET	=	Retail and Wholesale
HOT	=	Hotel
MAN	=	Manufacturing
SER	=	Retail and Wholesale + Hotel

In Fig.3 and 4 the legend refers to countries according to the following scheme:

DEN	=	Denmark
FRA	=	France
ITA	=	Italy
JAP	=	Japan
UK	=	United Kingdom
NEE	=	Finland
GER	=	Germany
USA	=	United States of America

8

Productivity Growth in Service and Non-Service Industries: Implications for Convergence

Henning Klodt
The Kiel Institute of World Economics

1. Introduction*

The resurrected interest in growth theory has put new life into the analysis of growth rate differentials across countries. Traditional growth theory predicts the convergence of per-capita incomes as a result of flows of physical capital and technical knowledge from rich to poor countries, whereas the new growth theory allows for permanently differing income levels across countries even in the absence of barriers to the flow of capital and technology. In this discussion, only limited attention has been paid to the question why the trend towards convergence (if there is any) was much stronger in the decades prior to 1973 than in the two subsequent decades. It seems not very convincing to assume that the weakening of convergence reflects an exhaustion of catch-up potentials, because the gap between rich and poor countries remains substantial. It is still an unsettled issue why poorer countries are less able than before to exploit the "advantages of economic backwardness" (Gerschenkron, 1952).
In this paper it is argued that the answer to this question is not to be found in a reduced capability of poor countries to attract capital and

* The author is grateful to Rainer Maurer for helpful comments.

technical knowledge, but in changing patterns of sectoral development within rich countries that reduced their growth disadvantage with poorer countries. In this context, at least part of the catch-up process of the past is attributed to the relative specialization of rich countries on service industries that exhibited lower productivity growth rates than manufacturing industries. As compared to poorer countries, rich countries are still specialized on services, but this specialization is apparently not associated with lower aggregate growth any longer.

Presumably, the introduction of new technologies and sectoral shifts within the service sector have enhanced the growth prospects of countries with high service sector shares, which may in turn have weakened the trend towards convergence.

Convergence never was a universal phenomenon throughout the world, but was more or less confined to groups of countries with rather similar basic economic conditions and institutional settings, i.e. to specific "convergence clubs" (Baumol, 1986). For instance, most western industrial countries seem to be members of one convergence club, whereas the Soviet-type economies of eastern Europe established another one. Convergence can be observed within each of these clubs, but there is no evidence for convergence between them.

This paper does not intend to explore the reasons for the existence of different convergence clubs or the nature and significance of the border lines between them[1]. Instead, it concentrates on the development within one of the biggest convergence clubs - the OECD area.

Section II presents some theoretical considerations and empirical estimates on convergence, whereas section III is concerned with structural adjustment and its implications for country-specific growth. Section IV concludes.

---

[1] Mankiw, Romer and Weil (1992) and Barro and Sala-i-Martin (1992) have tried to identify the determinants that establish different convergence clubs. When these determinants are properly included in the empirical estimates, "conditional convergence" for the whole set of countries can be observed.

2. Convergence

There are basically three hypotheses that can explain the convergence of per-capita incomes between rich and poor countries (Abramovitz, 1986):

According to the *technology transfer hypothesis,* poor countries catch up because imitation is in general less difficult than innovation. It should be noticed, however, that imitation does not automatically lead to convergence. If rich countries are innovating at a constant rate and poor countries are adapting the new technologies with a constant time lag, both groups of countries will tend to grow at the same rate for ever[2]. Convergence only occurs either if poor countries are able to reduce their time-lag to the best-practice technology or if the rate of invention in rich countries slows down. The worldwide increase in foreign direct investment, that fairly exceeds the increase in world output or world trade, can probably be interpreted as a main source of the reduction in the technological backwardness of poorer countries.

According to the *affluent society hypothesis*, poor countries grow faster because their marginal utility of income is higher. Here, convergence is attributed to an income elasticity of the demand for leisure time above unity. As a matter of fact, the reduction of average annual hours of work per employee was stronger in rich countries than in poor countries over the past decades[3]. Probably, convergence in per-capita productivity can at least partly be explained by saturation in rich countries.

According to the *structural adjustment hypothesis*, rich countries grow slower because productivity growth is lower in service activities than in industrial activities and because the share of services in total employment increases with per-capita income. This "productivity bias" has repeatedly been reported by several authors and has been used to explain why services tend to be relatively cheap in poor countries (Kravis, Heston, Summers, 1978; Bhagwati,

---

2 Such a growth pattern is described, for instance, by the product-cycle model of Krugman (1979).

3 Respective data for a broad range of countries are published by the International Labour Office (current issues).

1984). The implications of this bias for sectoral shifts in the course of economic growth are discussed in the following section[4].

All in all, each of these hypotheses seems suitable for explaining the convergence of income levels over time. It is not intended here to decide which one of them is more precisely on the mark.

An empirical test on convergence was carried out for the 24 OECD countries (excluding former Yugoslavia) and the period from 1960 to 1991 by the following OLSQ equation:

$$\hat{y}_i = a + b \ln y_i^o + u_i \qquad (1)$$

$\hat{y}$ denotes the average annual growth rate of GDP per head at 1985 prices, and y^o denotes the level of GDP per head at 1985 prices at the beginning of the period under consideration. The data on GDP were not converted into a single currency by official exchange rates for two reasons: firstly, the exchange rate markets of 1985 were quite disarrayed with a strongly overvaluated U.S.-Dollar. Secondly, per-capita income comparisons based on official exchange rates tend to understate the income level of poorer countries because long-term exchange rates can only reflect international price differences in tradable goods. As mentioned above, non-tradables (i.e. most services) are in general relatively cheaper in poor countries. In most cases, therefore, the relative income position of poor countries is better than the calculations based on official exchange rates would suggest. For these reasons the official exchange rates of 1985 were adjusted by the purchasing power price levels that are provided by Robert Summers and Alan Heston (1988). y^o therefore represents national income levels at 1985 prices expressed in "international dollars".

Equation (1) was estimated for the whole period from 1960 to 1991 and for two sub-periods. In a second step, the average percentage share of gross fixed capital formation in GDP (i/q) and the average

---

[4] Dowrick and Gemell (1991) examine the impact of productivity growth rate differentials between agriculture and other industries on aggregate growth and convergence for 78 countries. Within the OECD area, however, sectoral shifts between agriculture and industry seem less important, because the share of agriculture in economic activity is rather low.

growth rate of population (ê) as a proxy for employment growth were included in order to take account of national differences in capital deepening[5]:

$$\hat{y}_i = a + b \ln y_i^o + c(i/q)_i + d\hat{e}_i + u_i \qquad (2)$$

The results presented in Table 1 are indicating that convergence was merely a phenomenon of the sixties and early seventies.

The weakening of convergence since the early seventies has also been reported in various other studies[6]. If it were to be explained in the framework of the technology transfer hypothesis, one would have to suppose that transborder flows of technology were more difficult to achieve in the period since 1973 than in the period before. The empirical evidence on increased international flows of goods and capital and the reduced costs of transmitting information across long distances suggest, however, that the barriers to the international transfer of technology are declining rather than rising in the course of time. Hence, the technology transfer hypothesis may well explain convergence itself, but it fails to explain the slowdown of convergence.

The same applies to the affluent society hypothesis. There is no doubt that average working times tend to be lower in rich countries than in poor countries. But there is no evidence that the reduction of working time in rich countries was primarily a phenomenon of the pre 1973 era. In most industrialized countries working hours per head are declining at a rather stable trend over time. In West Germany, for instance, the average working time in the industrial sector (including mining and construction) was reduced from 2089 hours in 1960 to 1829 hours in 1973 and to 1604 hours in 1990[7].

---

5 Dowrick and Nguyen (1989) have demonstrated how equation (2) can be derived from a Cobb-Douglas production function with exogenous technical progress and additional technical progress resulting from catch-up.

6 See, e.g. Abramovitz (1986), Heitger (1987), Baumol and Wolff (1988), Dowrick and Nguyen (1989), Crafts (1992), Levine and Renelt (1992).

7 Institut fur Arbeitsmarkt - und Berufsforshung, unpublished data.

Table 1 Determinants of GDP per capita growth in OECD countries

Period	Constant	ln yo	i/q	ê	$\bar{R}^2$	Observations
	12.98	- 1.19			0.43	24
1960-91	(47.5)*	(4.27)*			(18.21)*	
	11.01	- 1.13	0.08	- 0.50	0.56	24
	(3.65)*	(4.06)*	(1.79)o	(1.98)o	(10.82)*	
	21.90	- 2.09			0.43	24
1960-73	(29.50)*	(4.30)*			(18.52)*	
	17.76	- 1.81	0.10	- 0.61	0.54	24
	(3.74)*	(3.96)*	(1.47)	1.50)	(10.17)*	
	7.01	- 0.56			0.06	24
1973-91	(32.83)*	(1.56)			(2.43)	
	5.97	- 0.61	0.07	- 0.28	0.10	24
	(1.34)	(1.38)	(1.55)	(0.83)	(1.85)	

Absolute t-values and F-value of regression in brackets. Levels of statistical significance: *=1 percent; +=5 percent; o=10 percent.

Data sources: OECD(a); Summers, Heston (1988).

Moreover, the weakening of convergence also shows up in those estimates that are based on hourly labour productivity (Abramovitz, 1986), whereas the affluent society hypothesis would predict no convergence in these data.

In the following section, it is discussed whether the structural adjustment hypothesis is capable to solve the puzzle of the diminishing importance of convergence. For this purpose, a simple model is presented that establishes a relationship between structural adjustment and international growth rate differentials.

3. Structural Adjustment

According to the well-known "three-sector-hypothesis" of Colin Clark and Jean Fourastié, the share of the industrial sector in the economy increases at early stages of industrial development and decreases as the economy matures. It has repeatedly been shown that this hypothesis is very powerful in explaining cross-country variations of sectoral shares in nominal output and employment (Kuznets, 1957, 1966; Chenery, 1960; Fels, Schatz, Wolter, 1971; Donges, Klodt, Schmidt, 1989). The underlying determinants are probably the productivity bias in favour of the industrial sector and the demand bias in favour of the service sector[8].

The empirical evidence on the development of sectoral shares in real output is less unequivocal. If one looks for the stylized facts of sectoral adjustment in real terms, the assumption of constant shares seems to be more appropriate than the assumption of permanent shifts between sectors (Kravis, Heston, Summers, 1983).

Figures 1 and 2 present the empirical evidence on service sector shares in nominal output and employment for 21 OECD countries[9]. As in the regression analysis of the preceding section, per capita incomes were calculated by purchasing power parities. Apparently, the shares of services tend to rise with real income.

This relationship seems to be somewhat stronger for employment than for nominal output, although both correlations are statistically significant.

The construction of a similar diagram on real output shares as provided by national accounts statistics would not make much sense, because national statistical offices are calculating real output by deflating nominal output with the national price structure of a base year. Even if the base year is identical for all countries, service output will be valued at a higher relative price in rich countries than in poor countries.

Hence, the available information from OECD statistics on "real" output shares of services is strongly biased by international differ-

8 For a graphical illustration of the impact of these biases on structural adjustment and an empirical evaluation for the West German economy see Klodt (1988).

9 Countries are identified by their car plate signs. Due to the lack of appropriate data, New Zealand, Iceland and Turkey are excluded from the diagram on employment. The service shares of the United States, Canada, Ireland, Portugal and the United Kingdom refer to the latest available year.

ences in relative prices that are systematically related to per capita income[10].

In the following, a simple two-sector model is developed that reproduces these stylized facts of structural adjustment. It assumes that real output (x) per worker (L) in services (s) and in manufacturing (m) grow at a constant rate over time, where the increase in service productivity is a constant fraction (r) of the increase in manufacturing. For convenience, it is assumed that the productivity levels at t=0 are equal in both sectors.

$$\frac{x_s}{L_s} = A\, e^{r\lambda t} \quad ; \qquad 0 < r < 1 \tag{3}$$

$$\frac{x_m}{L_m} = A\, e^{\lambda t} \tag{4}$$

As a consequence of the productivity bias, the relative price of services will increase over time. If wages in services and in manufacturing are identical within countries and if markets are competitive, the price ratio (p_s / p_m) will be determined by the productivity ratio.

$$\frac{p_s}{p_m} = e^{\lambda t(1-r)} \tag{5}$$

With homothetic preferences of consumers, the relative price changes would result in an increase of the share of manufacturing in real output. In this model, however, it is assumed that preferences are non-homothetic, i.e. that the income elasticity of the demand for services exceeds unity[11]. In accordance with the above cited empirical evidence, it is assumed that this demand bias just offsets the productivity bias. In this case the share of services in aggregate real output remains constant over time.

10 International price comparisons for goods and services are available from the various publications of Kravis, Heston and Summers, but it should be noted that their disaggregated data refer to the expenditure side of GDP, i.e. to the prices of gross output and not of value added.

11 Due to the adding-up conditions, the elasticity must asymptotically decline towards unity as the economy grows.

Figure 1 Share of services in GDP in OECD countries 1990

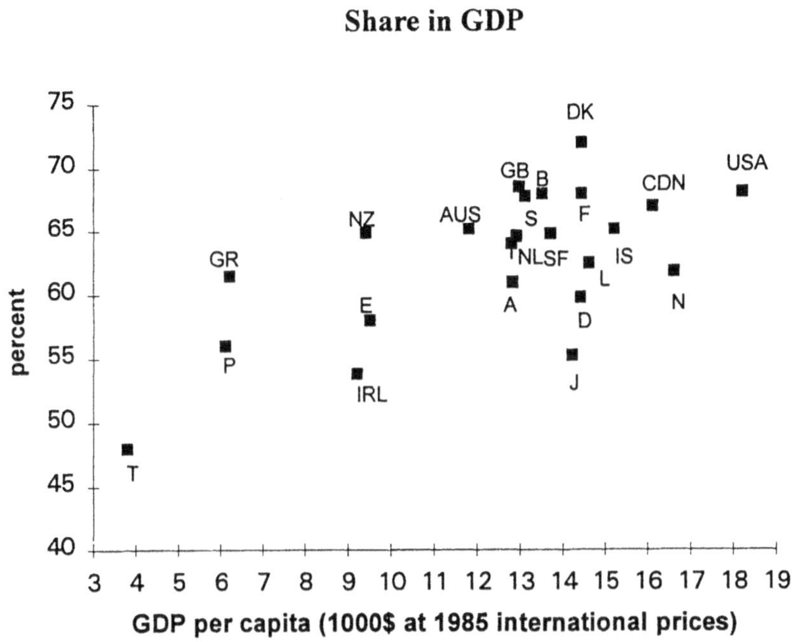

Data sources: OECD (a, b); Summers, Heston (1988)

Figure 2 Share of services in employment in OECD countries 1990

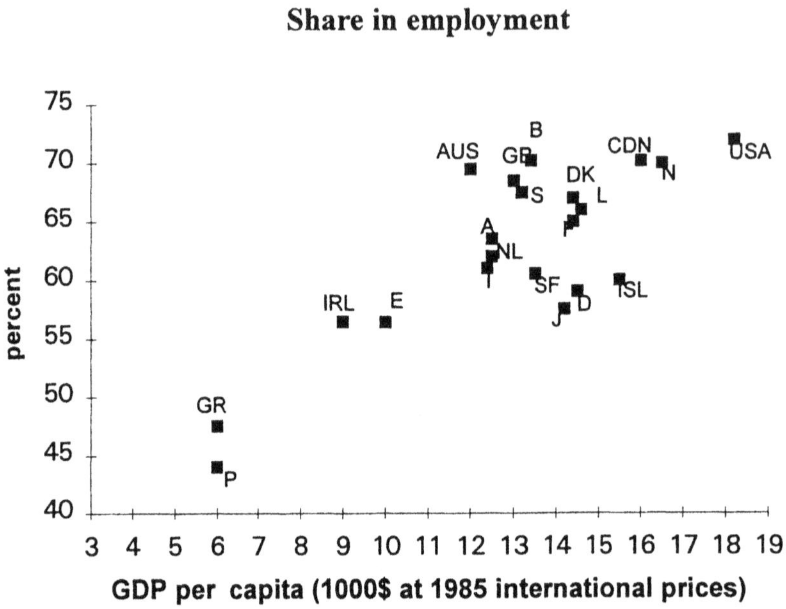

Data sources: OECD (a, b); Summers, Heston (1988)

$$x_s = cx; \qquad 0 < c < 1; \qquad x = x_s + x_m \tag{6}$$

When the price of manufactured goods is taken as numéraire, the share of services in nominal output can be calculated as follows:

$$\frac{p_s x_s}{p_s x_s + x_m} = \frac{1}{1 + (\frac{1}{c} - 1)e^{(r-1)\lambda t}} \tag{7}$$

With uniform nominal wages across industries, the share of service employment in total employment (ℓ_s) is equal to the service share in nominal output.

In this one-factor model, international differences in per-capita income can only result from technology differences. These differences can be expressed as a time lag (d) between the technology levels in rich and poor countries. When rich countries are producing with a technology available at time t, poor countries are still utilizing the technology of time (t-d). Hence, the share of service employment in total employment in a rich country (j) as compared to the corresponding share in a poor country (k) can be written as

$$\frac{\ell_s^j}{\ell_s^k} = \frac{1 + (\frac{1}{c} - 1)e^{(r-1)\lambda(t-d)}}{1 + (\frac{1}{c} - 1)e^{(r-1)\lambda t}}; \qquad 0 < d < t \tag{8}$$

This ratio is greater than unity; i.e. the employment share of services in rich countries is higher than in poor countries. Equivalently, the model predicts an increasing share of service employment over time for individual countries.

The growth rate of per-capita income ($\hat{y}$) equals the weighted average of productivity growth in services and manufacturing. When real output shares do not vary over time (as postulated by (6)), the sectoral employment shares can serve as the weights.

$$\hat{y}^k = \ell_s^k r\lambda + \ell_m^k \lambda \tag{9}$$

Because ℓ^k_s is smaller than ℓ^j_s, per capita income in the poor country k grows faster than in country j. Hence, the model explains convergence by the growth disadvantage of rich, service-intensive countries.

Table 2 Productivity bias between service and non-service industries in OECD countries (a)

	1960-73	1973-90
Canada	0.705	0.910 (b)
United States	0.724	1.039 (c)
Japan	0.815 (d)	0.953
Australia	0.905 (e)	0.969
Belgium	0.714	0.939
Denmark	0.859 (f)	0.887
Finland	0.725	0.972
France	0.746 (g)	0.976
Germany (h)	0.558	0.786
Greece	0.639	0.937
Italy	0.563	1.035
Norway	0.728 (g)	0.631
Portugal	0.747	1.059 (i)
Spain	0.794 (e)	0.816
Sweden	0.778 (j)	0.918
United Kingdom	0.870	0.931 (b)
Average (unweighted)	0.742	0.922

(a) Ratio of productivity growth in services to productivity growth in the remaining industries. - (b) 1973-88. - (c) 1973-87. - (d) 1961-73. - (e) 1964-73. - (f) 1966-73. -(g) 1962-73. -(h) Calculated from national sources at 1985 prices. - (i) 1973-89. - (j) 1963-73.

Data sources: OECD (b, c); Statistisches Bundesamt (1992).

The key parameter in this model is the productivity bias between service industries and other industries (r). Table 2 gives an impression of this bias for those countries where sectorally disaggregated data on output and employment are available from OECD statistics. Unfortunately, it was not possible to calculate sectoral productivity data on a single price base. The only exception is West Germany, where the Federal Statistical Office provides information on real output at 1985 prices for about 60 branches for the whole period from 1960 up to the present.
Table 2 shows that the productivity increase in West German non-service industries almost doubled the increase in services prior to 1973. In the following years, the productivity bias was still there, but the gap was closed to about one quarter.
The data for the remaining OECD countries were calculated at current prices. Only in Norway the gap between service and non-service industries widened after 1973 - a development that can presumably be attributed to the high productivity level in the oil sector. In all other countries the productivity bias strongly diminished, and in three countries it even disappeared.
According to equation (9) a decline in the productivity bias will reduce the speed of convergence. Hence, the structural adjustment hypothesis seems suitable for explaining the observed weakening of convergence since 1973.

4. Conclusions

The convergence of per capita income levels between rich and poor countries can be explained by several hypotheses, but most of these hypotheses are not able to explain why convergence was much stronger prior to 1973 than in subsequent years. In the context of the structural adjustment hypothesis, the weakening of convergence is not a puzzle any more, because convergence will only emerge if the productivity increase is exceptionally strong in those industries that exhibit an above-average employment share in poor countries. A levelling of productivity growth rates across sectors will result in a corresponding levelling of growth rates across countries.

It would surely be ill-considered to attribute the whole process of convergence to sectoral productivity differences and structural adjustment. The structural adjustment hypothesis probably explains only part of convergence, but it may well explain a substantially larger part of the slowdown of convergence.

In a sense, however, the structural adjustment hypothesis merely replaces one puzzle by another, as the diminishing of the productivity bias is left unexplained. This paper has not addressed the question why service industries have lost their productivity disadvantage in recent years. The answer can probably be found in two directions:

Firstly, the service sector itself is far from homogenous, and some service industries have never been low productivity industries. The prospects for introducing productivity enhancing technologies in banking and insurance or in communication services, for instance, are much better than in most personal services. Structural adjustment within the service sector is dominated by significant shifts from traditional, low productivity activities to modern activities with rich opportunities for productivity improvements.

Secondly, technical progress has probably lost its traditional bias in favour of the manufacturing sector. In a broad sense, many service activities are concerned to generating, collecting and disseminating information. Designers and sales-promotion agents create new information about products, financial institutions collect and distribute information about capital markets, lawyers provide information about the legal system to laymen, and the PTTs ship information from one place to the other.

All these activities are strongly facilitated by modern, microelectronics based information and communication technologies that became available in the post 1973 era.

It should be recognized, however, that sectoral biases of technical progress are no natural phenomenon. It is difficult to assess, therefore, whether the favourable impact of technical progress on productivity in the service sector will continue in the future.

The microelectronics revolution is not completely over and will probably continue to reduce the productivity disadvantage of service industries in the years to come. But it can not be ruled out that newly emerging technologies will again be concentrated on the industrial sector. For instance, the main area of application for biotechnology seems to be the improvement of industrial production processes. If biotechnology will turn out to be the dominant technology of the future, the industrial sector may regain its productivity advantage and convergence may speed up again.

References

Abramovitz, Moses, (1986), "Catching up, Forging Ahead, and Falling Behind" *Journal of Economic History*, vol.46, , 385-406.

Barro, Robert J., Sala-I-Martin Xavier, (1992), "Convergence", *Journal of Political Economy*, vol. 100, no.2, 223-251.

Baumol, William J., (1986), "Productivity Growth, Convergence and Welfare: What the Long-Run Data Show", *American Economic Review*, vol. 76, no. 5, 1072-1085.

Baumol, William J., Wolff Edward N.,(1988), "Productivity, Growth, Convergence, and Welfare: Reply". *American Economic Review*, vol. 78, 1155-1159.

Bhagwat I, Jagdish N.,(1984), "Why are Services Cheaper in the Poor Countries?", *Economic Journal*, vol. 94, 274-286.

Chenery, Hollis B.,(1960), "Patterns of Industrial Growth", *American Economic Review*, vol. 50, 626-654.

Crafts, Nicholas, (1992), "Productivity Growth Reconsidered", *Economic Policy*, no. 15, 388-426.

Donges, Juergen B., Klodt Henning, Schmidt Klaus-Dieter, (1989), "Perspective Structural Changes in the West German Economy", in Wilhelm Krelle (ed.), *The Future of The World Economy, Economic Growth and Structural Change*, Luxenburg, 385-398.

Dowrick Steve, Gemmell Norman, (1991), "Industrialisation, Catching Up and Economic Growth: A Comparative Study across the World's Capitalist Economies", *The Economic Journal*, vol. 101, 263-275.

Dowrick Steve, Duc-Tho Nguyen,(1989), "OECD Comparative Economic Growth 1950-85: Catch-Up and Convergence", *The American Economic Review*, vol. 79, no. 5, 1010-1030.

Fels Gerhard, Schatz Klaus-Werner, Wolter Frank,(1971), "Der Zusammenhang zwischen Produktionsstruktur und Entwicklungsniveau. Versuch einer Strukturprognose für die westdeutsche Wirtschaft", *Weltwirtschaftliches Archiv*, vol. 106, 240-278.

Gerschenkron Alexander, (1952), "Economic Backwardness in Historical Perspective", in Bert F. Hoselitz (ed.), *The Progress of Underdeveloped Areas*, Chicago.

Heitger, Bernhard, (1987), "Corporatism, Technological Gaps and Growth in OECD Countries", Weltwirtschaftliches Archiv, vol. 123, 462-473.

ILO, "Yearbook of Labour Statistics", Geneva, current issues.

Klodt Henning,(1988), "De-Industrialization in West Germany", *Jahrbücher für Nationalökonomie und Statistik*, vol. 204, no. 6, 531-540.

Kravis Irving B., Heston Alan, Summers Robert,(1978), *International Comparisons of Real Product and Purchasing Power*, Baltimore.

Kravis Irving B., Heston Alan, Summers Robert (1983), "The Share of Services in Economic Growth", in Adams F.G., Hickman B.G. (eds.), *Global Econometrics*, Essays in Honor of Lawrence R. Klein, Cambridge.

Krugman, Paul, (1979), "A Model of Innovation, Technology Transfer, and the World Distribution of Income", *Journal of Political Economy*, vol. 87, 253-266.

Kuznets, Simon, (1957), *Quantitative Aspects of the Economic Growth of Nations: II. Industrial Distribution of National Product and Labour Force. Economic Development and Cultural Change,* Supplement to vol. 5, no. 4.

Kuznets, Simon, (1966), "Modern Economic Growth Rate", *Structure and Spread*, New Haven.

Levine Ross, Renelt David, (1992), "Sensitivity Analysis of Cross-Country Growth Regressions", *The American Economic Review*, vol. 82, no. 4, 942-963.

Mankiw N. Gregory, Romer David, Weil David N, (1992), "A Contribution to the Empirics of Economic Growth", *Quarterly Journal of Economics*, vol. 107, 407-437.

OECD (a), "National Accounts. Main Aggregates" vol. I, Paris, current issues.

OECD (b), "National Accounts. Detailed Tables" vol. II, Paris, current issues.

OECD (c), "Labour Force Statistics" Paris, current issues.

Statistisches Bundesamt (1992), Fachserie 18: "Volkswirtschaftliche Gesamtrechnungen. Reihe S.15: Revidierte Ergebnisse 1980 bis 1990", Wiesbaden.

Summers Robert, Heston Alan, (1988), "A New Set of International Comparisons of Real Product and Price Levels: Estimates for 130 Countries, 1950-1985", *The Review of Income and Wealth*, vol. 34, 1-25.

9

The Comparative Performance of Industrial and Service Firms in the Eighties: An Italian Story

Pasquale L. Scandizzo
University of Rome "Tor Vergata"

1. Introduction

The importance of the growth pattern of the modern economies has long been an issue in economic research. The increasing weight of the service sector and the evolution of both services and industries have been the object of specific inquiries by Chenery (1960, 1979), Kuznets (1971), Chenery and Syrquin (1975), Baumol (1967) and Baumol et al. (1985). Earlier theories of development through progressive increases of the secondary over the primary sector and the tertiary over the secondary are due to Clark (1940) and Rostow (1960).

More recently, a number of studies (Petit, 1986, Baumol et al. 1985, Milana and Scandizzo, 1991) have examined the possibility that the growth of the service economy may foster a dual development and ultimately cause de-industrialization and generally the establishment of an undesirable pattern of production.

Under the circumstances of the Italian economy in the eighties, the policies of tight money and fixed exchange rate pursued in conjunction with the entrance in the ERM has fostered fears that dualism and de-industrialization might cause a regression of the production base toward a particularly inefficient industrial structure highly dependent on mature goods and non market services.

In this paper, I propose to look at the question of de-industrialization by directly considering the measure of comparative advantage of the industrial sector versus the service sector. For this purpose, I use microeconomic data from the Mediobanca panel for the period 1980-1991, to first investigate the evolution of economic performance for firms producing respectively industrial goods and services. I then analyze the financial performance for the same panel of firms, bringing into consideration the difference between *competitive advantage*, as determined by both economic and financial opportunities, and *comparative advantage*, which is defined as the consequence of the differences in the economic rates of return of the different sectors.

2. The Measure of Performance

In order to measure the performance of a firm for a given period of time, I use a method based on the discounted cash flow (DCF) and, more specifically, on the so called economic and financial net present value. This method, typically used to evaluate investment projects, can be extended to the evaluation of the performance of any enterprise, if we consider its initial value as an investment and its value at the end of the period considered as a resale value [1]. More precisely, if we denote with CF_t the enterprise "real" cash flow at time t (excluding all financial flows), the economic net present value (ENPV) between period t_0 and t_1 is defined as follows:

$$ENPV_{t_0,t_1} = \sum_{t=t_0}^{t_1} \frac{CF_t}{(1+r)^t} - V_{t_0} + \frac{V_{t_1}}{(1+r)^{t_1}} \tag{1}$$

where V_{t_0} and V_{t_1} measure the capital value of the enterprise respectively at time t_0 and at time t_1 and r is an appropriate rate of dis-

[1] For earlier applications of this method see Pera and Scandizzo (1988) and Scandizzo, Quaglione (1992).

count. The financial net present value is defined in a similar way, but financial flows are now excluded in the cash flow while V measures the net worth of the firm.
Because the capital value of a firm is nothing but the net present value of all its future cash flows, from (1) it follows that:

$$ENPV_{t_0,\infty} = \sum_{t=t_0}^{\infty} \frac{CF_t}{(1+r)^t} = V_{t_0}, \quad ENPV_{t_1,\infty} = \sum_{t=t_1}^{\infty} \frac{CF_t}{(1+r)^{t-t_1}} = V_{t_1} \qquad (2)$$

Thus, if all information were known at time t_0, from (1) and (2) it would follow that:

$$ENPV_{t_0,t_1} = 0 \qquad (3)$$

i.e. it would not be possible to make money by purchasing an asset if its cost were exactly equal to the present value of its future cash flows and both the purchases and the seller knew it.
In practice, expression (3) will not hold true if compared with book values and actual resale values of firms. The discrepancy is due to the fact that transaction values reflect a prediction about future cash flows and thus do not coincide with actual values.
If we distinguish predicted from realized values, we can write:

$$ENPV_{t_0,\infty} = \sum_{t=t_0}^{\infty} \frac{\hat{CF}_t}{(1+r)^t} = V_{t_0} \qquad (4)$$

where the sign ^ indicates that the value of the firm at time t_0 is based on a forecast of its future cash flows. Similarly:

$$ENPV^*_{t_1,\infty} = \sum_{t=t_1}^{\infty} \frac{CF^*_t}{(1+r)^t} = V_{t_1} \qquad (5)$$

where the star indicates that the same value at time t_1 is based on a different forecast than the one used at time zero.

Substituting (4) and (5) into (1), we obtain:

$$ENPV_{t_0,t_1} = \sum_{t=t_0}^{t_1} \frac{(CF_t - \hat{CF}_t)}{(1+r)^t} + \sum_{t=t_1}^{\infty} \frac{(CF^* - \hat{CF}_t)}{(1+r)^t} \quad (6)$$

Assuming that the forecast errors in (6) are additive, i.e. $CF_t = CF_t + u_t$ and $CF_t = CF^*_t + v_t$, expression (6) can be written as follows:

$$ENPV_{t_0,t_1} = \sum_{t=t_0}^{\infty} \frac{u_t}{(1+r)^t} - \sum_{t=t_1}^{\infty} (1+r) \frac{V_t}{(1+r)^t} \quad (7)$$

Expression (7) states that the economic net present value between two arbitrary periods of time t_0 and t_1 is the difference between the cumulated present values of two estimation errors: the over or under-evaluation of future cash flows at time t_0 and the over or under-evaluation of future cash flows at time t_1. If the two errors are in the same direction, e.g. they both tend to overvalue the firm, they also tend to offset each other.

If they are in the opposite direction, on the other hand, they tend to aggravate each other. In particular, the NPV will be negative in three cases: (i) if an initial overvaluation at t_0 is not compensated by a sufficiently large under-evaluation at t_1, (ii) if an initial under-evaluation is more than compensated by a final over-valuation and, (iii) if an under-evaluation at t_0 is followed by an overvaluation at t_1. In what sense, then, the ENPV can be used as a measure of the firm performance? To answer this question note that expression (8) measures at the same time how much better the firm has performed in the period under consideration vis a vis the original expectation both in terms of the difference between actual realization and original estimate $(CF_t - \hat{CF}_t)$ and in terms of the difference between the new estimate of cash flow and the previous on $(CF^*_t - \hat{CF}_t)$.

Expression (1) and its counterpart for the financial net present value can thus be used to measure the economic value of the firm between any two periods of time. If the firm is not actually bought at the beginning of the period and sold at the end, of course, the values V_{t_0} and V_{t_1} can only be taken from the balance sheet and they may understate or overstate the "true" value of the firm depending on a number of circumstances. Nevertheless, the interpretation given by the above analysis will apply, because V_{t_0} and V_{t_1} in any case are only estimates of future cash flows.

Moreover, if the ENPV measure is performed for different periods of time, varying both t_0 and t_1, one obtains a time series of net present value measures that can be organized in a triangular matrix:

$$\text{ENPV} = \text{W} = \begin{bmatrix} \mathbf{W}_{21} & & & \\ \mathbf{W}_{31} & \mathbf{W}_{32} & & \mathbf{0} \\ \mathbf{W}_{41} & \mathbf{W}_{42} & \ddots & \\ \vdots & \vdots & & \ddots \\ \mathbf{W}_{T1} & \mathbf{W}_{T2} & & \mathbf{W}_{T,T-1} \end{bmatrix} \qquad (8)$$

This matrix is triangular because it contains an "arrow of time", i.e. the NPV can only be calculated from t t_0 t+Δt and not viceversa. Each of its columns represents a series of performance measures which have in common the initial value of the firm and part of the cash flow. Each element of the column, compared with the previous element, thus measures an improved or deteriorated performance.

Consider one of the column of the matrix: an increase from one of the terms with a lower time subscript to one with a higher one denotes an increase in the profitability of holding the firm. Viceversa, a decrease denotes that it would have been better to sell the firm since the profitability of holding it one more unit of time has decreased. Each element of the column, therefore, indicates two things: first, whether the firm has created real wealth in the interval of time under consideration and, second, compared with the following term of the column, whether it was better to hold the firm or to sell it. This is equivalent to consider the value of a "put" option, i.e. an option to sell the firm for a given (strike) price, having as a "strike" price the current NPV and as a market prices the following NPV's. If the option is "in the money", i.e. the strike price is below the market price, the performance of the firm is improving. Viceversa, if the current NPV is above the future NPV's, the performance is deteriorating. In the first case one should exercise the option to sell in the current period. In the second, one should hold it.

What is the interpretation of a row of the matrix? Rather than considering the problem of holding a firm whose value may be decreasing, looking at the performance along one of the rows implies a retrospective question: having given up (i.e. ceased to hold) the firm in a given period, how much did the investment in the firm yield? The answer to this question depends on the retrospective time horizon, i.e. on the beginning date of the entrepreneur's involvement in the firm. Each element of the row corresponds to a different such a date and is equivalent to the strike price of a "call" option, while all the preceeding elements correspond to its market price. If the NPV at a date preceeding the one considered is higher, the firm should have been started in that date rather than in the one considered, i.e. the "call" should have been exercised. Also in this case, therefore a falling value of the option over time implies a deterioration in performance, while an increasing value implies that the firm has been doing better in more recent years, than in earlier ones.

The measures based on NPV can thus be used to evaluate firms and sectors of the economy and they convey additional information with respect to the usual applications to project evaluation. As for project evaluation, moreover, they can be generalized in two directions: first, rather than a single rate of discount, a different appropriate rate can be used for each year. In this case equation (1) becomes:

$$ENPV_{t_0,t_1} = \sum_{t=t_0}^{t_1} \frac{CF_t}{R_t} - V_{t_0} + \frac{V_{t_1}}{R_{t_1}} \tag{9}$$

where $R_t = \prod_{t=1}^{t} (1 + r_t)$

Second, the NPV measure can be normalized to account for the fact that the firms to be evaluated are of different size. Two types of normalization can be used: the first one consists in dividing the NPV by an appropriate indicator of firm size, for example, V_t. In symbols:

$$EY_{t_0,t_1} = \frac{ENPV_{t_0,t_1}}{V_{t_0}} \qquad (10)$$

where $EY_{t_0,t}$ denotes the economic yield of the investment V_t.
The second type of normalization consists in defining the rate of return of the firm to one of the resources used. The best known measure of this kind is the so called internal rate of return (IRR), defined as:

$$IRR_{t_0,t_1} = [r;\ NPV_{t_0,t_1}] = 0 \qquad (11)$$

i.e. as the rate of discount such that the NPV between t_0 and t_1 is just zero. The IRR measures the return to an average unit of capital invested in the firm under the hypothesis that the same return can be reinvested at the same rate. Notice, however, that while expression (10) incorporates the information on the discount factor, expression (11) does not. In order to take into account the opportunity cost of capital, it has to be modified by defining the differential internal rate of return (DIRR):

$$DIRR_{t_0,t_1} = IRR_{t_0,t_1} - R_{t_0,t_1} \qquad (12)$$

where $R_{t,t}$ is an appropriate rate of discount.

What is the interpretation of the yield (Y) and the DIRR? While the IRR broadly measures the profitability of a group of firms in a particular period of time, the Y and DIRR measures are relative indicators of the resource pull of a group of firms or of a sector. They offer a measure, in other words, of the extent to which capital is drawn preferentially into the sector examined vis a vis all other sectors of the economy. As resource pull variables, therefore, Y's and DIRR's belong to the family of the indicators, that are used to measure comparative advantage and effective protection [2].

[2] For a recent survey of such measures, see Scandizzo (1989).

More specifically, the economic yield and the economic DIRR measure the extent to which capital is attracted to a particular sector regardless of the way in which investment is financed. Viceversa, the financial yield and DIRR measure the capital pull for shareholders, that is, taking into account the degree of financial leverage of the firm and the difference between the rate of interest paid on loans and the discount rate. The financial indicators, therefore take into account the fact that borrowing and lending activities may allow a firm to exercise market power and skills to improve its performance.
The financial indicators can be also estimated “before” tax, in which case they show the firm's performance in economic and financial activities, and "after tax", incorporating tax smoothing and tax avoidance behavior in the financial results of the firm.
In a Modigliani & Miller world without taxation and with perfect capital markets, economic and financial indicators would of course coincide. Market imperfections and taxation, however, cause a double wedge to be inserted between economic returns to investment and after-tax return to capital owners. Capital is thus supplied to each sector as a consequence of its after-tax returns, while it is object of demand from investors on the basis returns, while it is demanded on the basis of before taxes or of economic returns.

Consider now the matrix of IRRs corresponding to (8), i.e. the matrix defined as:

$$\mathrm{EIRR} = [\mathrm{R};\ \mathrm{ENPV} = 0] = \begin{bmatrix} \mathbf{r}_{21} & & & & \mathbf{0} \\ \mathbf{r}_{31} & \mathbf{r}_{32} & & & \\ \mathbf{r}_{41} & \mathbf{r}_{42} & \ddots & & \\ \vdots & \vdots & & \ddots & \\ \mathbf{r}_{T1} & \mathbf{r}_{T2} & & & \mathbf{r}_{T,T-1} \end{bmatrix} \qquad (13)$$

The diagrammatic representation of R can take four basic forms, which are shown in Figures 1-4.

Figure 1 shows the first pattern where each curve represents the evolution of the IRR's relative to a firm whose evaluation is performed from a given period (the index of the curve) to each of the periods considered from 2 to T (reported along the horizontal axis).

Figure 1

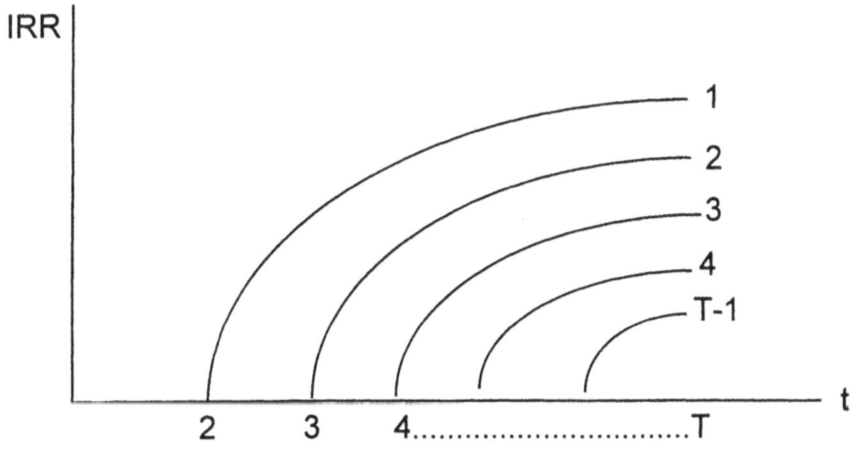

Each curve, thus, corresponds to a column of the matrix of expression (13), and describes how the IRR's relative to a particular starting period evolve as the duration of the firm activity becomes longer and longer.

In other words, Figure 1 shows a family of "yield curves" with the property that longer lived projects (or firms) yield higher returns than shorter ones. With the shape hypothesized in the figure, higher returns are associated both to projects that are started at the same period of time, but end up later (which are ordered along the curve), and to projects that are started earlier, but end up at the same period of time (these projects are ordered across the curves along vertical lines). Thus, if the curves are shaped as in Figure 1, both longer projects and older projects are favored, an indication that there is an established pattern of comparative advantage which is upheld through time.

Figure 2 shows an alternative pattern for the yield curves, where it is still true that longer projects are favoured over shorter ones, but newer projects now yield, for a given duration, higher rates of return. This pattern thus suggests not only that the existing pattern of comparative advantage can stand the test of time, but also that it is being strenghtened by the more recent projects and/or performances.

Figure 2

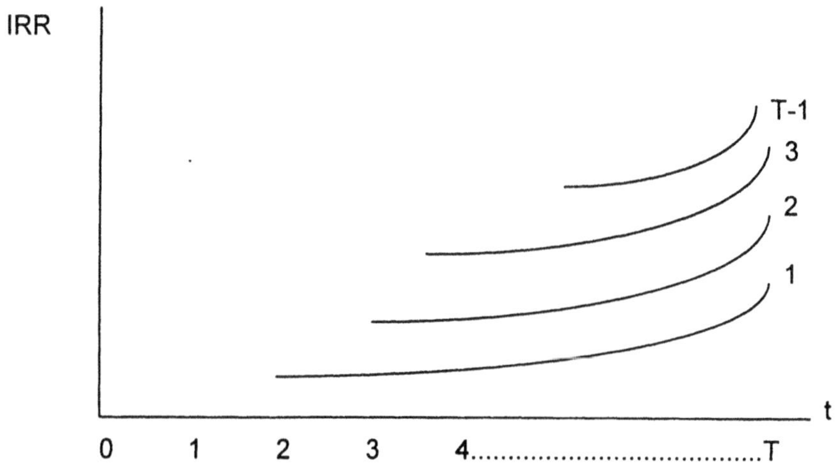

Figure 3

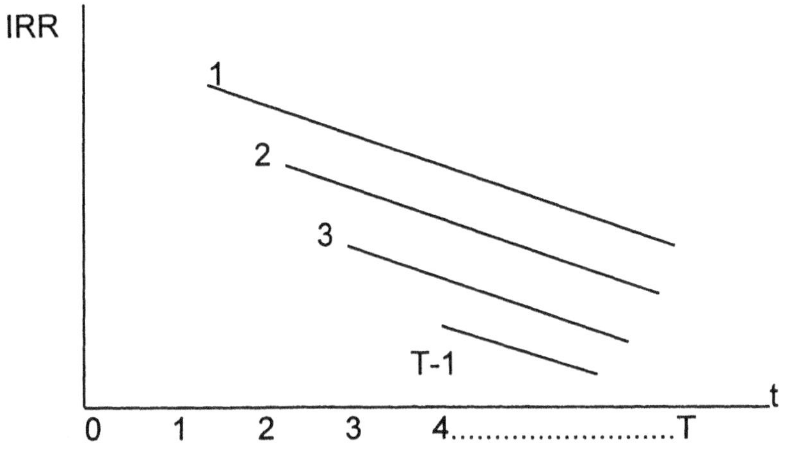

Figure 3 shows the case of a family of inverted yield curves. Here projects with longer duration are penalized with respect to shorter lived projects, while at the same time older projects yield higher returns than newer ones. The sectoral advantage appears to be eroded and declines with time both for a forward looking and a backward looking observer.

Figure 4

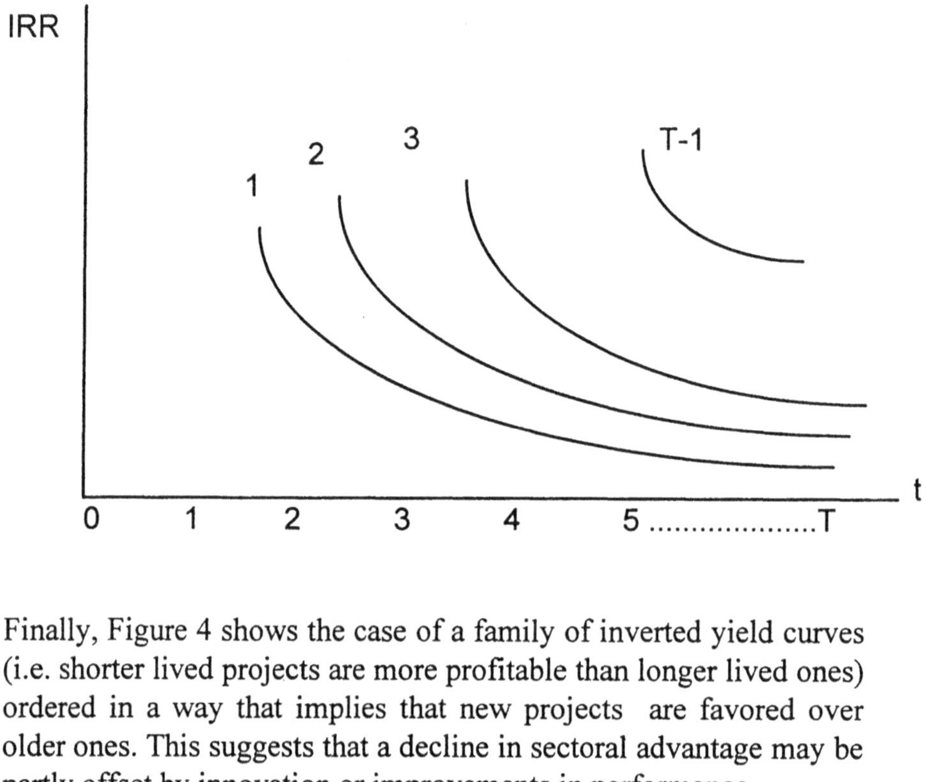

Finally, Figure 4 shows the case of a family of inverted yield curves (i.e. shorter lived projects are more profitable than longer lived ones) ordered in a way that implies that new projects are favored over older ones. This suggests that a decline in sectoral advantage may be partly offset by innovation or improvements in performance.

The four patterns described are by no means exhaustive. In particular "yield" curves need not be monotonic and non intersecting. In general, however, as I will show later, the cumulative nature of the DCF indexes will tend to converge to one of these basic patterns.

3. The Economic Performance

The discounted cash flow (DCF) analysis illustrated above has been applied to the aggregated accounts of the 1790 firms of the Mediobanca yearly panel from 1982 to 1990. Net present values have been estimated for the whole period 1982-1991, together with internal

rates of return both from the economic and the financial point of view.
Table 1 shows a first set of results for the whole sample of firms. These results point to a rather gloomy picture of the performance of Italian firms in the 80's. On one hand, in fact NPV's, which are computed using as discount rates the rates of return on Treasuries of similar maturity, are uniformly negative over the period considered. Moreover, the NPV values tend to fall in an accelerated way in the early years and keep falling, even though at a slower rate, in the more recent years. Economic rates of return, accordingly, are negative or, if positive, well below a reasonable opportunity cost for capital. Financial rates of return are always negative.

Table 1 Economic indicators of performance for the 1790 firms of the Mediobanca Panel

	NPV	IRR	REAL IRR	DIRR	ROI	AVERAGE INFLATION
1982-84	-16.160	11,22%	-2,78%	-8,01%	4,34%	14,00%
1982-85	-21.836	10,56%	-2,19%	-7,53%	4,84%	12,75%
1982-86	-23.957	10,48%	-0,92%	-6,47%	4,15%	11,40%
1982-87	-22.787	10,75%	0,42%	-5,16%	4,14%	10,33%
1982-88	-23.221	10,75%	1,18%	-4,49%	5,72%	9,57%
1982-89	-23.591	10,95%	1,83%	-3,97%	4,86%	9,13%
1982-90	-23.580	11,11%	2,34%	-3,52%	3,28%	8,78%
1982-91	-23.880	11,15%	2,65%	-3,20%	1,36%	8,50%

Note: brackets indicate negative values

What are the reasons for such a gloomy picture of the performance of the Italian firms in a period where, by all accounts, (see, for example, Savona, 1993), they were widely believed to fare better than their counterparts in many other countries?

As argued in the theoretical analysis above, the reasons why NPV's may turn out to be negative may reside in a performance of the firm, less positive than anticipated in its assets values at the beginning of the period. A negative NPV, therefore, does not necessarily mean that the firm has fared badly in absolute terms or in comparison to its competitors. Rather, it indicates a disproportion in value between its stocks and its flows. Such a disproportion may be only temporary, as for instance in the case of an investment whose productivity is not yet recognized in a sufficiently larger values of the assets or the cash flows, or it may be more persistent. In this latter case, the performance of the firm may be considered worrysome.

A negative NPV, on the other hand, may be caused by negative cash flows, at least in some of the years under consideration. In this case, the asset performance may be satisfactory, but the creation of wealth is hampered by the bottom line results of the firm's activity.

A negative cash flow, on the other hand, must eventually be recognized in a fall of the capital value of the firm, unless it is temporary because it is due either to transitory random shocks or to temporary resource committments to capital accumulation (i.e. real or financial investment).

Table 2 shows that in the case of the whole sample, the phenomenon of negative NPV's can be imputed to negative cash flows only for four out of the 10 years considered. For all other years, the main reason of the negative aggregate performance of the Italian firms appears to reside in the cited disproportion between assets, whose value did not increase sufficiently at the end of each period, and flows, which incorporated costly investments not sufficiently recognized in revenues and/or asset values.

If we consider a scale free indicator, such as the economic internal rate of return, the performance of the firms in the sample appears more encouraging.

The economic IRR (second column of Table 1), in particular, is basically constant at 11% per every year under consideration. Given the decreasing rate of inflation (last column of Table 1), this implies an increasing real rate of return. It is only because of the size of the return on Treasuries, therefore, that the results of firm activity may be judged negatively.

Table 2

1982-91 Whole panel: some characteristics of economic performance

	billion Lit.				yearly increments			
	Turnover	Cost of labour	Net investment	Cash flow	Turnover	Cost of labour	Net investment	Cash flow
1982	214.175	36.495	11.696	(3.339)				
1983	234.094	40.372	11.324	2.286	9,30%	10,62%	-3,18%	-168,46%
1984	264.578	43.113	13.629	1.326	13,02%	6,79%	20,35%	-41,99%
1985	292.927	47.297	15.220	5.501	10,71%	9,70%	11,67%	314,86%
1986	272.225	49.911	15.876	7.439	-7,07%	5,53%	4,31%	35,23%
1987	292.402	54.366	15.362	7.052	7,41%	8,93%	-3,24%	-5,20%
1988	322.172	59.136	19.651	5.329	10,18%	8,77%	27,92%	-24,43%
1989	360.193	64.900	25.057	(1.217)	11,80%	9,75%	27,51%	-122,84%
1990	380.121	69.305	25.263	(7.210)	5,53%	6,79%	0,82%	492,44%
1991	394.242	74.801	28.510	(1.513)	3,71%	7,93%	12,85%	-79,02%

As shown in the fourth column of Table 1, the difference between the rate of return of the firm and of a government bond of similar maturity over the same period of time, though always negative, decreases in absolute value.

For purposes of comparison, the Table shows also the series of ROI, the rate of return on investment, which corresponds to the internal rate of return over one year of operations, and is declining in the last four years.

Consider now the economic results as disaggregated in the two components: industry and services (Table 3) [3]. Even though the NPV is still always negative, the rates of return appear positive and healthy and exhibit a tendency to increase both in nominal and in real terms. Accordingly, the difference between the IRR and the risk-free rate on a government bond of similar maturity, though negative, is decreasing in absolute value and almost null for the whole period 1982-1991.

Table 3 Economic indicators of performance for industrial firms

	NPV	IRR	REAL IRR	DIRR	ROI	AVERAGE INFLATION
1982-84	(10.743)	11,97%	-2,03%	-7,26%	5,14%	14,00%
1982-85	(13.143)	11,80%	-0,95%	-6,29%	5,34%	12,75%
1982-86	(12.224)	12,25%	0,85%	-4,71%	4,52%	11,40%
1982-87	(9.167)	12,77%	2,44%	-3,13%	3,94%	10,33%
1982-88	(7.368)	12,95%	3,37%	-2,30%	6,52%	9,57%
1982-89	(5.257)	13,32%	4,19%	-1,61%	5,47%	9,13%
1982-90	(3.494)	13,50%	4,72%	-1,13%	3,08%	8,78%
1982-91	(3.021)	13,40%	4,90%	-0,95%	0,25%	8,50%

[3] The component "industry" includes firms in the energetic, mining and all manufacturing sectors, while under the denomination of services only three sectors are included: (i) retail trade, (ii) public services, highways and water and gas supply and, (iii) transportation services (see Mediobanca, 1981-1992).

In the years under consideration, therefore, the economic performance of industrial firms in Italy has been roughly matching the return of government bonds, and their performance appears to be improving over the period. The "catching up" with the government bonds, which is helped by the decline in inflation, appears to be gradual and continuous, and is completed only in the last year of the series.
The main reason for the time profile of this result, however, appears to be due to the negative real rate of return for the first two years of the investment in the firm. If we take the point of view of the option to buy rather than the option to sell as a measure of firm performance, i.e. we consider the last row of the matrix in (8) and of the corresponding matrices of IRR's, we obtain the results exposed in Table 4. These results indicate that, except for the period 1982-91, which shows a slight negative difference between the industry IRR and the government rate, the performance of industrial firms has always been positive. The "retrospective" IRR's in Table 4, corresponding to the returns accrued by excercising an option to buy the firm at a strike price variable with the beginning year of the series, are uniformly higher than the "perspective". IRR's in Table 3. This suggest that "new" firms have tended to perform better than "old" ones, and that short-lived projects may have been met with higher success than long term ones.

Table 4 Economic performance of industrial firms: Retrospective view

	NPV*	IRR	DIRR %	YIELD
1982-91	6,508	13,4	(0.70)	1,0
1983-91	4,826	14,34	0,89	6,4
1984-91	10,853	14,5	1,75	9,5
1985-91	19,475	15,52	3,38	13,5
1986-91	23,224	16,34	4,51	14,5
1987-91	18,116	16,14	4,34	10,4
1988-91	15,187	16,43	4,18	7,9
1989-91	8,999	13,52	2,66	4,3

* Billion lires

Consider now the performance of all firms producing services included in the sample. Table 5 shows that, seen from the perspective of the base year 1982, the economic results for this group have been dismal. Not only NPV's have been negative, but they have also been declining throughout the period, more markedly so if compared to inflation rates or rates of return on government bonds. These results are confirmed by the "retrospective" indicators in Table 6 that show, however, a difference with respect to the analysis of industrial firms.

Table 5 Economic indicators of performance of firms producing services

	NPV	IRR	REAL IRR	DIRR	ROI	AVERAGE INFLATION
1982-84	(5.416)	9,12%	-4,88%	-10,11%	2,32%	14,00%
1982-85	(8.691)	7,13%	-5,62%	-10,96%	3,56%	12,75%
1982-86	(11.730)	5,60%	-5,80%	-11,36%	3,18%	11,40%
1982-87	(13.617)	5,15%	-5,19%	-10,76%	4,68%	10,33%
1982-88	(15.851)	4,64%	-4,93%	-10,60%	3,58%	9,57%
1982-89	(18.331)	4,27%	-4,86%	-10,66%	3,21%	9,13%
1982-90	(20.676)	4,00%	-4,78%	-10,64%	3,83%	8,78%
1982-91	(22.199)	4,20%	-4,30%	-10,15%	4,36%	8,50%

For services-producing firms, in fact, it appears that the "retrospective" indicators are generally worse than the "perspective" ones, indicating a somewhat less dismal performance of older firms and/or projects.The aggregation of all firms producing services can be objected to because of their inherent heterogeneity with respect both to the nature of the products and the so called "mission" of the enterprise. In particular, the public nature of many services-producing firms appears to be a characteristic which has to be taken into account, given the public nature that both the product and the property may assume.

Table 6 Economic performance of firms producing services: Retrospective view

	NPV Billion lires	IRR	DIRR %	YIELD
1982-91	(22.035)	4,2	-9,9	(0.39)
1983-91	(29.663)	2,04	-11,41	(0.50)
1984-91	(25.818)	2,47	-10,28	(0.42)
1985-91	(22.705)	2,74	-9,4	(0.35)
1986-91	(20.950)	2,65	-9,18	(0.32)
1987-91	(18.870)	2,72	-9,08	(0.27)
1988-91	(16.977)	2,32	-9,93	(0.24)
1989-91	(16.291)	-0,21	-12,87	(0.21)

Tables 7, 8 and 9 report the results of the DCF analysis carried out respectively for three groups of services - producing firms: (i) retail shops, (ii) public services other than transportation and, (iii) transportation. The figures reported clearly show that it is not the public nature of the goods produced that is the main cause of the negative economic performance at market prices. In fact, the retail shops (Table 7), which are invariably private concerns, display the worse results, with a negative real return to capital only gradually improving over the longer term.
In comparison, the firms producing public services (Table 8), even though also characterized by a generally negative economic performance, show much higher rates of return and more substantial improvements over the longer term, where the real rate is approaching zero (-1.63%). The worse performance is offered by the transportation firms (Table 9), whose uniformly negative results show only a slight improvement and are well below those of all other groups in the sample.

Table 7 Economic indicators of performance for retail firms

	NPV	IRR	REAL IRR	DIRR	ROI	AVERAGE INFLATION
1982-84	(599)	-3,62%	-17,62%	-22,85%	0,41%	14,00%
1982-85	(768)	-2,56%	-15,31%	-20,66%	0,03%	12,75%
1982-86	(912)	-2,13%	-13,53%	-19,08%	-0,37%	11,40%
1982-87	(1.026)	-1,71%	-12,04%	-17,61%	-0,56%	10,33%
1982-88	(1.167)	-1,76%	-11,34%	-17,01%	-0,89%	9,57%
1982-89	(1.301)	-1,39%	-10,51%	-16,31%	-1,02%	9,13%
1982-90	(1.487)	-1,99%	-10,77%	-16,63%	-1,76%	8,78%
1982-91	(1.568)	-0,95%	-9,45%	-15,30%	-2,01%	8,50%

Table 8 Economic indicators of performance for public services

	NPV	IRR	REAL IRR	DIRR	ROI	AVERAGE INFLATION
1982-84	(2.921)	12,40%	-1,60%	-6,83%	3,61%	14,00%
1982-85	(5.545)	9,52%	-3,23%	-8,57%	3,85%	12,75%
1982-86	(7.892)	7,67%	-3,73%	-9,29%	3,94%	11,40%
1982-87	(9.167)	7,11%	-3,22%	-8,80%	4,27%	10,33%
1982-88	(10.790)	6,51%	-3,06%	-8,73%	4,36%	9,57%
1982-89	(12.570)	6,13%	-3,00%	-8,80%	4,41%	9,13%
1982-90	(13.558)	6,32%	-2,46%	-8,31%	4,55%	8,78%
1982-91	(13.796)	6,87%	-1,63%	-7,48%	4,68%	8,50%

Table 9 Economic indicators of performance for transportation firms

	NPV	IRR	REAL IRR	DIRR	ROI	AVERAGE INFLATION
1982-84	(1.895)	-9,71%	-23,71%	-28,94%	-15,29%	14,00%
1982-85	(2.373)	-6,89%	-19,64%	-24,98%	-13,85%	12,75%
1982-86	(2.918)	-6,91%	-18,31%	-23,87%	-13,12%	11,40%
1982-87	(3.419)	-7,38%	-17,71%	-23,29%	-12,84%	10,33%
1982-88	(3.886)	-7,47%	-17,04%	-22,71%	-12,88%	9,57%
1982-89	(4.443)	-8,41%	-17,54%	-23,34%	-13,01%	9,13%
1982-90	(5.015)	-9,24%	-18,02%	-23,87%	-13,28%	8,78%
1982-91	(5.469)	-9,03%	-17,53%	-23,38%	-13,39%	8,50%

4. The Financial Performance

4.1 "Before Tax" Results

In considering the results achieved by the firms under the broader profile of both the economic and the financial management of their resources, we have to distinguish between "before" and "after tax" performance. "Before tax" results point out the return to capital from the demand side, i.e. the willingness of entrepreneurs to pay for capital services. "After tax" results are instead supply data and show the incentive for capital owners to supply capital services to the production process. Taxation thus creates an externality, in the form of a wedge between prices of investors, who are willing to pay a higher value as they receive a larger benefit, and of savers, who are motivated by the tax to offer an amount of capital shorter than the equilibrium value.

"Before tax" results of economic and financial activities are also suggestive of what we can call the "full price" performance of the firm. Part of the financial activities of the firm are in fact a consequence of its ability to gain a financing margin through a positive difference between the timing of its monetary receipts and of its outlays. This ability may be the result of market power or of its capacity to play an intermediation role with its customers and/or suppliers. It can also be compounded by a good portfolio management of the firm's financial assets. On the other hand, a good financial performance may be the main result of investment opportunities in highly remunerative government bonds.

"After tax" results, on their part, in addition to all the factors accounted for in the "before tax" results, testify the relative advantage that the firm may have acquired in minimizing its tax outlays for any given level of profit. With regard to government bonds, in particular, a good "after tax" performance is often the consequence of a successfull disintermediation activity, whereby the firm borrows from the banks to finance the purchase of Treasuries, which for many years were tax-deductible (see Scandizzo, 1992).Tables 10 and 11 show the first set of results, concerning respectively the "before tax" yields and the differential rates of return. Both tables suggest that industrial firms and, within the service sector, retailers, have performed relatively well in the eighties. The perspective rates, however, are lower than the retrospective rates for the industrial firms, and suggest more profitable conditions for newer projects, while the opposite appears to be true for retail firms.

The negative yields and IRR's for Public Services and Transportation in Tables 10 and 11 for public enterprises can be interpreted as indicators of the degree of subsidy provided to them by allowing a return below the opportunity cost of capital. Such a degree of subsidy is based on a virtual transfer rather than on an actual one, since it measures the amount that would have been necessary to convince a private entrepreneur to stay in business in the sectors indicated. But even discounting to some extent the virtual nature of these transfers, they appear to be large, up to 15% for public services and to 47% for transportation. These two sectors, therefore, appear to be totally dependent on government subsidies both in the sense that they would produce little output without substantial public support and because, paradoxically, such a support has to be larger the larger are public debt and the related rates of interest.

Table 10 "Before tax" financial yields

Perspective (%)

	All firms	Industrial	Services	Retail	Public services	Transportation
1982-84	-1.4	2.2	1.6	2.3	1.1	-22.5
85	-1.5	1.9	-0.3	2.4	-1.8	-24.8
86	-0.7	0.2	-2.4	6.8	-4.5	-29.4
87	0.5	1.7	-3.6	7.2	-5.7	-33.6
88	1.1	2.8	-5.1	7.2	-7.3	-36.4
89	1.8	4.1	-6.3	6.1	-8.5	-40.3
90	2.4	4.9	-7.0	7.3	-8.6	-42.6
91	2.8	5.2	-7.0	5.9	-8.0	-43.7

Retrospective (%)

	All firms	Industrial	Services	Retail	Public services	Transportation
1982-91	2.8	5.2	-7.0	5.9	-8.0	-43.7
83-91	2.1	6.3	-13.6	7.8	-15.5	-46.7
84-91	3.3	7.3	-11.9	6.5	-13.2	-44.4
85-91	5.0	8.9	-9.9	6.4	-9.7	-38.0
86-91	4.7	8.5	-9.7	-0.3	-8.5	-38.8
87-91	5.2	9.1	-9.6	2.4	-6.5	-33.0
88-91	5.0	7.0	-3.5	1.9	-4.2	-30.0
89-91	2.7	4.0	-3.6	3.6	-3.0	-19.2

Table 11 "Before tax" differential rates of return

Perspective (%)

	All firms	Industrial	Services	Retail	Public services	Transportation
1982-84	-5.92	-8.70	6.16	7.21	2.09	-54.11
85	-4.87	-5.58	-1.90	5.15	-4.39	-38.1
86	-2.49	-1.53	-6.83	11.42	-7.76	-35.96
87	-0.40	1.29	-8.29	9.74	-8.41	-34.67
88	0.33	2.53	-10.02	8.57	-9.44	-32.12
89	1.13	3.66	-11.14	6.76	-10.14	-32.47
90	1.27	4.23	-11.54	7.55	-9.49	-31.96
91	2.05	4.37	-10.72	6.12	-8.24	-29.64

Retrospective (%)

	All firms	Industrial	Services	Retail	Public services	Transportation
1982-91	2.05	4.37	-10.72	6.12	-8.24	-29.64
83-91	1.28	5.41	-14.83	8.80	-12.01	-29.28
84-91	2.64	6.62	-13.83	6.95	-10.94	-28.71
85-91	5.34	9.67	-12.64	7.58	-9.13	-27.66
86-91	5.98	10.76	-13.33	-0.50	-8.81	-28.77
87-91	8.97	15.71	-14.91	4.06	-7.88	-29.01
88-91	11.03	14.68	-8.54	4.33	-6.73	-31.82
89-91	7.40	10.40	-10.08	11.27	-7.29	-31.45

Where was comparative advantage located during the years examined? Clearly, the supported sectors showing negative returns failed to attract non subsidized capital. But between industry and retail, the edge seems to be always for the latter. In the period 1982-86, in fact, industrial firms have low yields and negative differential rates of return, while retail firms show comparatively large returns by both

indicators. Between '86 and '91, however, industry improves its performance somewhat, but even though at declining rate, retail mantains a comparatively better record. It is only in the most recent years, contrary to what is generally believed, that industry seems to enjoy substantially higher returns.
From the investment demand point of view, it does not appear therefore that a de-industrialization pattern is reflected in the differences in return to capital, except perhaps for a few years and certainly not in the later years of the EMS and the overvalued exchange rate.

4.2 The "After Tax" Results

The competitive advantage of the firm can be seen, under the aspect of the "resource pull", from the point of view of the return after taxes to the capital invested by the shareholders (or by the owners when the limited liability condition does not hold). This point of view considers the financial performance of the firm as ultimately determining the incentive to retain the support of its owners, by remunerating adequately its capital and stock of entrepreneurship.

Table 12 Financial indicators of performance for the firms of the Mediobanca Panel ("after tax")

	YIELD	IRR	REAL IRR	DIRR	ROE	AVERAGE INFLATION
1982-84	(5.0)	2,15%	-11,85%	-17,08%	-6,47%	14,00%
1982-85	(6.1)	3,11%	-9,64%	-14,98%	-4,18%	12,75%
1982-86	(6.2)	4,87%	-6,53%	-12,08%	-2,44%	11,40%
1982-87	(5.6)	6,40%	-3,94%	-9,51%	-1,40%	10,33%
1982-88	(6.0)	6,40%	-3,17%	-8,84%	-0,54%	9,57%
1982-89	(6.1)	6,93%	-2,20%	-8,00%	0,38%	9,13%
1982-90	(5.8)	7,65%	-1,13%	-6,98%	0,78%	8,78%
1982-91	(5.6)	8,08%	-0,42%	-6,27%	0,75%	8,50%

As Table 12 shows, by and large, the performance of the sample of firms considered has been consistently negative for the capital owners, if compared with the "riskless" returns provided by government bonds over comparable periods of time or even simply to inflation rates.
While the "after tax" results have been slowly improving in the later years of the series, the data show clear evidence that high interest rates, high inflation and oppressive taxation have resulted in a particularly deadly combination for Italian firms.
Tables 13 and 14 show that the overall dismal performance is shared by industrial and services firms. Of these, the retail trade (Table 15) is only sector which has succeeded in duplicating the performance of government bonds and has not seen its capital eroded by inflation. The returns realized in this sector, however, have been declining in the more recent years, despite of the fact that its terms of trade have been improving because of the overvaluation of the currency (Milana and Scandizzo, 1991).
Because of their negative performance, public services and transportation firms have not been much affected by taxation, as a comparison of the data of Tables 16 and 17 with Tables 10 and 11 readily show. As before, the negative returns recorded for these sectors can be considered measures of the degree of support ensured by the taxpayers. Such a support appears to be somewhat decreasing, although the indicators are not unequivocal on this, in the later years.

Table 13 Financial indicators of performance for industrial firms ("after tax")

	YIELD	IRR	REAL IRR	DIRR	ROE	AVERAGE INFLATION
1982-84	(6,4)	2,15%	-11,85%	-20,89%	-6,97%	14,00%
1982-85	(7,1)	3,11%	-9,64%	-16,60%	-4,39%	12,75%
1982-86	(6,4)	4,87%	-6,53%	-11,97%	-2,40%	11,40%
1982-87	(5,3)	6,40%	-3,94%	-8,63%	-0,78%	10,33%
1982-88	(5,1)	6,40%	-3,17%	-7,49%	0,06%	9,57%
1982-89	(4,8)	6,93%	-2,20%	-6,31%	1,03%	9,13%
1982-90	(4,4)	7,65%	-1,13%	-5,27%	1,40%	8,78%
1982-91	(4,2)	8,08%	-0,42%	-4,76%	1,26%	8,50%

Table 14 Financial indicators of performance for services ("after tax")

	YIELD	IRR	REAL IRR	DIRR	ROE	AVERAGE INFLATION
1982-84	(0,4)	19,13%	5,13%	-0,10%	-4,04%	14,00%
1982-85	(2,6)	10,09%	-2,66%	-8,00%	-2,93%	12,75%
1982-86	(5,4)	4,36%	-7,04%	-12,60%	-2,27%	11,40%
1982-87	(7,0)	2,24%	-8,09%	-13,67%	-3,28%	10,33%
1982-88	(9,0)	0,13%	-9,44%	-15,11%	-2,43%	9,57%
1982-89	(10,6)	-1,19%	-10,32%	-16,12%	-1,89%	9,13%
1982-90	(11,7)	-1,90%	-10,68%	-16,54%	-1,41%	8,78%
1982-91	(11,9)	-1,29%	-9,79%	-15,64%	-0,98%	8,50%

Table 15 Financial indicators of performance for retail firms ("after tax")

	YIELD	IRR	REAL IRR	DIRR	ROE	AVERAGE INFLATION
1982-84	(0,4)	16,59%	2,59%	-2,64%	13,47%	14,00%
1982-85	(1,1)	14,03%	1,28%	-4,06%	14,07%	12,75%
1982-86	1,9	18,89%	7,49%	1,93%	13,43%	11,40%
1982-87	1,8	16,69%	6,35%	0,78%	13,08%	10,33%
1982-88	1,3	15,23%	5,66%	-0,01%	12,16%	9,57%
1982-89	(0,2)	13,15%	4,03%	-1,77%	11,92%	9,13%
1982-90	0,7	14,12%	5,34%	-0,52%	11,76%	8,78%
1982-91	0,9	12,27%	3,77%	-2,08%	12,04%	8,50%

Table 16 Financial indicators of performance for public services ("after tax")

	YIELD	IRR	REAL IRR	DIRR	ROE	AVERAGE INFLATION
1982-84	(0,2)	17,41%	3,41%	-1,82%	1,92%	14,00%
1982-85	(3,7)	9,74%	-3,01%	-8,35%	2,16%	12,75%
1982-86	(6,6)	5,48%	-5,92%	-11,48%	2,23%	11,40%
1982-87	(8,1)	3,94%	-6,40%	-11,97%	2,56%	10,33%
1982-88	(9,9)	2,26%	-7,31%	-12,98%	2,87%	9,57%
1982-89	(11,5)	1,32%	-7,81%	-13,61%	3,09%	9,13%
1982-90	(11,4)	1,76%	-7,02%	-12,88%	3,25%	8,78%
1982-91	(11,3)	2,77%	-5,73%	-11,58%	3,39%	8,50%

Table 17 Financial indicators of performance for transportation firms ("after tax")

	YIELD	IRR	REAL IRR	DIRR	ROE	AVERAGE INFLATION
1982-84	(23,6)	-37,62%	-51,62%	-56,85%	-40,37%	14,00%
1982-85	(26,6)	-23,22%	-35,97%	-41,31%	-35,98%	12,75%
1982-86	(31,6)	-22,16%	-33,56%	-39,11%	-32,62%	11,40%
1982-87	(38,0)	-21,56%	-31,89%	-37,47%	-30,13%	10,33%
1982-88	(39,0)	-19,41%	-28,98%	-34,65%	-27,89%	9,57%
1982-89	(43,0)	-19,64%	-28,77%	-34,57%	-26,90%	9,13%
1982-90	(45,3)	-19,21%	-27,99%	-33,85%	-25,78%	8,78%
1982-91	(46,5)	-17,00%	-25,50%	-31,35%	-24,86%	8,50%

5. Some Conclusions

The performance of firms producing industrial goods and services can be analyzed from the comparative advantage point of view, or from the point of view of the greater or lower benefit assured by their ability to compete in financing, tax-avoidance and securing government support.

The comparative advantage perspective considers gross returns to investment the main measure of market success, regardless of their distribution among creditors and share holders. On this base, industry and public services both fared reasonably well in Italy during the past 10 years, showing a comparatively positive performance vis a vis all other subsectors of the economy and in particular retail trade and transportation.

Between industry and public services, however, the performance of industry is certainly superior and improving over time.

The data considered appear to provide clear evidence, in other words, of the fact that industrial growth has been more desirable than growth in all types of services, including public ones.

Because the higher economic returns of industrial firms may be the result of a shrinking sector, it is important to look at financial returns both "before" and "after taxes" to see whether their potential advantage has translated itself into an adequate "resource pull" both on the side of investment demand and capital supply.

"Before tax" returns displayed by the firms in the panel according to a variety of indicators again show a positive performance of industrial firms. Retail firms, however, appear to hold the hedge in this respect, with much better results both in the shorter and in the longer run. Even though their capacity to obtain high returns has somewhat declined in recent years, one should thus expect that the retail sector has expanded beyond what would have been desirable on the basis of its "ex ante" economic advantage.

"After tax" returns dramatize this conclusion in that only retail trade emerges as a sector with positive returns, once taxation is taken into account. The combination of debt and tax financing has thus condemned most of the Italian economy to operate in a substantially subsidized regime.

Retail firms appear to have been the only sizable group which has been able to escape from this situation, but there are signs that they may also be forced to succumb soon.

References

Baumol W.J., (1967), "Macroeconomics of Unbalanced Growth: The Anatomy of Urban Crisis", *American Economic Review*, no. 57, 415-426.

Baumol W.J., Batey Blackman S.A. and Wolff E.N., (1985), "Unbalanced Growth Revisited: Asymptotic Stagnancy and New Evidence", *American Economic Review*, no. 75, 806-817.

Chenery H.B., (1960), "Patterns of Industrial Growth", *American Economic Review*, 50 (3).

Chenery H.B. and Syrquin M., (1975), *Patterns of Development 1950-70*, Oxford University Press, London.

Chenery H.B., (1979), *Structural Change and Development Policy*, Oxford University Press, London.

Clark C.G., (1940), *Condition of Economic Progress*, MacMillan, London, revised ed. 1957.

Kuznets S., (1971), *Economic Growth of Nations: Total Output and Production Structure*, The Belknap Press of Harvard University Press, Cambridge, Mass.

Mediobanca, (1981-1992), *Dati Cumulativi di 1790 Società Italiane.*

Milana C. and Scandizzo P.L., (1991), "Settori Esposti e non Esposti e Politica dei Redditi in Italia", *Economia e Lavòro*, no.3, 19-37.

Milana C. and Scandizzo P.L., (1991), " Il Prezzo del Petrolio e i Suoi Effetti in Italia: Un'Analisi di Equilibrio Economico Generale", *Rassegna Economica*, no.2, 209-260.

Pera A. and Scandizzo P.L., (1988), "La Valutazione della Performance delle Imprese Pubbliche", *Rivista Internazionale di Scienze Sociali*, 1, 84-107.

Petit P., (1986), "Full Employment Policies in Stagnation: France in the 1980s", *Cambridge Journal of Economics*, 10 (4), 393-406.

Rostow W.W., (1960), *The Stages of Economic Growth*, Cambridge University Press, Cambridge.

Savona P., (1993), "Riflessioni sulla Ripresa Economica degli Anni Ottanta e sulle Prospettive per gli Anni Novanta", *Sviluppo Economico*, no. 1, 29-58.

Scandizzo P.L., (1989), "Measures of Industrial Protectionism: Relevance for Trade and Labour Policies", *Labour* 3, no.3, 129-167.

Scandizzo P.L., (1992), *Il "Sistema Italia" e le Banche Locali*, Banca Popolare di Belpasso, Belpasso (Catania).

Scandizzo P.L. and Quaglione D., (1992), *Le Imprese Italiane negli Anni 80: Performance, Fattori di Successo e Trasferimento delle Tecnologie e delle Innovazioni*, University of Rome "Tor Vergata" and Institute of Studies for Economic Planning (ISPE), Rome.

10

The Productivity Differential Between Manufacturing and Services in Italy: Technical Progress or Competition Deficit?

Guido Pellegrini
Bank of Italy

1. Introduction*

The gap in the labour productivity growth of services in the last two decades was in Europe positive (excluding Germany), ranging around the two per cent per year (Table 1). In the same period, the productivity differential was more than double in Italy. This was not only due to the very rapid growth of the per capita product in the manufacturing sector, but also to the slower than average productivity dynamics in the service firms.

This empirical evidence is at the basis of the recent debate in Italy on the sources of the productivity gap between manufacturing and services: the difference is not imputed only to the factors that explain the existence of a gap in almost all the countries (as the difference in the sectorial technological development), but other sources linked to the structure of the products and the markets are often proposed.

*Some paragraphs of this paper were written while I was visiting the University College of London, Department of Economics. A similar study was carried out on a panel of English firms (Pellegrini, 1993b). Any view expressed and all errors are mine.

Table 1 Per capita value added growth per year (at market price): 1970 - 1989 (percent changes)

Country	Manufacturing	Services
Belgium	5.5	1.5
West Germany	2.4	2.8
France	3.1	2.3
Italy	4.5	1.0
Netherlands	3.8	1.7
United Kingdom	3.3	1.7

Source: Eurostat (1992).

The "technological" explanation of the productivity gap origins from the seminal paper of Baumol (1967), recently extended and reformulated by Inman (1985)[1] . According to Baumol, the gap has to be attributed to the different technological structure, that affects the introduction of technological innovations, and therefore the total factor productivity (TFP) and the labour productivity in the two sectors. One reason is that the introduction of technological improvements is often incorporated in the capital equipment, higher in manufacturing. Another reason is that, in some service sectors, the substitution between labour and capital is very low. The empirical estimates of TFP in Italy and in other industrialized countries are in line with this hypothesis: the gap in TFP growth in manufacturing and services is close to the gap in labour productivity, and only a small portion of the difference can be attributed to the different growth of the production factors in the two sectors[2]. The strong heterogeneity inside services is reflected on the Baumol gap by sector: in some branches, like communications, some transportation services, some business services, the growth rate of TFP has been faster than in the manufacturing ones.

In Italy, the debate has been focused on two explanations that, even though not in contrast with the Baumol hypothesis, either criticize its viability, if the national account data are used, or support new

[1]See also Baumol, Blackman and Wolff (1985).

[2] See Pellegrini (1993a) for the estimates of TFP in Italy and a brief survey of some empirical analysis in other countries.

integration, taking into account the institutional characteristics of some service markets.

A heterogeneous group of studies have argued that the estimates of service productivity growth are not very reliable, because of the strong measurement problems of the services output[3]. The problems derive from the fact that it is often not clear *what* it has to be measured (for instance, in medical care services or in some personal services). Output in service sector is in general immaterial and multidimensional, changing with respect to several qualitative attributes. A typical example is transportation: the output is not only the changing in the space position of a good or a person, but also the attributes like the punctualness, the comfortableness, the timetable etc. Usually, multidimensional outputs are presented also in manufacturing, but these are by large referred to a basket of physical attributes. In this case, the techniques used in the national account allow to derive some measure of output quantity. The same cannot be said for the qualitative attributes, that often are not measured at all.

The problem is usually overcome by measuring the product at current prices by the firm total revenues or sales or receipts[4]. The different product characteristics are aggregated by an implicit price system that reflects the consumer preferences. Actually, the measurement problem is only shifted on the estimation of the service deflator. The output at constant price is properly determinated only if the price index used for deflationing the revenues takes into account the multidimensional output characteristics and the quality variety. The estimate of the appropriate index in services is also very complex because the markets are strongly differentiated, by location and by product. These evidences lead some authors to conclude that not only the output and the productivity in service sectors are probably underestimated, but also the same notion of "product" for the service sector is so evanescent that some doubts are risen on the

[3] See Fuà (1993) and Alvaro and Erba (1993).

[4] In some sectors (banking, insurance, trade) the service has not an explicit price, but it is estimated as a margin over the product prices. In this case the services are estimated by an "imputation" procedure.

inclusion of the services output in the estimate of the national product.

This conclusion appears, in my view, too pessimistic. I do not minimize the measurement problems in the service sector, but I note that the difference with the same problems in the manufacturing sector cannot be imputed to the concept of product that is used in both branches[5]. Therefore, the problem depends on the empirical ability to collect information on the multidimensional quality variability of the service products. Moreover, this problem can affect directly the level of the service productivity, but only marginally the dynamics. The reason lies in the plausible positive correlation, in some service sectors, between identifiable and unidentifiable output characteristics. The idea is that improvements in the managerial and productive efficiency are associated to improvements in the quality of the service. therefore, if the relation between "intensive" and "extensive" improvements is fairly constant, the dynamics of 'extensive' productivity is a good proxy of the "qualitative" one.

The main limit of this view, that imputed the productivity differential to a underestimation of service output, is that it cannot explain the divergence of Italy from the other European countries. This difference cannot be attributed to the different data collection and estimation techniques, because Italy uses the SEC methodology.

A recent group of studies has instead proposed another hypothesis, that is not alternative but complementary to the Baumol model, in order to interpret the italian case[6]. The theoretical foundations lie in the analysis of the factors relating to the organization of production, and their links with the TFP growth[7]. The production rules and the management structure affect the effort of worker and management, and so the TPF, if the quantity of labour is measured in hours and not in "effort" unity. One factor that affects the "effort" is the product market structure. Monopoly power generates some rents, that can be partially captured by managers and workers in the form of reduced effort. In this cases, changes in competition can be

[5] See also Solow (1993).

[6] See Barca and Visco (1993), CER (1992), Pellegrini (1993a).

[7] For a general overview of the problem see Nickel, Wadhwani and Wall (1992) and Pellegrini (1993b).

translated in changes in the level of TFP. Other factors affecting the effort of workers and managers are the degree of union power, that can influence the distribution of the rent and the level of work effort, and the presence of financial distress, that increases the probabilities of bankruptcy and therefore presses managers and worker for posing more effort on the job.

The productivity gap in this view comes from the different structure of service market. Actually, the service sectors in Italy are characterized by a competition deficit with respect to the manufacturing sectors and also to the service ones in other European countries. The different degree of competition can be attributed to the presence of barriers to entry and to growth, especially due to regulation, and to the existence of public monopolies in some markets[8]. For instance, in Pellegrini (1990) the effects of regulation in retail sectors, that is in Italy very strict, on the market structure are described: per capita value added at constant price in the retail sector has grown in Italy at 0,4 per cent per year, 1,5 points less than in France and Germany, almost 3 points less than in U.K.

The impact of a reduction in competition on the productivity can be static and dynamic: it is static, because it reduces the incentives to an optimal use of the production factors. For instance, in the previous framework, the monopolistic rent is captured by the manager by means of a reduction in the effort of optimization of the production process, because the same effort is costly; it is dynamic, because it reduces the need for innovation. These effects can explain the productivity gap in the long run, but the low degree of competition can affect also the productivity growth in the short run. For instance, legal constraints to the growth, as in the retail sector in Italy, have reduced the competition between big and small firms, helping the small shops, and therefore have limited the exploitation of scale economies and the speed of the transition to a more efficient and productive system.

Also other theories on the cyclical behavior of the productivity differential between manufacturing and service sectors are more coherent if the presence of a competition deficit is presumed. An

[8] The characteristics of service market are described in Sapir (1990).

example are the theories that explain the productivity slowdown in the eighties as an effect of the robust expansion of the demand that, in presence of supply constraints, has allowed the staying on the market of the small inefficient firms[9]. These theories are better founded if they assume the presence of local monopolistic markets, that imply that the exploitation of scale economies is more costly and less profitable for the more efficient firms. Similar consideration can be applied also to the theories of services as "sponge sectors"[10].
The empirical validation of the different hypotheses is usually based on macro data. Actually, these seems to me unable to discriminate between the technical progress and competition deficit explanations, because: (i) the presence of a competition deficit must be analyzed at a very detailed level, being the service market strongly differentiated in the space and for the kind of output; (ii) the macro data often hide market composition effects.
These effects are very relevant in dualistic markets, where the dualistic structure is generated by the regulatory framework. Moreover the variability of per capita value added in service sector is usually larger than in manufacturing, because the service production structures are more flexible in the use of production factors, more affected by the condition in the local market, being the service output not transportable, more influenced by specific shock, being the services not storable. Therefore the aggregate analysis, being founded on averages, is less reliable. A more effective analysis requires a careful recognition of the factors that can affect the firm behavior at the sector or firm level. Therefore, the study should use firm data, with information on the degree of competition in the output and factors markets.
Moreover, the data should be organized in a panel, where each company is sampled for more years, and therefore it is possible to take into account firm fixed effects.

[9] See ISTAT (1993).

[10] See Pellegrini (1993a) for details.

TFP estimates at micro level have been recently carried on British firms, but they were mainly limited to the manufacturing sectors[11]. In these papers, the TFP dynamics has been related to market structure, unionization and financial position of the firms[12]. Actually, it is quite surprising that the productivity gap between manufacturing and services at firm levels has received so little attention in literature.

The aim of this paper is to analyze the TFP differential between manufacturing and service sectors, taking into account the disparities in the product market structure and in the financial and sectorial characteristics of production. The reason of the productivity differential is not explicitly investigated: the hypothesis is that the differential, after controlling for the factors that can affect the TFP growth, should be attributed residually to technical progress. The study breaks new ground by testing the presence of the TFP differential using a micro production function estimated on firm data. The analysis is carried on a panel of 3801 Italian companies in three manufacturing sectors (machinery, textiles and food) and three service sector (wholesale trade, retail trade, hotels and restaurants) for the period 1982-1990. The rest of the paper is as follows. Section 2 describes the data used in the panel, section 3 outlines the model used in the micro econometric analysis. Empirical results are presented in section 4, and the final section offers some concluding remarks.

2. The Data

The data panel consists of a set of information on 3801 Italian companies, that is derived from four different sources: (i) the database of company accounts, collected and standardized by

[11] Recent analysis are in Gregg, Machin and Metcalf (1992) and Nickell, Wadhwani and Wall (1992). See also Pellegrini (1993b) for a comparative analysis of the productivity gap among British manufacturing and service firms. Some cross-section estimates of service productivity on Dutch data are in Carree and Thurik (1991), van Dalen and Thurik (1991),

[12] See Gregg, Machin and Metcalf (1992). For some analysis on the productivity effects of competition and unionization see also Brown and Wadhwani (1990), Nickell, Wadhwani and Wall (1992) and Oulton (1990).

Centrale dei Bilanci, from which can be drawn firm-level variables (inputs and output) at current prices; (ii) the more disaggregated database of company accounts for a "close sample" of firms, collected also by Centrale dei Bilanci, from which are derived information on capital composition between machinery and constructions; (iii) the national accounts by sector, with information on output and capital deflators, and the share of independent workers; (iv) surveys on manufacturing firms, that have information on the rate of capital utilization (by ISCO) and on the overtime hours worked (by ISTAT).

The firms were sampled (from the 36000 that are on average in the database of Centrale dei Bilanci) according to two criteria: (i) a set of tests for excluding errors or extreme values. Therefore were chosen firms with more than 4 workers, with a complete balance-sheet in every year, not affected by mergers or acquisitions; (ii) the continuous presence of the firm (9 observations) from 1982 to 1990. The selection criteria can introduce some selectivity bias in the sample, if the average firm life is affected by some endogenous variables that are not uniformly distributed in the sample. As it is usual in panel data analysis, the lack of larger information set prevents us from further investigations. The build-up of a data panel based on the firm balance-sheet presents other different problems: (i) the sample is not very representative of the universe. Moreover, the firms are sampled in the Centrale dei Bilanci dataset if they have multiple relations with the banking system. Therefore, if there is a positive correlation between this characteristic and the efficiency of the company, our sample selects the firms that are more efficient. The effect is probably more important for the small firms, and can lead to the presence, in the sample, of a spurious negative correlation between dimension and productivity, that blurred the analysis of the scale economies; (ii) the transformation of balance-sheet data in economic variables. The problem is more complex for the capital evaluation, that in the balance-sheet depends on accounts criteria and not on economic ones; (iii) the absence of information on output prices and hours worked, that requires the matching with the national account data. The panel that we derived is a balanced one.

The sectorial composition of the 3801 sampled companies is the following: 1869 (49 per cent of the total sample) operate in services, the residual 1932 in manufacturing. In services, 546 firms (14.5 per cent) are in retail trade, 1316 (34.6 per cent) in wholesale trade, and 7 (0.2 per cent) in lodging and catering. Given the high number of firms in the wholesale trade, the sector is separated in two sub-sectors: wholesale trade of intermediate products (656 firms, 17.3 per cent), and wholesale trade of final products (660 firms, 17.4 per cent). The lodging and catering sector has an insufficient number of firms for econometric analysis, that therefore is not applied. In manufacturing, the firms are 823 (21.7 per cent) in machinery, 734 (19.3) in textile and 375 (9.9) in food sector. The sectors have been chosen by two criteria: a sufficient number of firms in all period for service sectors; for manufacturing, a productive structure spreads out on the territory, and a dimensional and technical variability comparable with the service sectors.

The use of balance-sheet for the evaluation of inputs and output leads to imperfections and measurement errors, that are less relevant if the first differences of the data are utilized. Output is measured by value added, because we want to estimate a production function with only labour and capital as productive factors. The estimated of value added that can be derived from account data is imperfect: the value added proxy (deflated sum of profit and wage bill) is affected by the accounting convention in profit evaluation (capital gain is included etc.). From the other side, other alternative measures of output, like deflated sale, are less correlated with the factor utilization. Employment is measured by "heads", because we do not have information on hours at firm levels. A better proxy of labour input can be derived, for manufacturing, by using the index of overtime hours worked at sectoral level, derived from the survey in the big firms. For service sectors, the same problem needs of a different solution, because the higher flexibility in the service labour market implies that demand shocks are accommodated by using the "intensive" and "extensive" margin. In order to capture these effects on the human capital composition, we have used the ratio of independent worker on the total employment by sector, that can be founded in the national accounts. Note that the overtime index and the share of independent workers are both positively correlated with the sectorial business cycle. A similar correlation is with profits, that will be used as "instrument" in the econometric analysis. Capital is measured by total tangible assets. We deflated with separated indexes the share of machinery and the share of construction, derived by using sectoral information coming from the "close sample".The financial structure of the firm is captured by the liquidity ratio (ratio between current assets and liabilities).

The sectorial distribution of the variables constructed as rough indicator of market competition is quite interesting. The first indicator is related to the share of export on sales. In the 1990, this share is null in the retail trade and lodging and catering, it is around 3 per cent in the wholesale trade, 5 per cent in the food sector, 23 per cent in the machinery and 17 per cent in the textile industry. Another indicator, based on the total sample of firms in the Centrale dei Bilanci database, is related to the share on the total sales of firms with less than 500 worker, by sector and region. This share should capture the degree of concentration at the regional level, and it is a measure of the competitive environment. The indicator is around 95 per cent in the wholesale trade sector, around 85 per cent in retail trade, from 85 to 76 per cent in manufacturing. The empirical presence of a productivity gap in the sample is confirmed in Table 2.

Table 2 Output, employment and labour productivity growth in the sample: 1982 -1990 (annual average) (*)

Sector	y	l	y - l
Retail trade	2.7	1.8	0.9
Wholesale trade (final goods)	3.9	2.0	1.9
Wholesale trade (intermediate goods)	2.4	1.2	1.2
Lodging and catering	3.9	6.3	-2.4
Machinery	3.3	-0.3	3.6
Textile	1.8	-1.1	2.9
Food	5.3	1.3	4.0

(*) y = real value added at 1985 prices.
l = employment.

The interesting result is that the gap between manufacturing and services is confirmed also at firm level, even if there are several reasons why the sample data can differ from the national accounts (for instance, lack in firm coverage, selectivity bias, measurement errors etc.). However, similarities in labour productivity growth suggest that the micro analysis can throw some light also on aggregate productivity behavior.

3. The Model

The model applied in this paper is based on the augmented production function. The productivity growth is residually determined after the estimation of a (Cobb-Douglas) production function, with labour and capital as productive factors but that takes into account also aggregate and firms fixed effects. The residual is considered as a function of "effort" of workers and managers, and therefore conditioned to product market and financial structure variables[13]. This framework allows a common treatment of different explanation of productivity growth, even if the introduction of non standard variables in the production function is quite *ad hoc* (König,1992).

The theoretical framework is close to the model presented in Pellegrini (1993b), that has partially modified the model proposed by Gregg, Machin and Metcalf (1992). For firm i at time t, the augmented Cobb-Douglas function is:

$$y_{it} = \alpha_i UFE_i + \alpha_t AGG_t + \beta k_{it} + \gamma l_{it} + \pi MIS_{it} + TFP_i \qquad (1)$$

where y is the log of real value added, k and l are capital and labour inputs (also in log), MIS are variables related to factor measurement, AGG is an aggregate cycle with common effects to all firms, and UFE captures all not observable firm-specific effects, that are constant in time.

TFP is the level of total factor productivity, that can be attributed to four factors: (i) change in "effort", captured by the variables

[13] See Nickell, Wadhwani and Wall (1992).

reflecting effects arising from the firm product market, from the competitive environment and from financial structure; (ii) technological progress, different for each sector, and described by a deterministic time trend; (iii) the structure of local product and market factors also approximated by a deterministic trend; (iv) firm idiosyncratic error term (u), that mainly incorporates measurement errors in factor variables and factor intensity shocks. The restriction on constant return of scale is not imposed to the model.

The firm fixed effects are eliminated from (1) by differencing the variables, that it is possible because we have not a simple cross section but a panel data. The direct estimation of labour productivity is given by the following equations:

$$\Delta(y_{it} - l_{it}) = \beta\Delta(k_{it} - l_{it}) + \gamma\Delta l_{it} + \pi\Delta MIS_{it} + \theta S_i + \psi TER_i + \phi\Delta COMP_{it} + \Delta u_{it} \quad (2)$$

where S is a sectorial *dummy* variable, TER a dummy variable by region and dimension, COMP a set of variables related to competition and other factors that can affect productivity. The model is basically static. A simple dynamic adjustment of factors and product can be inserted in the model by using as explicative variables the lagged (one period) values of output and factor inputs[14]. Finally, the estimated model is the following:

$$\Delta(y_{it} - l_{it}) = \lambda\Delta(y_{i,t-1} - l_{i,t-1}) + \beta_1\Delta(k_{it} - l_{it}) + \beta_2\Delta(k_{i,t-1} - l_{i,t-1}) + \gamma_1\Delta l_{it} + \gamma_2\Delta l_{i,t-1} + \pi\Delta MIS_{it} + \theta S_i + \psi TER_i + \phi\Delta COMP_{it} + \Delta u_{it} \quad (3)$$

In equation (3) the production factors are endogenous, because shocks to TFP can affect not only the level of output but also factor intensity. Moreover, the presence of a MA(1) error term (if u is a white noise) implies that also one-period lagged values of output,

[14] Nickell, Wadhwani and Wall (1992) demonstrate that this partial adjustment dynamics can be derived from a simple inventory determination model.

capital and labor are endogenous. In this case, estimation of (3) by OLS yields biased estimates of lagged dependent variables coefficient. A unbiased estimation technique is, in this case, the instrumental variables estimator, where valid instruments, under the hypothesis of absence of serial correlation in the error term, are not only the exogenous variable but also the endogenous variables lagged two periods and beyond. In the paper we adopt a 2-stage LQ estimator, using as instruments, apart from the exogenous variables, the per capita profit and the endogenous variables lagged two and three periods.

4. The Results

The estimation strategy of model (3) has been twofold: in the first place, the model has been estimated over the complete sample, under the hypothesis that the sectorial effect can influence only the constant, i.e. the estimation of TFP growth; secondly, the estimation has considered only the sectorial sub-sample, allowing the change of all coefficients by sector. In both cases, the econometric results are not very satisfactory. The labour productivity variance that is explained by the model is around 3 per cent, that is quite a low value also for cross-section analysis. There are several reasons for that: first of all, the labour productivity is affected by a relevant set of local and firm specific factors (for instance, presence and strength of the unions, human capital quality, the proximity of common infrastructure etc.) for which we have no information and are badly captured by regional dummies. The limited number of information can reflect also on the instrument choice. The low fit of the model can depend also by the measurement problems coming from the use of balance-sheet information. Another problem that affects both aggregate and sectorial estimates is the evaluation of scale economies. Previously we noted the plausible presence of a selection bias, because the sample criteria selects the more efficient firms, lower is the firm dimension. This effect can explain the decreasing return of scale that appear in the estimated model, also in the sub-samples. The problem can be amplified by the limited number of years of the sample, that affected the dynamic specification of the model.

The result of the econometric estimation of the model for the overall sample are set out in Table 3. Even if in presence of the previous problems, the coefficients are statistically significant, and their signs are correct. The residuals show a negative serial correlation, in line with the hypothesis of a white noise error in the productivity level.

The returns of scale are, in the long run and in the aggregate specification, negative and significant: the sum of long run coefficient for labour and capital is 0.77. However, the dimension coefficients show some positive effects. Strongly significant are also the effects of cyclical shock common to all sectors, that plausibly include also the effects of the business cycle on the measurement of productive factors. Among the variables related to the factor measurements, only the overtime hours worked are significant and correctly signed.

The most interesting aspect of empirical analysis is probably the estimation of technological and competition on sectorial TFP dynamics. The coefficient of the sectorial technological trend is positive and very similar in the manufacturing sector, close to zero in service sectors. From the other side, these coefficients are not significant at 95 per cent. Therefore, even if the results suggest a technical positive differential for the manufacturing sectors, the per capita output variability is so high that a more statistically consistent evaluation will require more information and a higher sectorial disaggregation. The impact of the other variables is clearer. The inverse relation between per capita output dynamics and degree of liquidity of the firm. This supports the idea that when there are some trouble for the firms, managers and workers give more effort, with a positive effect on firm efficiency, even if it is not possible exclude the presence of "window dressing" of firm accounts. The relation between concentration processes at regional level and productivity is negative and significant: in absence of economies of scale, when there is an increase in the share of larger firm sells, could be also an increase in the monopolistic rent, that can be transferred in a net reduction of the firm efficiency. The impact of the share of exports on sales is positive and significant, and therefore these variables can be considered a good proxy of the market exposition to foreign firms' competition. The effect of the fluctuation of this share in instead negative, probably capturing some cyclical effect: in presence of a steady demand growth, the firms concentrate the sales in the domestic market, where stronger is their competitive vantage and larger, usually, the share of their sales.

The results of sectorial estimation, that are not reported here for sake of brevity, are more ambiguous, because they are affected also by the reduction in the degree of freedom. The impact of liquidity ratio is significant for all manufacturing sectors, but only in the wholesale trade of intermediate inputs for the service sectors. The proxy of competitive environment is not significant in all sectors, and in some cases the sign is reversed.

The analysis on the econometric results is not easy, because there are measurement, estimation and interpretation problems for the coefficients and the variables of the model. The results show the large variability of the productivity dynamics at firm level that cannot be clearly captured by the quite simple model that we have used. The econometric framework we have implemented can only suggest same preliminary inferences drawn from our panel data. The effects of technical progress seems in line with the Baumol model, even if the related parameters are not statistically significant. The effects of competition are more consistent, especially in the manufacturing sectors. The results give some support to the idea that the Baumol model can only partially interpret the productivity differential. From the other side, the empirical analysis does not explain why the service firms are less reactive to changes in the competitive environment. Some considerations about that will be presented in the next section of the paper.

Table 3 Two stages least squares. Parameter estimates

Variable	Parameter Estimate	T-Statistic
INTERCEP	-0.428008	-0.351
V86	0.034798	3.403
V87	0.041061	3.207
V88	0.049817	3.329
V89	0.027374	2.535
L1VG	0.291533	8.671
D1LK	0.465855	2.574
D1OC	-0.825091	-0.673
L1LK	-0.363991	-2.514
L1OC	0.380930	4.087
S1	-0.006967	-0.717
S2	0.002792	0.316
S3	0.214733	0.936
S4	0.631327	0.636
S5	0.619062	0.625
S6	0.619434	0.616
R1	-0.001851	-0.096
R3	-0.003738	-0.209
R4	0.004407	0.172
R5	0.015070	0.506
R6	-0.003636	-0.188
R7	-0.002403	-0.102
R8	-0.004743	-0.253
R9	-0.007960	-0.414
R10	-0.002700	-0.089
R11	0.004385	0.174
R12	0.010792	0.502
R13	0.018114	0.426
R14	0.028704	0.259
R15	0.003348	0.126
R16	-0.012997	-0.513
R18	0.038270	0.419
R19	-0.008787	-0.395
D1M1	0.008226	0.716
D1M2	0.007589	1.034
D1M3	0.017501	1.892
D1M4	0.005954	0.592
D1M5	0.010886	0.372
QIND	1.454333	0.077
CTRA	-0.473772	-1.030
STRA	0.036549	2.961
D1LQ	-0.000221	-3.415
D1Q2	0.000040472	2.301
FATX	0.047824	2.554
D1FATX	-0.066203	-3.481

Durbin-Watson	2,710
(For Number of Obs.)	18680
1st Order Autocorrelation	-0.355

Note to Table 3

L1VG:	lag 1 of the dependent variable.
D1LK:	first differences of the log of the capital/labour ratio.
L1Lk:	lag 1 of the previous variable.
D1OC:	first differences of the log of total employment.
L1OC:	lag 1 of the previous variable.
Y86-Y89:	dummy variables for each years.
S1-S6:	sectorial dummy variables (retail trade, wholesale trade of final products, lodging and catering, machinery, textile, food)
R1-R19:	regional dummy variables.
QIND:	share of independent workers in the sector.
CTRA:	rate of capacity utilization for the manufacturing sectors.
STRA:	overtime hours worked for the manufacturing sectors.
D1LQ:	first differences of the ration between current assets and liabilities.
D1Q2:	share of total sales of larger firms (more than 500 workers) by rcgion and sector.
FATX:	share of export.
D1FATX:	first differences of the previous variable.

5. Conclusions

The presence of a gap in the productivity dynamics between manufacturing and service sectors is tested using firm-level data. The model discriminates between differences in the sectorial rate of growth of technological progress and differences coming from the competitive environment and financial distress of the firms, taking into account also the presence of firm fixed effects.

The presence of a large productivity variability is only partially captured by the empirical model. The measurement errors of the economic variables, that are probably related to the use of balance-sheet data, do not help the empirical analysis. The paper can give only some preliminary evidence, even if it sets the methodological underpinning for an appropriate productivity analysis. The principal results related to the technological effect and the impact of competition on productivity growth can be synthesized in two points: the sectorial effects on TFP have the sign that is coherent with the Baumol model, but are not statistically significant; the effect of "effort" variables are significant in the aggregate model, less in the sectorial ones.

For the first point, the scarce relevance of sectorial effects is attributed to the limited quality of our data and to the model, that is probably oversimplified, instead that to the absence of a sectorial impact of the technological progress. This hypothesis is supported by the results of an analogous study on British firms (Pellegrini, 1993b), where these effects are very significant. For the second point, the results show the presence of a competition deficit in the service sectors, that it is reflected on our estimates in three different ways: (i) the service firms in our sample are less reactive to liquidity crisis, suggesting that the existence of monopoly position at local level can affect the firm dynamism; (2) the different export shares is strictly linked with the competitive environment in the market; (3) the increase of the share of larger firms does not seem to affect the degree of competition in the market.

The structure of service markets appears to be deeply different from the manufacturing ones. The presence of a stronger dimensional and territorial segmentation increases the protection of the incumbents in the market and can reduce the competition among firms. The reason at the base of this segmentation are twofold: from one side, it depends on the specific characteristics of service production, that determine a high product differentiation in space and in quality, and therefore support the dimensional and local segmentation processes; from the other side, there is a distinctive characteristic of Italian service market that presents, especially for the trade sector, a strict regulation with legal barriers to entry and to growth, that facilitate the formation of rent positions (Pellegrini, 1994). Therefore, policy interventions that remove these barriers can have a positive effect on service productivity level and growth.

The principal contribution of the paper to the study of the productivity gap between services and manufacturing is mainly methodological: improvement in the analysis can be obtained using microeconomic data and studying the effect of competition at the firm level. The empirical analysis is a first step in this direction. More robust results can be achieved by increasing the available information and using more complete models.

References

Alvaro G. and Erba A., (1993), *Industrialismo e Post-Industrialismo*, mimeo.

Barca F. and Visco I., (1992), "L'Economia Italiana nella Prospettiva Europea: Terziario Protetto e Dinamica dei Redditi Nominali", *Temi di Discussione*, Banca d'Italia, no. 175.

Baumol W. J., (1967), "Macroeconomics of Unbalanced Growth: The Anatomy of Urban Crises", *American Economic Review*, 57, June.

Brown W. and Wadhwani S., (1990), "The Economic Effect of Industrial Relations Legislation Since 1979", *National Institute Economic Review*, 131, 57-70.

Carree M. and Thurik R., (1991), "Market Volatily, Entry Barriers and Retail Profit Margins", Econometric Institute, Erasmus University, mimeo.

CER, (1991), *Rapporto*, no. 5

EUROSTAT, (1992), *National Account ESA*, Luxembourg, 1992.

Fuà G., (1993), *Crescita Economica*, Il Mulino, Bologna.

Fuchs V. R., (1968), *The Service Economy*, NBER, Columbia University Press, New York.

Gregg P., Machin S. and Metcalf D., (1992), "Signals and Cycles? Productivity Growth and Changes in Union Status in British Companies, 1984-1989", *University College London Discussion Paper in Economics*, no. 91-15, revised June 1992.

König H., (1992), "Comments", *European Economic Review*, 36, no. 5, 1086-1092.

Inman R. P., (1985), "Introduction and Overview", in Inman R.P. (ed.), *Managing the Service Economy: Prospects and Problems*, Cambridge University Press, Cambridge (U.K.).

ISTAT (1993), *Rapporto Annuale . La Situazione Economica del Paese 1992*, Roma.

Nickell S., Wadhwani S. and Wall M., (1992), "Productivity Growth in U.K. Companies, 1975-1986", *European Economic Review*, 36, no.5, 1055-1085.

Ochel W., and Wegner M., (1987), *Services Economies in Europe: Opportunities for Growth*, Pinter, London.

Oulton N., (1990), "Labour Productivity in U.K. Manufacturing in the 1970s and in the 1980s", *National Institute Economic Review*, 132, 71-91.

Pellegrini G., (1993a), "La Produttività nei Servizi Destinabili alla Vendita: Nuove Evidenze per un Vecchio Problema", *Temi di Discussione*, Banca d'Italia, no. 212.

Pellegrini G., (1993b), "The Baumol Gap Revisited: An Econometric Analysis of the Productivity Differential between U.K. Manufacturing and Service Firms, 1982 - 1989", *Labour*, 7.

Pellegrini G., (1994), *L'impatto delle Barriere all'Entrata di Tipo Legale sulla Struttura del Settore Distributivo*, Banca d'Italia, in Dell'Aringa C., "Caratteri Strutturali dell'Inflazione Italiana", Il Mulino, Bologna, forthcoming.

Sapir A., (1991), "The Structure of Services in Europe: A Conceptual Framework", *CEPR Discussion Paper*, no. 498.

Solow R., (1992), "Introduction", *Scandinavian Journal of Economics*, Supplement, vol. 94.

van Dalen J., and Thurik R., (1991), "Econometric Analysis and Firm Diagnostics: An Example from the Dutch Exporting Flower Trade", Econometric Institute, Erasmus University, mimeo.

GPSR Compliance

The European Union's (EU) General Product Safety Regulation (GPSR) is a set of rules that requires consumer products to be safe and our obligations to ensure this.

If you have any concerns about our products, you can contact us on ProductSafety@springernature.com

In case Publisher is established outside the EU, the EU authorized representative is:

Springer Nature Customer Service Center GmbH
Europaplatz 3
69115 Heidelberg, Germany

Batch number: 10732714

Printed by Printforce, the Netherlands